Praise for Linda [Ellerbee]

"What can you say about Linda E[llerbee? She is] irreverent and writes like a dream."

"[*Move On* is] gut-honest.... Like G[od, Ellerbee has a] talent for seeing what is important in what appears to be minor, and for seeing what is absurd in what appears to be important. And for writing about both with clarity, grace and a healthy dash of Tabasco."

—*Atlanta Journal*

"Linda Ellerbee has a smart mouth. That she gets paid real money because of [and sometimes despite of] her smart mouth is both a joy and an inspiration, especially to the folks who thought up 'Murphy Brown.' "

—*Dallas Morning News*

"On screen, Linda Ellerbee is that startling thing, a network person with edge. In print she is even sharper and funnier, a natural writer with good stories and an unnerving message: TV is human."   —Roy Blount, Jr.

"Ellerbee's throwaway lines are better than most people's keepers."

—*Seattle Times*

"[*Move On* is] one from the heart."   —*Rocky Mountain News*

" 'A good time to laugh is anytime you can.' Ellerbee gives us that anytime in all her chapters."   —*Houston Chronicle*

"As the old saying goes, I wish I had written [*And So It Goes*]. Linda Ellerbee captures all the zaniness, as well as seriousness, of our business. It's literate, witty and lots of fun to read."   —Sam Donaldson

"In her first book, *And So It Goes*, Ellerbee treated us to an acerbic inside view of television that would make Edward R. Murrow roll over in his grave. [*Move On*] allows Ellerbee to get her licks in on such subjects as television programmers, Ban-Lon, middle age—and herself. And it allows her to show off her novelistic storytelling skill, which is considerable.... I have long believed that the reason Texans are sometimes hated by people from other states is that they are richer, smarter, funnier and louder than anybody else. Linda Ellerbee...is a Texan who confirms the stereotype, except that she's not rich.... She's smart, she's funny, and she's got a mouth on her, as my fellow Brooklynites would say. That's why this new volume of autobiographical reflections on her pre- and post-television experiences is a delicious read."   Grace Lichtenstein, *Washington Post*

"[*Move On* is] at once breezy and profound.... Linda Ellerbee surveys the tapestry of her life with uncommon wit and perception."

—*Cleveland Plain Dealer*

"Tough and funny."   —*San Francisco Chronicle*

"[*And So It Goes*] is more fun than flipping channels. Linda Ellerbee, a serious journalist, has written a funny book about TV news that serious people should tune in to."   —Lesley Stahl

"*And So It Goes* is funny, acerbic and, most of all, informed. Ellerbee writes deliciously and on target."   —Mike Wallace

"*Move On* is the story of how little Linda Jane Smith from Texas became Linda Ellerbee, TV personality, by growing up in a time of unparalleled social and technological change.... With unapologetic, wry honesty, Ellerbee [writes] a strong story about surviving, soul intact."

—*Buffalo News*

ALSO BY LINDA ELLERBEE

"And So It Goes": Adventures in Television

MOVE ON

Adventures
in the Real World

LINDA ELLERBEE

Harper Perennial
A Division of HarperCollinsPublishers
An Edward Burlingame Book

A hardcover edition of this book was published in 1991 by G. P. Putnam's Sons. It is here reprinted by arrangement with G. P. Putnam's Sons.

HarperCollins books may be purchased for educational, business, or sales promotional use. For information, please call or write: Special Markets Department, HarperCollins Publishers, Inc., 10 East 53rd Street, New York, NY 10022. Telephone: (212) 207-7528; Fax: (212) 207-7222.

First HarperPerennial edition published 1992.

LIBRARY OF CONGRESS CATALOG CARD NUMBER 91-57911

ISBN 0-06-097469-9

92 93 94 95 96 MB 10 9 8 7 6 5 4 3 2 1

ACKNOWLEDGMENTS

No one but me is to blame for what's in this book; however, Neil Nyren, my editor, is to blame *for* this book. He made me do it, for which I thank him. When I grow up I want to be a writer. This was good practice.

Also, I want to thank some people around Lucky Duck Productions who contributed and commented, constantly. Simon Rosenberg: "Gee, I don't know, there are an awful lot of commas." Cole Pleasant: "I don't see why you can't write country and western songs instead." Nadine Stewart: "Now *that's* funny."

My children helped, particularly Josh, who, not being as quick to leave a country as Vanessa, had to read more. I have written about my children here and sincerely hope they wait until I die to write about me; but Vanessa wrote her own section in "Mother and Child Reunion," and a letter from Josh is included in "Putting It Together."

I'm most especially grateful to Rolfe, who gave me love and strength to go through so many changes—in a book, in my life.

I have, in the book, taken some liberty with some names. In the chapter "We Reserve the Right to Refuse Service to You," none of the names but my own is real and at least one character is a composite of people who were actually there. The same is true in the chapter "Time in a Bottle." Other names have been changed throughout the book where I thought the use of real names might hurt someone's feelings unnecessarily. It is not my intention to do harm but to tell stories, good stories, I hope.

Finally, I should like to thank my agent, Lobster Newberg (thank you, Kinky), my higher power and my Macintosh.

New York
October 1990

To Joshua and Vanessa,
who made the trip worth taking,
and to Hallie and Ray, because.

Stop worrying where you're going.
Move on.
If you can know where you're going,
You've gone.
Just keep moving on . . .

—STEPHEN SONDHEIM

TRUCKIN'

I packed up his comic books, sold off the bunk beds, gave away
the last *Star Wars* sheet and threw out the beanbag chair that had
bled to death in 1975. I tore down the six *M*A*S*H* posters super-
glued to the wall between his room and mine. Next I tore down
the wall. After that, I ripped up the floor, raised high the roof
beam, put up a skylight big enough to bring the moon home, put
down a Jacuzzi big enough to do the backstroke across, planted
flowers so fragile they faint if you frown twice, painted everything else a lovely shade of Childless White and watched my son
go nuts.

"You turned my bedroom into a bathtub!"

"Try not to shout, Josh. You'll wake the magnolias."

"How could you do such a thing?"

"I have my reasons."

"Name one!"

"You don't live here anymore."

"What kind of reason is that?"

Change, like youth, is purely wasted on the young. My son was
living in his own apartment but that was different, that change
hadn't upset him, not like this one had; moving out had been

easy, a natural progression, a rite of passage, he'd called it. He was twenty; he didn't know the first thing about change. He thought change would always be easy. He thought change would always be a choice.

His choice.

So did I at his age. I couldn't wait to move on. I knew here could never be as sweet as there; going was a question, staying was an answer. Questions were better. I dreamed early and often of taking dangerous steps, making headlong rushes, and if I confused change with motion, and bigger with better, I had help. It starts when you're a child. I remember the Christmas my Aunt Alice Rose from Beeville gave me the puzzle map of the United States and the first thing I noticed was that "united" did not mean equal. Texas was hands down the best piece in the puzzle. California was bent, Michigan was broken and Colorado was Wyoming. Vermont was only an upside-down New Hampshire, Kentucky was merely the poor man's Virginia, and if you'd seen one Dakota, you'd seen 'em all. Other states were equally boring; most of them looked like, well, states (except for Florida. Any way you looked at Florida, it made you snicker). Texas, on the other hand, didn't look like a thing in this world but Texas.

The movies I saw, books I read, songs I heard, my teachers and life in general while I was growing up did nothing but reinforce my belief in the wonderfulness of Texas and, of course, Texans. I felt sorry for people who were only Americans, even though my mother said it was their own fault; that anybody who wasn't Texan didn't deserve to be. My Aunt Sister said this wasn't the Christian way to look at things; after all, somebody had to be from Arkansas. My Aunt Alice Rose from Beeville said she'd be damned if she could see why. My daddy said Praise Jesus, at least it wasn't us.

I was eighteen when I packed my guitar, clicked the heels of my ruby sneakers three times and left Texas the first time, and the one thing I knew for sure was that anything was possible; maybe everything was possible. If $2+2=4$ today, who knew but what tomorrow we might get up and find $2+2=5$? It could happen. I for one intended to keep my knees bent.

In the Andes, I taught Quechuan Indians to sing "Onward, Christian Soldiers" in Spanish, a second language neither they nor I spoke or understood very well, and thought about Che Guevara; I was *An Enlightened Missionary*.

In Memphis, I married the Junior Executive Trainee. We lived in garden-apartment hell. I cooked Burnt Orange dinners on our Avocado Green stove in our Harvest Gold kitchen, after which I often locked myself in our Arctic White bathroom and held my breath until I turned Wedgwood Blue; I was *A Model Wife*.

In Chicago, I worked for an FM station (*Career Girl*), formed a band (*Folk Musician*) and fell in love with a banjo player (*Fool*).

In Los Angeles, I wrote one-liners that were not funny for a television show that was not renewed; I was *In Show Business*.

In Texas, I married the cowboy-poet. He believed in Jesus Christ, Kahlil Gibran and Karl Marx. He believed in making love not war. We moved to the Mexican border and made two babies in two years; I was *The Mommy*.

In Alaska, I left the commune to write radio programs for a Republican politician after I lost my cowboy-poet to a Quaker vegetarian who didn't shave her legs or believe in cars unless they were ambulances. I was *The Earth Mother/Revolutionary* turned *The Working Mother/Hack Writer*.

In Dallas, I got my first job as a real reporter, bought a used Volkswagen, rented an apartment near the freeway and found a live-in baby-sitter I could trust. Two months later, I got fired and the live-in baby-sitter I could trust left town with the used Volkswagen; I was *The Failure*. In a rented apartment near the freeway.

During the next seventeen years, I was *The Television Journalist*. I traveled everywhere, covered everything and if I couldn't be in two places at once, at least I could be seen trying. For the last few years I have been, depending on whom you ask, a humorist, a newspaper columnist, a television commentator, a film documentarian, a book writer, an independent producer, a coffee huckster and/or *A Pain in the Ass*.

Sometimes I wish I didn't know now what I didn't know then. Every change was harder than the one before, it seems, and if they've confused me, these changes, they've sometimes confused those around me more. But that, too, is what I have written about in this book.

When people asked me was I going to write a second book about television, and I told them I wasn't, they said that despite the money I made off the first book, I was still a damn fool; at least I *knew* something about television. When I mentioned I might like to try fiction instead, close friends and people I hardly knew said take two aspirin and call them in the morning. Fiction? What in the world was I thinking of? I don't know; I guess I was just curious to find out if after so many years writing fact, I could, if pressed, write truth. That was, of course, too much to ask. I decided to write about change instead.

Changes.

Some of the stories are personal. Some are simpler than that. This is not a diary, not an owner's manual; it's not an autobiography or novel and it sure as hell isn't journalism. If anything, it's a time-travel book, a brief trip through some changes in and around me. In the last few years I quit a salaried job; started a company; renovated an old house; saw my mother die; saw my children grow up, move out, move back in, move out; watched my weight go up, down, up; and underwent other, sometimes more difficult changes, for the better, I hope. And while I believe the only thing harder than learning from experience is not learning from experience, I can sit right here and wish it had been different, some of it, all of it. I suspect that's the way most people feel about the past. As I said, this is not the story of my life, but some of these are stories from my life. Others are from other lives: my friends, my family, my bigger world—my changing world. This is about Bugs Bunny and Texas, revolutions, rock 'n' roll, finding a style, finding a job, five networks, four marriages and two children. And a couple of yellow dogs: Bo, the one hanging around now, and Magoo, the original yellow dog, from the commune. It's about being parent to one's parent, son, daughter and oneself; dreaming Roy would leave Dale and believing my Aunt Alice Rose, who almost ran away with the millionaire; learning from Gladys who said "gotohell," and Lucy who was eaten by a television; about Maxwell House, alcohol, feminism and the pain of learning what you are.

Be warned. They are not entirely in order, the stories in this book, but that's how they were written, not how they were lived, and if connections from one chapter to the next sometimes seem absent, there's nothing wrong with you; they often are absent. I have used song titles for chapter headings, and though you probably don't care in the least, I'll explain. Maybe it's my age, or the age that has been mine to live in, about which I have a great deal more to say later, but the fact is, music has informed my life. Like Nietzsche, I believe that without music, life would be a mistake. Nothing but silence says it better, and silence is not what I do best. The song titles are mostly familiar to you, I expect, with the possible exception of three by Stephen Sondheim. One might think I have an extraordinary respect for this man's work. I do. Stephen Sondheim's songs make you think with the heart and feel with the brain, and although I've never met the man, he has accompanied me for years in this writing tomfoolery, and in my life. It was Stephen Sondheim's genuinely inspiring song "Move On" that gave me the idea for this book.

Stephen Sondheim and Mabel Scott.

It was Mabel Scott who got me thinking about change.

I was planning a trip to Texas. There are many ways to go home. One of the best ways to go home is when your book is high on the best-seller list, you've signed a contract for a new book, cashed the check of the people who want to make a movie out of your first book, agreed to write and anchor a new prime-time weekly network television program about recent American history (it is to run opposite *The Cosby Show*, but at the time you think this is not an insurmountable problem, which goes to show what you still don't know about networks or much else) and lost twenty-five pounds. I tell you, I was in high cotton, especially when I got a call from my pal David Berg, self-effacing criminal lawyer to the rich and occasionally innocent, fresh from emceeing his own 25th high-school reunion ("I read *Fern Hill* to the football players, Linda Jane, reminded them that the only time that mattered in their whole lives was when they were children making

LINDA ELLERBEE

fun of debaters like me and you, and now they're all trying to
sell me life insurance"). He called to say he wanted to throw a
party for me when I got to Texas, and why didn't we invite
everybody in my high school who'd ever been rude to me?

Oh, my, what a *wonderful* idea.

But, I asked, could he also invite Mabel Scott? My high-school
English teacher.

"Your English teacher. Was she rude to you?"

Mabel Scott was not rude, I explained. Mabel Scott was special,
a world-class teacher. She'd led us, pushed, bullied, encouraged
and given me confidence when there'd been no reason for her
to do so. Certainly she could not have seen in me much to warrant
her attention, but give it she had, in abundance, five days a week.
Kafka, Shakespeare, Salinger, Steinbeck. If she liked them, she
was sure you would. She felt the same about Conrad, Melville
and Chesterton. She taught with a wry passion. She made words
catch fire; I loved it, and her, and had known for years that if,
in spite of an incomplete education and an uncommon lack of
talent for business, I had been able to support myself doing work
I loved and raise my children without asking others for help, then
I mainly owed five people: my parents, my children and Mabel
Scott. I'd told the other four thank you. Now I wanted to tell
her. David found Mrs. Scott, invited her, and when I went to
Texas, she came to the party.

For a girl who never was cheerleader and never will be Miss
Congeniality, a party whose purpose is you is heady stuff. Fifty
people said nice things to me. Two of them even meant it. I could
have danced all night and still wish my Aunt Alice Rose from
Beeville had; she, however, being mostly deaf and partly drunk,
began by inquiring of our host and anyone else slow enough to
wander into her range just exactly why it was we weren't selling
copies of Linda Jane's book at this party. Money was money,
wasn't it? There was an interesting moment when, in a mid-
harangue pause, she handed her drink to a well-known local
television anchorman, a dark and smoothly handsome fellow with
a Spanish surname who also happened to be wearing a dinner
jacket, and demanded, "Boy, bring me another." I was real glad
when the doorbell rang and even gladder to see Mabel Scott.

"Oh, Mrs. Scott," I gushed.

Then, standing in the hallway just inside the front door, not even letting the woman sit down, I told her the things I'd been wanting to about how I owed her for what I'd become. I was flush with myself, full up to here; they'd saddled me a high horse and I'd ridden it. I went on, gabbling at Mabel Scott, finishing up with the announcement that for me, having it all was finally being able to meet her again and say thank you.

There is a difference between having it all and reality. Reality is what happened next. Mabel Scott, my English teacher, smiled at me, shook my hand and then went to work teaching me again.

"Well, Linda," said Mrs. Scott, "I can't tell you how pleased I was to be invited to this party." She paused. "I always wondered whatever became of you."

By the way, some of this book is true.

SYMPATHY
FOR THE DEVIL

The August I was eight years old, a television ate my best friend. My *very first* very best friend. I took it personally. What if I never found a second? Lord only knew how long it might be before I met another little girl as qualified as Lucy, whose house was right across the street from mine and, no, I did not mind that Lucy was so much younger, because she was not like most people who lived near you when they were barely seven; she hardly ever whined, not even when all nine kids on our block played Cowboys and Cowboys and every one of us got to be Roy Rogers or Pat Brady or at least Gabby Hayes, except Lucy, who had to be Dale Evans. Lucy understood: someone had to be Dale Evans. Nor did she cry, not even when we played dodge ball and some big kid threw the ball so hard and fast that when Lucy finally was able to stand you could read "Spaulding" backwards on one or more of her legs. Best of all, she did not shy from telling a big lie when a big lie was what was called for. Lucy was world-class, and if the television hadn't eaten her, we would both be flying today. That summer we were so close to mastering the trick, the wonderful, magical, fantastical secret trick.

This, I swear, is gospel.

Understand, we were going to fly without being surrounded by aluminum or covered with feathers, and we knew that sometime before the day grown-ups who want to fool children call Labor Day (which children who will not be fooled know by its true name: The Day Summer Dies), we would succeed, because we had something to help us slip the surly bonds of earth. We had, praise Jesus, a Theory.

We discovered the Theory by accident, just like Columbus and America. We were in my backyard. Picture the perfect swing set: high, wide and handsome, built solid and grounded for life. There was a steel trapeze bar worn smooth from use and hung high enough to do tricks on but low enough to survive them. There were three swings, spaced right, with red wooden seats almost brushing the ground, which made all the difference in the air, the extra distance being so crucial. One day in June, somewhere out in the extra distance, something went wrong. I was swinging as high as I could and then I was swinging a little higher and then—the next time the swing started to come back down, I didn't. I just kept going up. And up. And up. And . . .

Believe me, it was a moment.

Then I began to fall. Know what? Know what? Lucy was yelling at me. No, I didn't know *what*. All I knew was, the way my left arm hurt, making a scene made sense. Lucy was unmoved and continued to yell at me. Know what? Know what? Linda Jane, for a minute there, you flew. *Linda Jane, you actually flew!* You seemed to, you know, catch the wind and—and soar! Right up to when you must have done something wrong, because you fell. Jesus, Mary and Joseph, did you fall and—broke your arm, it looks like from here.

Wearing the cast gave me time to work out our scientifics. Scientifics were important, although naturally they weren't as important as having a Theory. Our Theory was basically sound, even if we couldn't exactly say what it was. It had something to do with swinging just high enough and just straight enough so that if you jumped out of the swing at just the right moment and held your body in just the right position—*you just might fly.*

LINDA ELLERBEE

That much was possibly certain.

We spent July waiting for my cast to come off and practicing our walk-arounds. We ran our hands across the wooden seats, feeling for the odd splinter, which if not caught in time could flat out ruin your perfect takeoff. We pulled on the swing's chains, testing for weak links, but were prepared to sacrifice safety for the extra distance. We chewed Dentyne gum and stared off into space.

Out of nowhere, it was August. I loved that month almost as much as I hated it. My birthday was in August, but it was also the month that signified the end of summer vacation, and the beginning of another school year. I wasn't scared of third grade, especially when I didn't think about it. The worst part was that Lucy and I went to different schools. This had begun the year before and our parents had said it wouldn't make a bit of difference, since we weren't in the same grade anyway, but it had, the way it does when people come from two countries that are supposed to speak the same language, only half the time you can't understand what the other person is talking about. Like when an American tries to hold a conversation with somebody from England. Or Arkansas.

I went to River Oaks Elementary School, two blocks away, very old and public, while Lucy went to The Church of the One True Way School, which was clear across town, brand-new and Christian. The Church of the One True Way School was part of The Church of the One True Way, which was ten years old and had been Lucy's daddy's idea in the first place; he'd found ordinary churches very disappointing after a world war.

Lucy's daddy had been a sergeant in the United States Army (he wore his sergeant's haircut until the day he died). Ordinary churches were slack, he said: poorly supervised, undisciplined and way too merciful. Even the Baptists. Lucy's father suspected the Baptists of being soft on communism, which was pretty silly since everybody in the state of Texas knew Baptists were all for changing the flag to something with no red in it. Baptists didn't smoke, cuss, drink, play bingo, or fornicate. I don't know how there got to be so many Baptists. They didn't even dance. Yes, that's so, Lucy's daddy always said, but they sing. There were other people who agreed with Lucy's daddy, enough of them to form their own church where they could worship God according to their own ideas, which were the right ideas. Uncertainty did not raise the money to rent the hall. Doubt did not name their congregation The Church of the One True Way. And mercy did not enter into the matter at all.

Then two years before, Lucy's daddy had decided it still wasn't enough. He had another idea: The Church of the One True Way School, where their innocent lambs of school age would be free to learn everything they needed to learn about what was best for them to know. They would learn in The Lord's Own House, in Christian classes led by Christian teachers, where they would be safe from accidental exposure to dangers Lucy's daddy couldn't bring himself to name, but were well-documented plenty of places in the Bible, if you knew what to look for.

He asked the others to think. Did they really want their own little lambs thrown into the company of Baptists, or worse, Episcopalians? Did they want them around books—books that weren't the Bible, or if they were, sure as not they were the wrong Bible? What about music teachers? What about Democrats, for God's sake? And folk dancing? Had they thought about the dangers of folk dancing? No? One thing led to another, they ought to know that. One thing always led to another. Pretty soon their children would be believing in Santa Claus, reading comics, drinking cherry Cokes, eating Fritos and wearing lipstick. They'd meet atheists (if books were considered more dangerous than atheists, it was only that in Houston you could find a book a lot sooner than you could find an atheist). And if all that weren't enough to persuade them of their Christian duty, he'd saved the worst for last. Any time Lucy's daddy began talking about the worst, you would be sure where he was headed. In East Texas, the worst could mean only one thing.

Louisiana.

Anybody with half a brain knew that not one human being in the state of Louisiana ever spent a nickel's worth of a minute worrying about hell. And it did not matter whether they were

Catholics, Protestants, Cajuns, Negroes or from Shreveport, they were all the same: they saw sin in a whole different light. People from Louisiana had too much fun, too little shame and no fear anywhere in them. Were the Good Christian Families of The Church of the One True Way prepared to send their own flesh and blood to some school where people had fun? Lucy's daddy didn't think they were.

And so this band of fifty or so shepherds, each of whom had been saved several times, sat on folding chairs in the basement game room of the VFW hall just past the Conoco station on Old Alameda Road, where The Church of the One True Way met on Sunday mornings and Sunday nights. They listened while Lucy's daddy explained to them what had to be done, then they prayed three or four times, voted once or twice, and when at last they got up to go home, they'd made themselves a school. Lucy was the first to enroll. It wasn't her idea.

I was a Methodist. I sang, danced, spit, and on certain Sundays was invited to drink tiny cups of what they said we should pretend was Jesus' blood, but if I were Jesus, I wouldn't want people pretending I had Welchade for blood. As for the rest, I believed in Santa Claus when I wanted to, and although I'd never met an atheist or a person from Louisiana, I'd read about both in books belonging to my parents, who read and even bought books, but they were, after all, Democrats. They taught me to put up with other people's ways, and usually I found this an easy thing to do, as long as religious freedom didn't come between me and my best friend. So far it showed no signs of doing so, since we both hated all churches, Lucy and me, except once in a while, when I thought I might like to be Catholic so I could light a candle for a dead person, if I knew one, or lock myself inside a box and tell someone I couldn't see everything about me, starting from the beginning and leaving out nothing.

Most of the time, religion confused me, but so did almost everything else: schools, churches, mothers, fathers, friends, the future. I was grateful that once we were flying, once we were up there in the sky, we could finally see what it all meant.

Once we were up there.

Near the tail of the last week in August, two weeks after my birthday, we were ready. Today we would fly.

Betchurass.

Early that morning, we began, taking turns—one pushing, one pumping. All day we pushed and pumped, higher, higher, so close. It wasn't dark, but it was getting there when Lucy's mother hollered for Lucy to come home right this minute and see what her daddy and The Lord had brought them. This was strictly against the rules. Nobody had to come home in August until it was altogether dark. As for rushing to see what Lucy's daddy and The Lord had brought them, well, you had to know Lucy's daddy. He wasn't a man to be struck on his way home with an irresistible impulse to stop at the horse store and say golly, does my little girl love ponies! So does her best friend. Guess I better get two of them. No, Lucy's daddy was a man who made his whole family go to church on *Wednesday* night, when they had Bible Study Class. Lucy's daddy taught Bible Study Class. They had *tests* there. There wasn't going to be any pony.

And so we kept on swinging while she continued to pretend not to hear her mother calling her, until her mother dropped the *Luceee* part and got right down to *Lucille Louise.* Halfway through the fourth *Lucille Louise,* Lucy slowly raised her head; she tilted it as though she were straining to hear some woman who might just possibly be calling to her from the next county. Some woman she hardly knew.

"Oh? Were you calling me, Mother? What? I can barely hear you. Okay, okay, I'm coming. Yes, ma'am. *Right now.*"

Lucy and I walked together to the end of my driveway, where she had to start running because our black, tar street was high-summer sticky. When it got real hot, our street bubbled. Halfway across, Lucy risked getting stuck for the rest of her natural life in order to snag a lightning bug for company; once she was in her front yard she slowed to something between a meander and a lollygag, choosing a path that would take her straight through the sprinklers. Twice. I stood at the end of our driveway watching the glow go on and off inside Lucy's cupped hand. The darker it got, the better I could see the bug light up.

All this time, Lucy's mother was inside the house, looking out the screen door, talking. It didn't matter that I couldn't hear her words, I didn't have to. I knew exactly what she was saying. *Mother Stuff.* Every mother I'd ever met in my whole life could do ten to twenty minutes of *Mother Stuff* without once stopping to breathe or think, and every child I'd ever met in my whole life could, by the first syllable of the second word, turn clinically deaf. There was only one good thing about *Mother Stuff:* it neither required nor abided an answer. When at last Lucy sashayed her way to her front door (anything slower than a sashay was hard to distinguish from a full stop), you could tell it was not too soon.

Lucy turned back to look at me. I saw her grin. I saw her raise her right hand, make a hard fist and jab her thumb straight up into the air. The "go" sign used by pilots everywhere. *Awright.* So we'd fly tomorrow instead. So what? We'd waited all summer. We could wait one more day. Of course she slammed the door on her way in. I can hear that door slam today.

Bang!

In my memory, I've listened to that screen door shut beind my best friend a thousand times.

Bang!

It was the last time I ever saw her.

Bang.

I cried and cried, especially when nobody would admit to me that Lucy was dead. They lied to me, every last grown-up one of them. They said Lucy wasn't dead. They said Lucy was inside. Inside? I knocked on the door every day, but nobody answered, except for her mother who said Lucy couldn't come out to play because Lucy was busy. I dialed their number on our telephone, but nobody answered, except for her mother who said Lucy couldn't come to the telephone because Lucy was busy. Lucy was busy? Too busy to play? Too busy to fly? She had to be dead. Nothing else made sense. For one thing, tell me what, short of death, could separate such very best friends? No, if she were alive—if she were *breathing*—she'd have come back outside the next morning, or the morning after that. We were going to fly. Her thumb had said so.

My mother said I was behaving like a child (I was too insulted to point out what a stupid thing that was to say to an eight-year-old). My father took me to ride the ponies on South Main Street. He thought it would take my mind off losing Lucy. I used to love riding those ponies, making up stories to myself: I was a fierce cowgirl and the pony was a wild stallion, a pinto or a palomino named Thunder or Beowulf or maybe Rita. I was always renaming those ponies, because they usually had names like Pokey or Sweet Sal or, yuck, Old Bill, the slowest, and if the pony didn't want to be Rita, well, I'd be Rita and the pony could be Zeus. But I didn't want to ride those ponies anymore. They weren't wild stallions. I wasn't a fierce cowgirl. And nobody was named Rita.

Daddy's feelings were hurt, I could tell.

I might never have known the truth of the Lucy matter, if some weeks later I hadn't overheard my mother say to my father how maybe I would calm down about Lucy if we got a television, too.

A what? What on earth was a television?

This word was brand-new to me, but I was clever enough to figure out right then that what Lucy's daddy had brought home that night must have been a television. At last I knew what had happened to Lucy. It was as clear to me as homemade sin. The television ate her.

Sweet Baby Jesus, it must have been a horrible thing to see. I tried to imagine watching a television eat Lucy, wondering just how much more horrible a thing it might be to imagine if I knew what a television was. I was scared. Either my parents didn't understand about televisions or they were tired of putting up with their own little girl. I decided to give them the benefit of the doubt. It eats people, I said to my parents. Television eats people.

"What did you say, Linda Jane?"

They laughed and laughed. Oh, Linda Jane, they said. Oh, Linda Jane. You're the funniest thing. Television doesn't eat people. Television is good. Television will bring people together. Television is part of The Wonderful World of Tomorrow. You'll love it. Yes, Linda, you'll love television, just like Lucy, who, they said, was inside her house with her parents right this minute, watching television. They might even be eating popcorn.

The best part, they told me, was that one day every family in

America would have a television. I told them I would kill myself first. Mother smiled and shook her head at me in the way that said, Oh, Linda Jane, what am I going to do about you? Daddy told me to go find a book and read something until I was ready to be reasonable. I read in the chinaberry tree, I read under the oleander bush. I read sitting on each of the three red wooden seats of our perfect swing set, digging my toes into the ground so I wouldn't accidentally swing so much as an umpteenth of an inch. Labor Day came. Summer died. School started. The third grade was where we learned to write instead of print. We raised silkworms and listened to Miss Warner read from *The Secret Garden*. Halloween, I went to a party at Carol's house. Thanksgiving, I got to play an ear of corn in the school pageant. Long division ruined most of December. After a while, I forgot about flying. I did not forget about Lucy, and I did not look for another very best friend.

Santa Claus brought us a television for Christmas. See, said my parents, television doesn't eat people. Maybe not. But television changed people. Television changed my family forever. We stopped eating dinner at the dining-room table after my mother found out about TV trays. We kept the TV trays behind the kitchen door and served ourselves from pots on the stove. Setting and clearing the dining-room table used to be my job; now, setting and clearing meant unfolding and wiping our TV trays, then, when we'd finished, wiping and folding our TV trays. Dinner was served in time for one program and finished in time for another. During dinner we used to talk to one another. Now television talked to us. If you had something you absolutely had to say, you waited until the commercial, which is, I suspect, where I learned to speak in thirty-second bursts. As a future writer, it was good practice in editing my thoughts. As a little girl, it was lonely as hell. Once in a while, I'd pass our dining-room table and stop, thinking I heard our ghosts sitting around talking to one another, saying stuff.

Before television, I would lie in bed at night listening to my parents come upstairs, enter their bedroom and say things to one another that I couldn't hear, but it didn't matter, their voices rocked me to sleep. My first memory, the first one ever, was of my parents and their friends talking me to sleep when we were living in Bryan and my bedroom was right next to the kitchen. It was still in my crib then. From the kitchen I could hear them, hear the rolling cadence of their speech, the rising and falling of their voices and the sound of chips.

"Two pair showing."

"Call?"

"Check."

"Call?"

"Call." *Clink.*

"I raise." *Clink clink.*

"See your raise and raise you back." *Clink clink clink.*

"Call." *Clink. Clink.*

"I'm in." *Clink.*

"I'm out."

"Let's see 'em."

It was a song to me, a lullaby. Now Daddy went to bed right after the weather and Mama stayed up to see Jack Paar (later she stayed up to see Steve Allen and Johnny Carson and even Joey Bishop, but not David Letterman). I went to sleep alone, listening to voices in my memory.

Daddy stopped buying Perry Mason books. Perry was on television and that was so much easier for him, Daddy said, because he could never remember which Perry Mason books he'd read and was always buying the wrong ones by mistake, then reading them all the way to the end before he realized he'd already read them. Television fixed that, he said, because although the stories weren't as good as the stories in the books, at least he knew he hadn't already read them. But it had been Daddy and Perry who'd taught me how fine it could be to read something you liked twice, especially if you didn't know the second time wasn't the first time. My mother used to laugh at Daddy. She would never buy or read the same book again and again. She had her own library card. She subscribed to magazines and belonged to The Book-of-the-Month Club. Also, she hated mystery stories. Her favorite books were about doctors who found God and women who found doctors. Her most favorite book ever was *Gone With the Wind*, which she'd read before I was born. Read it while she vacuumed the floor, she said. Read it while she'd ironed shirts. Read it while she'd fixed dinner and read it while she'd washed up. Mama sure loved that book. She dropped Book-of-the-Month after she discovered *As the World Turns*. Later, she stopped her magazine subscriptions. Except for *TV Guide*. I don't know what she did with her library card. I know what she didn't do with it.

Mom quit taking me to the movies about this time, not that she'd ever taken me to the movies very often after Mr. Disney let Bambi's mother get killed, which she said showed a lack of imagination. She and Daddy stopped going to movies, period. Daddy claimed it was because movies weren't as much fun after Martin broke up with Lewis, but that wasn't it. Most movies he cared about seeing would one day show up on television, he said. Maybe even Martin & Lewis movies. All you had to do was wait. And watch.

After a while, we didn't play baseball anymore, my daddy and me. We didn't go to baseball games together, either, but we watched more baseball than ever. That's how Daddy perfected The Art of Dozing to Baseball. He would sit down in his big chair, turn on the game and fall asleep within five minutes. That is, he appeared to be asleep. His eyes were shut. He snored. But if you shook him and said, Daddy, you're asleep, he'd open his eyes and tell you what the score was, who was up and what the pitcher ought to throw next. The Art of Dozing to Baseball. I've worked at it myself, but have never been able to get beyond waking up in time to see the instant replay. Daddy never needed instant replay and, no, I don't know how he did it; he was a talented man and he had his secrets.

Our lives began to seem centered around, and somehow measured by, television. My family believed in television. If it was on TV, it must be so. Calendars were tricky and church bells might fool you, but if you heard Ed Sullivan's voice you *knew* it was Sunday night. When four men in uniforms sang that they were the men from Texaco who worked from Maine to Mexico, you *knew* it was Tuesday night. Depending on which verse they were singing, you knew whether it was seven o'clock or eight o'clock on Tuesday night. It was the only night of the week I got to stay up until eight o'clock. My parents allowed this for purely patriotic reasons. If you didn't watch Uncle Milty on Tuesday nights, on Wednesday mornings you might have trouble persuading people you were a real American and not some commie pinko foreigner from Dallas. I wasn't crazy about Milton Berle, but I pretended I was; an extra hour is an extra hour, and if the best way to get your daddy's attention is to watch TV with him, then it was worth every joke Berle could steal. Later I would find another solution, far more bizarre but ten times as effective.

Television was taking my parents away from me, not all the time, but enough, I believed. When it was on, they didn't see me, I thought. Take holidays. Although I was an only child, there were always grandparents, aunts, uncles and cousins enough to fill the biggest holiday. They were the best times. White linen and old silver and pretty china. Platters of turkey and ham, bowls of cornbread dressing and sweet potatoes and ambrosia. Homemade rolls. Glass cake stands holding pineapple, coconut, angel food and devil's food cakes, all with good boiled icing. There was apple pie with cheese. There were little silver dishes with dividers for watermelon pickles, black olives and sliced cranberry jelly. There was all the iced tea you'd ever want. Lord, it was grand. We kids always finished first (we weren't one of those families where they make the kids eat last and you never get a drumstick). After we ate, we'd be excused to go outside, where we'd play. When we decided the grown-ups had spent enough time sitting around the table after they'd already finished eating, which was real boring, we'd go back in and make as much noise as we could, until finally four or five grown-ups would come outside and play with us because it was just easier, that's all. We played hide-and-seek or baseball or football or dodge ball. Sometimes we just played *ball*. Sometimes we just played. Once in a while, there would be fireworks, which were always exciting ever since the Christmas Uncle Buck shot off a Roman candle and set the neighbor's yard on fire, but that was before we had a television.

Now, holiday dinners began to be timed to accommodate the

kickoff, or once in a while the halftime, depending on how many games there were to watch; but on Thanksgiving or New Year's there were always games so important they absolutely could not be missed under any circumstances, certainly not for something as inconsequential as being "it" and counting to ten while you pretended not to see six children climb into the backseat of your car.

"Ssshhh, not now, Linda Jane. The Aggies have the ball."

"But you said . . . you promised . . ."

"Linda Jane, didn't your daddy just tell you to hush up? We can't hear the television for you talking."

Over the years, our TVs and our TV trays got bigger and better; at one point both were covered with a maple veneer and nobody but me seemed to see anything funny about an Early-American TV set and six Early-American TV trays. Where could you go from there, I wondered. The answer was an Early-American color TV. The first time I saw a color TV was at Susan's house. We were ten and she was my good friend, even if she did like to watch television. Susan was blonde, pretty and rich. And sweet. And happy. If you live in a mansion with a cook, a chauffeur and a golden retriever named Foots, if you belong to a yacht club because that's where your yacht lives, if you have two free passes to any movie theater in Texas, well, happiness is possible, I decided. Susan's mother was the one who first made me understand what it was like to be rich, and how it really wasn't mansions or servants or boats or even a big dog. It was all of it and something more. The moment I fully grasped rich was the night I heard Susan's mother call the drugstore and order a case of Kotex.

A case? I mean—why? I knew then that no matter how much money I ever had, I still wouldn't be rich. I didn't *think* rich.

TV was something Susan and I used like trade beads. If I would watch a TV show with Susan, she would go to movies with me. Thanks to her passes, Susan and I had been known to see three movies in a single Saturday, or if we weren't feeling up to the hard work of being driven by Susan's chauffeur from one theater to another, we'd watch one movie three times. Susan's daddy bought a color television as soon as there was a color television to buy. Susan invited me over to watch *The Wizard of Oz*. We sat in her mother's bedroom wiggling ourselves deep into the goose-down cushions of her mother's blue silk sofa, fortified with these special and, I was sure, expensive olives Susan's daddy had imported from California, some Dentler's potato chips and a few Dr Peppers. Awright, I said to myself, bring on your miracle. The movie began. The black-and-white part at the beginning of *The Wizard of Oz* was still black and white, but when Aunt Em's house landed on the wicked witch of the East and Dorothy opened the door, sure enough, she stepped right out of Kansas and into The World of Compatible Color! Living Color, it was called then. Only there was this one teeny, weeny problem. In real life, there are more than two colors. On the television that night, there was red and there was green, and they were everywhere, even in places they didn't belong such as in the yellow-brick road and on Toto. The red and green were bleeding outside the lines like a coloring book done by a three-year-old, or a boy. One more thing. The red and the green—they *glowed*. Susan was disappointed even though we'd already seen this movie in a genuine movie theater and therefore were perfectly able to remember how it was supposed to look before the television dyed everything red and green. Susan's daddy was angry. He wasn't used to spending money on things that would turn on you. I, on the other hand, was giddy with joy; any TV that made people want to hurt it was a friend of mine. It seemed that everybody in the whole world liked to watch television more than I did, although nobody ever came close to Lucy.

Lucy.

Maybe the TV hadn't actually eaten her. But she may as well have been dead; once they pointed her in the direction of that box, she never looked up and she never looked back. Every afternoon when she got home from school, she'd sit down on the floor in their living room and watch whatever there was to watch. Every Saturday morning, she'd watch cartoons. I'm not kidding when I say I lost my best friend. I really did. I had no interest in sitting still when I could be climbing trees or riding bikes or annoying the neighbors or practicing my damn takeoffs just in case one day she woke up and remembered we had a Theory. And Lucy had no interest in doing any of those things when she could go home and take a bath in *My Friend Flicka*. Maybe it was because that was about as close as she was going to get to having her own pony. Maybe it was because her daddy hadn't caught on yet that TV was more dangerous than a busload of Catholics from Louisiana. Maybe if they'd allowed her real world to stretch, she wouldn't have been satisfied with a nineteen-inch world. Maybe if they'd allowed her to read comic books . . .

Who knows? All I know is, Lucy was bewitched by the black-and-white shapes that flickered back and forth in front of her. I don't know if it had to do with Lucy or if it was *me*, but for whatever reason, I hated watching television. There I was, part of the first television generation, only I wasn't part of it at all. It didn't matter what my friends thought. I didn't think Howdy Doody was cute. I thought *Howdy Doody* was for morons. *My Friend Flicka* was the same story every week. *The Lone Ranger, Superman* and *Sky King* were the same man in different clothes. I cannot hum the theme to *The Andy Griffith Show, The Twilight Zone* or *Mr. Ed.* I never once said, away we go, just the facts, ma'am, or scoobee-doo-bee-doo. I loved Walt Disney enough to hate *The Mickey Mouse Club.* Later I loved Chuck Berry enough to hate *American Bandstand.* And I loved Christmas enough to hate Macy's (I hated Andy Williams even more). When television was being authenticated culturally by my peers, I was absent without excuse. Arrogance had nothing to do with it, not really. Years later, I finally found my way to the couch and even came to love dearly certain pieces of television, and to believe they required no apology and no explanation. Good was good, I discovered; no matter where you found it. *All in the Family* was nothing less than a longer version of *Our Town.* Frank Capra could have written *The Mary Tyler Moore Show.* H. L. Mencken would have loved hosting the early *Saturday Night Live.* And Shakespeare, I'm positive, would have been a Trekkie.

And I was right all along.

Television really does eat people. I know, because it ate me.

You may have noticed. It isn't so bad. There are advantages. I'm sorry I didn't see them sooner. If I were inside the television, I didn't have to watch it. If I were inside the television, maybe my parents would notice me more. And if I'm inside the television, one day I might get lucky and find Lucy. I never had another *first* best friend. I never learned to fly, either. But Labor Day is a long time from now. And it's not dark yet, not here in my new backyard, the one inside the television set, not dark now, not dark ever, unless somebody turns the set off. Which means there's plenty of time.

I just keep practicing my takeoffs.

MY HEROES HAVE
ALWAYS BEEN COWBOYS

And they still are, it seems.

—*WILLIE NELSON*

People said Gladys had spunk. What she had was style. Maybe if she'd been taller they'd have called it courage. She swore she wasn't as short as she looked, but Gladys was always swearing; her second favorite word was "gotohell." Her favorite word was shorter, began with an "s" and ended with an exclamation point. Mama said cursing wasn't ladylike. Gladys said she didn't curse, she cussed, and cussing didn't count.

Oh, Gladys, said Mama.

They were two good friends, Gladys and Mama. Gladys drove my mother to the hospital the night I was born, and if it was Mama who gave me my first nest, it was Gladys who gave me my first wings.

I was three years old. We were in a car somewhere in downtown Bryan, Texas; Gladys was driving, looking through the steering wheel instead of over it. I was sitting in my mother's lap, wiggling, impatient to get home and take off my dress, which was, like all the dresses Mama made me wear, spotless, starched and painful. Mama hated dirt. As for wrinkles, well, all you need to know is that my mother ironed my diapers. That day my dress, shoes, socks and hair ribbon were white. Mama loved me in white: it was so beautifully inappropriate.

Gladys said if I weren't wearing all that white, she'd have suggested buying me some ice cream. Mama said I was much too young for ice cream. Gladys hit the brakes. Hallie, do you mean to tell me the child has never tasted ice cream? Without waiting for an answer Gladys made a sudden, thrilling U-turn right in the middle of an intersection and, never taking her tiny foot off the accelerator or her tiny hand off the horn, made for the drugstore, cussing all the way. My mother said nothing, realizing, I suspect, that it was too late, or maybe she was busy praying; Mama often prayed when Gladys drove. After bringing the car to a stop at least a foot before it was actually inside the drugstore, Gladys yanked me off Mama's lap, carried me inside, sat me on a stool, threw a nickel on the counter and told the man to give me a chocolate ice-cream cone *thisverydamnminute,* another of Gladys's favorite words. I looked at what they put in my hand. I looked at Gladys. I didn't know what I was supposed to do.

Lick it, said Gladys.

Tentatively, I put my tongue to the brown, cold ball, then, babbling incoherently, did my three-year-old best to become *one* with that ice-cream cone. Gladys held Mama back and stood, watching me, laughing at the terrible mess I made. Gladys laughed quicker, harder and longer than other people, especially at herself. Pretty soon I was laughing, too. Finally, even Mama began to smile. This was a heady moment. I had ruined my clothes and my mother hadn't killed me dead where I stood. Mama even looked as though she still loved me, except for the funny noise she was making. Gladys reached in her purse and took out a handkerchief. I thought she meant to wipe my face, but she handed it to my mother and told her to blow her nose and stop that sniffling; everybody had to grow up sometime.

Oh, Gladys, said Mama.

My first taste of freedom was my first introduction to style, and it was as memorable as my first taste of ice cream. *Style,* not styles. Styles, like everything else, change. Style doesn't. Funny thing about style: never once was I accused of having any until I abandoned all attempts to get me some. Part of the problem was that for years I concentrated on the pursuit of style under the mistaken impression that I knew what it was. There was a time when all I asked of life, apart from a horse of my own, were blue, piercing eyes, skin that tanned, silky, obedient blond hair, and a voice that would stop the show. It didn't seem like much to ask. What I got instead were eyes that weren't really brown, hair that wasn't really anything else, freckles, a tin ear and a (consequently) useless memory of every lyric I heard. But I got two more gifts, and they changed my life.

I got a library card and movie money. That's how I came to find out about style. It helped that it cost nine cents to see a movie. Along with so many other Americans, I was in love with the movies and took from them more than they gave, intentionally. This is, I believe, one thing I have in common with Ronald Reagan. Come to think of it, with the exception of age, gender, background, occupation, credit rating, marital status, sexual preference, politics and place in history, Ronald Reagan and I are a lot alike. We went to the movies together separately. For example, when the former President, talking about *Mr. Smith Goes to Washington,* a motion picture by Frank Capra, said, "I began to realize, through the power of that motion picture that one man can make a difference," well, I knew what he meant, for once.

The first movie I ever saw was Walt Disney's *Song of the South,* and it left such a dent in my five-year-old brain that forty years later I still can't tell the difference between a cartoon rabbit and a real person. From *Gone With the Wind,* I learned Margaret Mitchell had a lot in common with Walt Disney. From *To Kill a Mockingbird,* I learned that where bigotry was concerned, tomorrow wasn't always another day. I also learned that bigotry didn't necessarily have anything to do with race, or the South. Generally being different was enough.

I learned a lot about women from the movies, too, and not all of it had to do with style. Some of it had to do with the consequences of style. In *Annie Get Your Gun,* Betty Hutton taught me if there's anything he can do that I can do better, I'd better not do it better in front of him. *Funny Girl* taught me that in spite of what you've been told about where and when nice guys finish, the truth is that funny girls finish last first. Shane, Butch Cassidy and John Wayne (all of his movies, even when he didn't play a cowboy) taught me that my heroes have always been cowboys, and then there was *It's a Wonderful Life*. You see, to paraphrase Mr. Reagan, that's when I first began to realize, through the power of *that* movie, not that one man *can* make a difference, but that one man *does* make a difference. Especially if he has style. Oh, I saw a lot of movies. And through all the other messages I got from them, one still came through the clearest. *Style* compensated for a lot in this life.

Take *Little Women*. Amy was beautiful, Beth was kind, Meg was competent, but it's Jo you remember, because Jo had style, or did until she married that old man with a beard, but that was later when she had style enough to spare or maybe sense enough to need none. Bogart. He wasn't handsome, didn't sing or dance, and was, worse luck, short, but he had style. That's why Ingrid truly didn't want to get on that plane out of Casablanca. And that's why he made her do it. *Casablanca* showed me what happens when somebody trusts nobody once too often. As a result, I have all my life avoided falling in love with those sad-eyed, softhearted (and often soused) cynics who, no matter what they say about all the gin joints in all the world, end up choosing Claude Rains over Ingrid Bergman. Actually, that's a lie. I should have learned to avoid falling in love with those guys, but I didn't, not entirely, which is why every so often I still ask Sam to play it again, for me. But it was only a movie, and later it was only my heart.

I began to understand that style didn't guarantee happiness. Still, who cared? Sure, Snow White, who had no style, lived happily ever after, but Auntie Mame lived. I paid attention. I saw that Bette Davis had style. Jimmy Cagney had style. Seymour Glass had style. Annie Oakley, Robin Hood, Joan of Arc, Jesse James, Mildred Pierce and Huckleberry Finn had style. The whale in *Moby Dick* had style. All I needed was some style of my own.

First, my looks (talent, seeming harder to fake, could wait). For most of my life, I did battle with The Clothes Rules. To me, dressed is jeans, a shirt (T- for summer, sweat for winter) and shoes (sneakers for summer, boots for winter). Anything else is costume. As bad fortune would have it, where I grew up, everybody was into costume, my mother most of all and most notably every September. Forget what the government and the calendar tell you about January first, governments lie and calendars are made by governments. The new year does not start in January. The new year starts in September. Even little children know this. Nobody makes you wear new clothes in January.

There were all these rules: The Clothes Rules. Many of them were silly and some were what, for lack of a better word, we will call stupid. Take the matter of color. As a child, I was not allowed to wear lavender, because the Negroes wore lavender. I couldn't wear orange, because the Mexicans wore orange. I couldn't wear blue and green together, because the Jews wore blue and green together. I couldn't wear black, because the Catholics wore black. On the other hand, I could wear white only after Easter and before Labor Day. You figure it out. I never could. Was she a bigot, my mother? Yes and no. Mostly, like many in the postwar South, she was a woman of her time and place. Later, when her times changed, Mama changed, but not before learning a clothes-rule lesson herself, the hard way.

We lived in Houston, Texas. I went to Vanderbilt University, which is in Nashville, Tennessee (Mama told all her friends I went East to school, which, geographically speaking, I suppose I did). Neither of my parents, both of whom came of age during the Depression, had been able to go to college, and therefore were very proud to be able to send their only child, their daughter, Linda Jane, to college. Mama was determined I would have The Right Clothes to begin my great endeavor, which, to Mama, was not so much a search for knowledge as for a husband, although I was encouraged by her to get myself some education, so that if my husband died or left me in some less honorable manner, I would have, in the words of my time, *something to fall back on*. It was 1962.

Over the summer Mama worked hard at shopping. She dragged me from store to store, making me try on absolutely everything. She said just because one sock fit, it didn't mean the other would. Dresses were the worst. After she found one to her liking, I would have to stand still for hours (stop fidgeting, Linda Jane) while the alterations lady transferred ten thousand and twelve straight pins straight from her mouth to the soft parts of my body. At last I was ready for college, but now Mama was worried because, she said, what would happen to all those pretty clothes when she wasn't there to take care of them? *Lord knows Linda Jane won't.* Lord knows Linda Jane didn't. In fact, what Linda Jane did was to hide most of them in the bottom of her closet. You see, Mama's clothes rules weren't the only clothes rules. Nashville was a step ahead of Mama when it came to discrimination. A red blouse, Linda? Nobody wears colored blouses but poor white trash. Loafers with socks? How low-rent. A nylon slip? No silk? Don't you have any cashmere? Oh, *Ban*-Lon? Oh. Oh.

When I told Mama, three things happened. First she said what did they know in Nashville; any Tennessean with brains had long since moved to Texas. Like Davy Crockett. Next she sat down and cried with shame. My mama, who'd saved and worked so hard and tried so hard to give me the things she never had, cried because some eighteen-year-old twits a thousand miles away said she had no taste. The third thing Mama did was grow. Mama, you might say, outgrew her clothes, and the rules that went with them. She never looked at what people wore quite the same way after that. What I hate most about telling this story is the memory of being ashamed of my mother for buying me the "wrong" clothes. I owed that woman better.

Besides, my own search for some style has been marked by a singular lack of direction, with numerous side trips into the downright silly. My task, as I saw it, was not to dress well, but to find the costume that would make people tell each other I had style. Back then, dressing differently meant dressing weird. I was prepared. If everyone wore the same style, no one had any style. Yes, I remember thinking that. At ten, I took my cue from my heroes and for a couple of years wore nothing but cowboy (all right, cowgirl) shirts, the kind with fringe on them. At fourteen, I began wearing low-cut necklines until, at fifteen, I developed breasts and a keen sense of embarrassment about having done so. That summer I worked as a lifeguard—in a sweatshirt. At twenty-one, I bought my first bottle of French wine, opened my first savings account, and discovered plastic clothes. I was "mod." My earrings were bigger and uglier than anybody's. My skirts were short, primary-colored and responsible for the death of uncounted thousands of baby polyesters. My lipstick was pink and only a little darker than that particular shade of off-white they used to paint garden-apartment living rooms.

Then came the Movement. Style scooted over to make room for political commitment, which included, along with beads, flowers and bright colors, more fringe than Roy Rogers ever dreamed of. Being a hippie was hard work. Often I was worn out from the effort required to dress in a way that would defy the rules of established fashion, while conforming to the equally strict rules of revolutionary fashion. The Movement was followed by reality, which was followed by a job in television, which was when, after looking at all the polyester pantsuits with the lapels that could open envelopes, I recovered my determination to find, invent, develop or steal my own style, at least where clothes were concerned. As a result I began auditioning trademarks. The first was the scarf: I owned dozens of them, and each day I wore a different one tied around my neck. It was supposed to be my signature, a practice I gave up when a man I lusted after asked me if I was related to Dale Evans.

By the time I turned thirty, I started to run out of ideas and energy, and fell back on Katharine Hepburn. One dozen pairs of slacks—one design, twelve colors. One dozen blouses—one design, twelve colors. Two pairs of shoes—same design, same color. No frills would ensure no failure. Each morning I needed only to pick two colors that didn't clash. It was too much to ask. I clashed with myself at least twice a week. Finally I gave up: when it came to style, all I knew, all I'd ever known, was how to get dressed. The sneakers, the blue jeans, the T-shirts and sweatshirts—they returned from exile and remain in power still. I have no style, but I am comfortable. I am dressed.

Meanwhile, there was my writing, which was to me more worthy of my attention. (Mama said I became a writer just so I could dress badly. Once I told her there was an old Spanish proverb which said God helps the badly dressed. Mama was unimpressed. Later, somebody told me I'd made a mistake in translation. Apparently, what the old Spanish proverb says is that *nobody but* God helps the badly dressed.) And she was wrong about why I write. I'm a writer because I'm a reader. The thing is, my grandmother Dovye used to say, if you don't read, you can't write, and if you can't write you must work for a living. And, she usually added, you don't know how to do anything, Linda Jane.

Partly I'm a writer because of my grandmother Dovye, my Aunt Sister, my cousin Shirley Jean and yes, my mother. And Trinity, Texas. Not too long ago I went back to Trinity to dedicate the town library. It's Trinity's first library, but to me *Trinity* was a library, and although I did not live there, I grew up there. In the summer, the tar on the road from my grandmother Dovye's house to town was, like that in front of our house in Houston, often too hot to walk on barefoot, and if you had to put on shoes, well, you might as well stay home and read something. In winter, the children who lived in Trinity all year round were in school, and if there wasn't going to be anyone around to play with, you might as well stay home and read something. Fall and spring are vague in my mind. It's possible they didn't have those seasons in Trinity, or maybe they did but I was home reading something. I was always home reading something, especially at night, much to the dissatisfaction of my cousin Shirley Jean, who was ten years older than me, and perfect. Shirley Jean was often forced to share her bed with me and could not get over the shame of a perfect person being asked to sleep with a family mistake. She told everybody how I had dirty little feet, from which she surely would catch a dreadful disease and die before she got to get married or even go to the Cotton Bowl.

My cousin Shirley Jean lied.

She could not have known my feet were dirty, because the minute she got into bed she turned off the light. I forgave her that, even though it meant I could not read—probably nothing tires out a person more than being perfect—but what I could not forgive my cousin Shirley Jean for was that she came to bed with peanut-butter breath. I preferred sleeping with my Aunt Sister, who always brought a book to bed, and Sister's bed had two reading lights, one for her and one, I proudly assumed, for me. Sister read novels, and when she was done with them Sister let me read novels. They were unsuitable novels. When my mother was in Trinity, I got to lie in her bed and be read poetry by her. It wasn't like the poetry my daddy liked; it all rhymed. Even my grandmother Dovye, who had a good Methodist hold on right and wrong, gave in when I was around; she let me read comics and once, just once, she bought me a movie magazine. In my grandmother's house, nobody ever told me to read something because it was right for me. Anything I could read, I was allowed to read, which explains why, in one summer, I went through the first four books of the New Testament, *Forever Amber,* Walt Whitman's *Leaves of Grass,* eight issues of Archie comics and my cousin Shirley Jean's diary.

It does not explain why, so many years later, the citizens of Trinity, Texas, having finally built and stocked their first public library, asked me to dedicate it. I suspect the invitation had more to do with television than books. I didn't care. I went, and it was at my Aunt Sister's house, the night before the ceremony, that my cousin Shirley Jean sat me down and told me the truth after all these years, which was that my aunt, mother and grandmother had urged reading on me, not to broaden my horizons, not because they especially believed in reading, although they did, but because it was the only way they knew to shut me up. I was crushed, but stood up and did the right thing at the dedication. As part of my speech, I read aloud from my cousin Shirley Jean's high-school diary. How did I remember the words after so many years? I didn't. I made it all up, and was able to do so in a way guaranteed to embarrass her in front of Trinity only because I really had read all of her diaries years ago. As my grandmother Dovye always said, if you don't read, you can't write.

Books were always telling you how important style was, when it came to writing, which is how I came to write so much trash. Remember Ferlinghetti? It's his fault my poems made no sense (on purpose, too) for years, even if he did not, as e. e. cummings did, bear responsibility for my forsaking capital letters, commas and iambic pentameter in general. I blame Hemingway for the stories I wrote about brave, true fish who died but were, you understand, good and fine to think about later when the days were shorter. Because of Tom Wolfe, I switched to elaboration, determined to see how many unrelated, puce-scented, platinum-toned, tinselated, by God, perfectly droll, invent-a-babble adjectives I could stuff into one sentence or, better yet, the title. Tom Robbins and Ken Kesey taught me how unlikely it was that I'd write anything worth a damn unless I went crazy first. Sylvia Plath set even tougher rules.

Except for suicide, I tried their tricks, aped their styles and absorbed none of their art. My writing had no more style than my clothing. But at some point in my life, style and me, we made a truce. I promised to stop trying to get any. To hell with Bette and Sylvia, and Helen Gurley Brown. I would not dress up, I would dress. I would not decorate, I would furnish. I would not write, I would tell stories. The matter was settled, and remained settled until recently, when for no good reason people began to write about my style. I tried to explain. There was no style. There was only the relief of having quit the chase.

However, when I came across Alfred Hitchcock's definition of style, I got to laugh the only laugh that counts, which is the one you have on yourself. If I hadn't finally been too lazy to care about whether I had style, I wouldn't finally have understood what the man was trying to tell me. Style, wrote Alfred Hitchcock, is self-plagiarism.

That is a brave, true and cowgirl-fringed fish worth stealing.

Gladys could have told me that all along, I suspect. My mother's friend Gladys, with her ice-cream cones and wings, was a self-plagiarist of the first rank, a woman of style *and* courage. To the end. Two years ago Gladys died, the same way she made a U-turn: fearlessly, noisily and without warning.

The last time I'd seen her had been that August, when my eighteen-year-old son and I were in Bryan. She hadn't seen Josh since he was born. I wanted to show her how much better he looked with teeth. We had a fine visit and, walking us back to our car, Gladys pointed out the bump in her sidewalk where she'd tripped and broken her hip the year before. Gladys stopped to cuss the bump awhile. She was seventy-five, but she still knew how to talk to a bump. I asked her why on earth she didn't get the bump fixed. Gladys laughed. Fix the bump? *Let the bump win?* I swear, Linda Jane, the older you get, the more you remind me of your mother.

Those were her last words to me. My last words to her were "Oh, Gladys."

Mama would understand. How I miss both those good, strong women. What I wouldn't give if they were here now. Why, we'd be laughing and eating ice cream *thisverydamnminute*. And with such style.

DIAMONDS ON THE
SOLES OF HER SHOES

Well that's one way to lose these walking blues.

—*PAUL SIMON*

Alice Rose was the baby in my mother's family, and so in a way it didn't matter how old she got, because she still would be the baby and babies are always new, aren't they?

New and filled with possibility.

There are so many possibilities.

That's what my Aunt Alice Rose used to tell me.

I have a photograph of her. She's not a baby in this picture, not a real one anyway; she's a woman, no, make that a *girl*, because that is how she referred to herself in the stories she told me about her life before she married Uncle Buck and moved to the oil camp outside Beeville, Texas.

"When I was a girl . . ."

Most of her stories began that way. I loved her stories. My favorite and hers was the one about the photograph and how it had been made when she was seventeen years old and had run away from home, away from Trinity, Texas, run all the way to Galveston with the millionaire. Maybe he wasn't quite a millionaire, but he *was* from downtown Dallas and he was madly in love with Alice Rose, who was blonde and thin and, when the light hit her a certain way, looked a little bit like Carole Lombard, only younger. And this almost-millionaire from downtown Dallas meant to take her all the way to Paris, France, where they would be married just as soon as she could find the right wedding dress, a French wedding dress, genuine satin, with a train and a princess waist and a veil with so many seed pearls sewn on it anybody who saw her would swear she was a movie star or a debutante or something exotic, a Piscopalian, maybe. She wouldn't mind it if people took her for a Piscopalian; Piscopalians were different. Alice Rose was not one, but she knew, for example, that Piscopalians got real wine at communion. And Piscopalians had priests, like Catholics only better, because Piscopalians were still Protestants.

So there they were, Alice Rose and the millionaire from downtown Dallas, in Galveston, all set to take a boat, a big one with beds on it, to New York City, where they would stay in a hotel five or maybe forty stories tall and then they would get on an even bigger boat and sail to Paris, France. Alice Rose very much wanted to see Paris, France, and New York City, but most of all she wanted to see a hotel because all she'd ever seen so far was a tourist court—the one south of town outside the Trinity city-limit sign just past the Paper Moon on the road to the state prison farm. The Paper Moon was a honky-tonk, *the* honky-tonk, actually, and naturally she had never been inside the place. She was a nice girl, and nice girls didn't go to honky-tonks until after they were married and weren't nice girls anymore. Then they could go to the Paper Moon, but not too often, and only if they went with their husbands and didn't talk to other men or dance with other men or drink anything but Coca-Cola, or speak to girls who weren't married and weren't nice girls or they wouldn't be there. Married girls could even go to the tourist court with their husbands. Only, if you were a married girl, why, wondered Alice Rose, would you want to go to a tourist court unless of course you were at the Grand Canyon or someplace?

New York. Paris. Downtown Dallas.

Galveston.

It was all out there.

The world was waiting and Alice Rose was ready.

When my Aunt Alice Rose would get to this part of the story she would always stop and light a cigarette and then sigh.

"If only . . . if only," she'd say. If only her daddy hadn't found out where they'd gone, and come to Galveston and forced her to go back with him to Trinity before she got to stay in a hotel or see the inside of a honky-tonk or a boat big enough to have beds in it.

The only thing Alice Rose got was a chance to spend one perfect afternoon sitting on a log, by the sea, with the wind blowing her hair and the sun on her face, watching birds fly, but that afternoon changed everything, she said, because it was her first adventure, *only* her first, that's all, and the very perfection of that one afternoon proved what she'd always suspected: she was born for adventure. Even if her daddy had other notions, it was proof enough. Would I like to see the photograph of her, the photograph taken that very perfect afternoon on that very perfect beach?

Look at it.

Couldn't I feel the sun? Couldn't I hear the wind? Smell the sea? Couldn't I taste the possibilities? There were so many possibilities.

There were always so many possibilities.

She was nearly twice seventeen when she first showed me this photograph, which had been blown up, surrounded by a gold-plated frame and protected by glass, and was sitting on her bedside table next to her glasses, her alarm clock, her ashtray, her copy of *Reader's Digest*, her small package of Kleenex and her family-size bottle of aspirin. All of it was on the table on her side of the bed she shared with my Uncle Buck in the company-owned house they paid almost no rent for, because the company paid Uncle Buck to add and subtract and do whatever else was necessary to do in order to keep accurate account of what it cost the company to pump the oil and pay the salaries of the people who kept this small piece of the company running. They lived, all of them, with their families on this company-owned land, a dozen dusty miles outside Beeville, Texas. Beeville wasn't Dallas. It wasn't even Galveston.

She told me her story and showed me her photograph so often, and it was not until the summer I was eleven years old that I first began to notice certain things about the picture, such as the fact that the log, on which she was more perched than seated, was perfectly shaped, impossibly smooth and a little saddle-broken. This was the log that had just happened to wash up to precisely the right place on the beach, not too far from, nor too near to, what Aunt Alice Rose always called "the sea," but which map-makers and the rest of us generally called the Gulf of Mexico. I wasn't bothered by what name we were going to give this water, I was bothered by the troublesome notion that there was some-thing wrong with the water in the photograph, too. It looked— almost as if it weren't real water at all. It looked like a painting of real water, and if the water was fake, what about the log and the sand and the sun and the wind and the birds? What about the possibilities? I thought it over and decided I was wrong. Of course the water was real, because the picture was real, and if everything in the picture now seemed to me to be almost too perfect to be real, it was only more proof that Aunt Alice Rose's story was true: it was, after all, a picture of a time and a place when everything *was* perfect. My doubts vanished, but my ques-tions had given me an idea of a way I could impress my Aunt Alice Rose, whom I desired to impress, because she was the glam-orous one in our family and indeed the only one who, when she was young, had ever sought adventures or tasted possibilities or even so much as tried to run away.

I had recently finished six weeks at summer camp, where I had spent every Tuesday, Thursday and Saturday morning between the hours of nine and ten in a class in basic photography. Now I'd found a way to make use of what I had learned; Aunt Alice Rose would surely be, could not help but be, impressed by my incredible grasp of what I believed to be the carefully guarded secrets of illusion.

And so one afternoon in late August, when my Aunt Alice Rose, whom I still called Rosie back then because she didn't like people to think she was old enough to have a niece my age, and I were passing the time of day with some of her friends at the Beeville Country Club, to which she and my Uncle Buck almost belonged, I announced to one and all that I had discovered something about her cherished, if not sacred, picture.

It could, I said, be a trick photo.

It could be faked. The sea. The sky. The sand. The sun. It could all be done *in a studio*. That's what a camera could do, I said, smugly. A camera could make anyplace look like some other place. A camera could even make anybody look like somebody else. Proud and loud, I went on and on, but then I looked at my Aunt Alice Rose and she wasn't looking at me. She wasn't looking at anybody else, either. She was just looking. Hey, Rosie, come on. I didn't mean your picture is phony. No way. We all know, I said, and believed what I was saying, that your picture is a classic record of one perfect moment. The kind of moment most people never get.

Of course she'd run away. Of course there had been a millionaire and a boat to New York City which she would have taken if her father, my grandfather, hadn't snatched her from—from who knows what? Who knows what her life might have been like? It couldn't possibly be a lie, her story.

All I'd meant to do was to show off for her in front of her friends. My Aunt Alice Rose liked me to show off. She liked it that I could swim faster than most boys and do a jackknife off the high board and sing the words to songs from back before I was born, when she was a girl and George Gershwin was still alive, still writing the s'wonderful songs she loved so. They were the best songs, she said. She liked it that I read more than she did, as long as I didn't fall asleep reading at night and waste electricity, which wasn't free and money didn't grow on trees, but, she said, I couldn't be expected to know about electricity and how much a watt costs, because I lived in Houston, which was nearly as expensive as downtown Dallas, and if they built that freeway they were talking about, Lord knows what it would cost to live there, but then Lord knows why anybody would want to live in Houston or even downtown Dallas, these days. It just went to show you. There I was in that big city in a house where I had my own bedroom and a mother and father who spoiled me rotten, just throwing their money away on pony rides and summer camp and movies and books and drawing paper and crayons, all for me, not to mention (she always mentioned) the television set my father bought my mother or the fact that my mother, my father and I ate dinner out every single Sunday at Weldon's cafeteria, which everybody knew served overpriced ham.

No wonder I was a brat, said my Aunt Alice Rose.

My Aunt Alice Rose had no children to raise and so she knew better than anyone else how to raise them. A long time ago before I was born, Alice Rose and Buck had had a baby of their own. Her name was Carol. She'd died when she was two days old, and everybody had sworn it would be a miracle if Alice Rose lived herself, because she was so torn up inside from the baby coming out sideways and early. The doctor said he could have done more but when Alice Rose began to turn blue and then white and then a color of green he'd never seen anybody turn before, and stayed that color for close to ten minutes, there was nothing to do but what he had done. The doctor told Alice Rose she ought to be damn grateful he'd been there at all and wasn't that worth more to her than all those female plumbing things he'd removed, just to make sure (he'd made real sure).

They never adopted a baby. Sometimes my Aunt Alice Rose would talk to me about Carol and tell me how old Carol would have been now, and what kind of dresses she would have liked and where she might have wanted to go to college and what a good cheerleader she would have made, and every year on Carol's birthday Aunt Alice Rose would drink most of a bottle of vodka and sit in her chair and look across the room at Uncle Buck and say nothing. Uncle Buck never talked about Carol to me or to anybody else in the family, but he cried easier than any man I've ever known. I loved them both, although they were not soft, nor easy to love, but they were kinder to me than they were to each other. As the years passed and they were more and more un-happy, it got harder for them to be kind to anybody at all, but with me, they tried. They usually tried.

I liked going to stay with them in the summer when I was little. I knew Alice Rose liked it, too, and I knew that while I was there she could pretend, sort of, that I was her little girl and she could make up stories to herself about what a better little girl I would be if I were hers and not her sister Hallie's. That's why I never minded showing off for her. Also, I liked showing off.

Until that day at the country club. Once I began babbling about her photograph and camera tricks and studios, I couldn't seem to stop, even after I saw my Aunt Alice Rose's face. I finished by assuring her that nobody doubted her photograph (or her story) for a single moment; I was merely trying to say it would be possible—it would be *possible*—for somebody who'd never done what she did, never gone to Galveston when she was seventeen or had a millionaire who loved her and wanted to take her places and show her things—it would be possible for somebody to fake such a picture. Without ever once leaving Trinity, Texas.

JUNE 1987

My Aunt Alice Rose died today. She was seventy-five years old and whatever organs she had left had all seemed to come to the same conclusion at once: it was quitting time. My cousin Billy was there; he'd gone to Beeville to see about getting her to go someplace where there were more and probably, he thought, better doctors, but when he brought up the subject she said if you think I'm a bitch in Beeville you wait and see what a bitch I can be in Houston, and then she died. Tonight I looked until I found that picture, her photograph, which she had taken out of its frame and given to me so many years ago on the night of the day I showed off what I knew, or thought I knew. At the time, I did not understand what I had done or why she no longer wanted something she had loved so much and so long. Two days after my revelations at the country club, I went home to Houston so that my mother and I would have time to shop for new clothes for me before school started the next week. I did not see my aunt until Christmas, when the whole family got together as usual, and as usual we made enough noise that nobody actually had to sit down and talk to anybody else. Alice Rose made more noise than the others, but I thought nothing of that: she always had. The next summer, I went to camp and then to Pennsylvania to visit my mother's other sister. I'd never been to Pennsylvania. I'd never seen houses that were attached to one another. My mother said the experience would be good for me, and I did not argue, nor did I argue the following summer when my mother said I should stay in Houston for once.

I never went back to Beeville again, except when I positively had to go for one family thing or another. Aunt Alice Rose and I stopped being close, but we never stopped loving one another, I know that. I kept the photograph, but I kept it packed away all these years until now, and as I sit here looking at it, I, too, can feel the wind and the sun and the sand and hear the birds and smell the sea. I, too, can almost taste the possibilities.

Almost.

WE RESERVE THE RIGHT TO REFUSE SERVICE TO YOU

When we came into the canyon I was sitting in the Vista Dome of the California Zephyr, thinking about Natalie Wood—Natalie in *West Side Story,* so beautiful it didn't matter that she was a mediocre actress, maybe even a silly person—she was Natalie Wood, whose popularity coincided with my adolescence, informing it, her particular "look" looming large enough to remind me constantly that there was no justice. Luckily, I was practically a college freshman, a traveler, and above childish envies. The train was itchy hot. We'd been coming into or going out of one canyon or another for a long time now, and while they were very interesting (they had two sides and were made of rock), it did not take me long to look at a canyon. Then I saw the green river.

People warned me about Colorado. My father said it was tall. Mama had said it was cold; I might need a sweater, she'd said, even though it was June, and she'd spent three days asking people what kind of sweater was right for June but of course nobody in Houston knew. Other people had spoken of other surprises they said were waiting for me in Colorado: bears and Colorado drivers. A more well-traveled cousin had told me to pay no attention to living Christmas trees, they were vulgar, and everybody had warned me about the air there; they said you couldn't see it. But nobody had said anything about green rivers. Texas rivers ran to brown, when they ran, which wasn't as often as you'd expect—except when it was too much all at once (always more often than you'd expect). I didn't know in the summer of 1962 how reckless magic could be. All I knew was, where rivers ran green, magic must be.

Magic was what I wanted. I'd been graduated from high school for nearly a week and was on my way to be the Junior Hostess at the Hotel El Dorado, "The Spa in the Heart of the Rockies," my first summer job away from home, from Texas, away from my parents and my numbingly steady boyfriend. For someone who was ready to be taken seriously, my new job had its flaws. *Junior* Hostess? That sounded like Child Bride, or a very small cupcake. I would ask Frank to change my job title. Frank King ran the Hotel El Dorado and he was my pal. Well, really, he was my father's friend, they did some business together, but when he and his wife came to visit us, Frank always kidded around with me and was much less nerdy than most of my parents' friends, even though he was as old as they were, which was very old indeed; they were all over fifty. I remember my father saying this was a new job for Frank, and wasn't it amazing the way people in the hotel business were always moving around, not like the insurance business, no ma'am.

When he asked my father if I would like a job for the summer, my parents talked it over and decided I couldn't get in too much trouble (translation: get laid) as long as Frank and his lovely wife Helen were there to keep an eye on me. I looked forward to working with Frank; it wouldn't be like having a real boss. It wouldn't be like a real job, like work or anything; me in my new black Jantzen, reading romance novels by the pool, waving to my small charges at their sweet play. What was so difficult about that?

. Although I'd never seen a photograph of it, I knew the Hotel El Dorado was a big and famous resort, although I'd never seen a resort. Hadn't Frank King told me the President stayed there? It must be when he isn't at Hyannisport. The Hotel El Dorado was probably like the new all-green-and-gold Shamrock Hotel in Houston, only on a mountain. The Shamrock had the fanciest bathrooms; there were mirrors with gold speckles all over the silver, and you couldn't see yourself very well but it was worth it.

The train slowed. Outside the dome, more rock and narrow sky, and still, the green river. Good. I put down the book I'd been not really reading; it was called *Catch-22*, and I didn't quite get it—what *was* this fellow Yossarian's problem? And what kind of name was "Yossarian"? Armenian? I'd never met an Armenian; were they *all* nuts? I'd been lost in the first chapter when the green river first caught my attention. Checking my watch, I stood up, tugged my girdle down, checked my stocking supporters and straightened my dress, a dark blue Lanz with white eyelet trim and empire waist, and put on my high-heeled pumps, pointy-toed, painful and dyed to match, all very Texas Deb, which I wasn't, but Mama admired the look. Now we were in a tunnel. I sat back down and took out my compact, waiting for the light to come back, not that I needed to; I knew what the mirror would show: brown hair in a bubble haircut, round face, too much eyebrow, too many freckles, not enough neck. *Ordinary*. Using a lip brush, I applied two firm coats of Revlon's Persian Melon matte finish to my mouth, which I liked, but only when I didn't smile. I powdered the freckles and curled some eyelashes, suddenly squinting as the train came out the other side of a mountain. The canyon walls receded, and land spread out and sunlight hit the green river, exploding it into glittering gold and silver shards, a million broken mirrors flashing back at me from every direction at once.

At the station, I looked for Frank but he wasn't there. Nobody was there to meet me; in fact, nobody was there at all. This was not beginning well. I sat outside the station on a wooden bench, alone, a child waiting to be fetched. After a while, I decided to walk. The resort couldn't be far. I was a grown-up. I didn't need any help. Someone could bring my luggage later.

Ironwood Springs, I saw, was in a valley surrounded by mountains, some red, others black. The red ones had a sparse cover of gray-green brush, sage probably, and on the black mountains were great patches of green, spruce and fir and what looked like a scattering of ponderosa. In the distance, I could see meadows, cottonwoods and tall white clouds drifting in blue. I could see cattle. By the time I'd walked up the street that led from the train station to town, my feet hurt. Reaching down, I picked gum off the bottom of one blue pump, but when I stood back up, it made the stocking on that leg sag at the knee. To fix it, I would have to pull the stocking up and re-snap it to the supporter and that would mean lifting my skirt above my, oh, hell, let it sag, girl. Downtown Ironwood Springs was three blocks long; it ended at the Colorado River and there, across the bridge, between the river and a spruce-dotted mountain, was the Hotel El Dorado.

Was I supposed to laugh or what? In the foreground there was this ridiculous stone affair with cupolas on top. I decided that this was the mineral spa Frank had told me about, mainly because it was next to a swimming pool that must have covered more than an acre. The hotel itself was partway up a slope, and huge, way out of scale to anything else in town. The building, all five towered-and-belfried stories of it, had been constructed around three sides of a courtyard, and I'd have bet money the man who designed it was personally responsible for introducing the sixteenth-century Italian look into the Rockies. Whatever else you might say, in its own way the Hotel El Dorado, like Mount Selena, its partner and consort at the opposite end of the valley, had set itself above the rest.

As I got closer, I noticed something else. The Hotel El Dorado was real old. Entering through a great porte cochere for carriages, I realized the porte cochere wasn't for show, wasn't a replica of sixteenth-century Italy, as I'd thought—it was a modern convenience of nineteenth-century America—*when it had been built*. A large hall ran the length of the building. To my right was a door with a sign on it. THE SUNDRIES SHOPPE. I could not imagine. Ahead was the lobby; pure Victorian to start, it had been—what?—bombed? Almost everything in the room—ceiling, walls, rugs, sofas—was brown, layers on layers of unrelieved, light-absorbing, shit-brown. Furniture, what there was of it, was predominantly fake wood covered with fake leather. There were lamps from the forties, shades from the fifties and the sixties, and (my final clue that this was not the Shamrock) there was the wallpaper behind the reception desk: it was contact paper, large daisies, electric blue.

A Negro who looked to be about my age was arguing with the woman behind the desk, who was making a great show of going through her files. He looked extremely agitated.

"I'm one of the actors. You *have* to have a room for me. *Ma'am*."

The woman looked as if she had to have no such thing. Seeing me, she ignored him and came out from behind the desk, smiling.

"Are you Linda Jane?"

"No, I'm Linda. No Jane." *A baby name, Linda Jane.*

"That's good, because I am."

"Linda?"

"No, Jane."

Jane wasn't much older than me and was tall and blonde, and beautiful in the way perfect health is, but was dressed very plainly; she wore a navy-blue cotton jumper hemmed three inches below her knee, over a white blouse with long sleeves that came down past her wrists to cover part of her hands. Her hair, cut short and held back on the right side of her forehead by a bobby pin, was neither teased nor curled. She wore no makeup, no jewelry, and smiled the whole time she talked. The whole time.

"You're Linda Jane Smith, the Junior Hostess? You're late." She had a smile like a dead angel.

"How can I be late, I just got here. Where's Frank?"

"Who's Frank?"

"Frank King."

"*Mr.* King? The manager? He's managing the hotel. And don't call him Frank. Why are you late?"

"Uh, nobody met me. I had to walk." I slipped one foot out of its pretty pump and rubbed a blistered heel. Jane was unimpressed.

"Met you? That's funny. Grab your bag and follow me. Do you wear those shoes all the time? How do you get your toes inside the points—braid them? You won't need shoes like that here. Come on, what are you waiting for?"

"My bag—bags. Plural. I have several. I left them at the station. Shouldn't we send someone?"

"Who?" She seemed genuinely bewildered.

"Hey, what about me, lady? What about my room?" Jane stopped and turned to the guy who was still standing at the desk. She stared at him, as if considering something, then shook her head slightly, and started down the hall.

"They just don't understand," said Jane, as though I did.

We went up a pair of broad double stairs that met at a landing above. The hall one flight up was almost as wide and tall as the one below, but then we turned right, into a small, uncarpeted alcove, and stopped in front of a fire door. Jane had to use both hands to get it unstuck. I followed her onto a catwalk over the alley behind the kitchen, in the rear of the hotel. Below, I could see somebody leaning on a mop, wiping sweat from his forehead with a bandana. Jane looked where I did.

"You know how Mexicans are," she said, but I did not. I knew how Negroes were. There weren't so many Mexicans near where we lived, which was in East Texas and more like the South than the West. I'd been raised by and around Negroes and loved Willie Pearl as much as I loved other members of my family, who, in the tradition of Southern families, were never all related to me. I thought Negroes were very fine people, the ones I knew. When I thought about them at all.

We came to a two-story gray-brick bunker I assumed to be the garage, and in this I was correct; that is, it had been the garage back when cars were horses. Now both floors were used, as Jane put it, "to house *you* summer help."

When she showed me my room, it was so dirty I leaned against the wall in shock, and stuck there. The sucking noise when I pulled away woke up a roach, who crawled from under the chest of drawers, up the iron bedstead and into the rolled mattress, familiarly.

"You're down for dinner service. You have seventeen to feed ten minutes from now. That's the first shift, the droolers. Bedtime and potty list are in the office. The animals—that's the second shift, you know, the older kids—make them stop asking for extra water. Don't be fooled by the mountains; this is the desert and God's too generous with His blessings as it is. Melodrama on the patio at eight, followed by group sing, but that could change, the Colonel's been drinking. Anyway get yourself downstairs in"— she looked at her watch—"under ten minutes."

It was 4:30 in the afternoon.

I stood in the middle of the room, a huddle of one, afraid to touch anything, wanting to hold my nose. My acquaintance with mildew and roaches up to now had been brief and confined mostly to the rotting toolsheds and abandoned shacks of the migratory workers who picked cotton every September near where my grandmother lived. I thought about my resort wardrobe waiting at the station. Mama hadn't been sure about what people wore at resorts, so we'd gone first to the "Cruise Clothes" section at Neiman-Marcus, then to the "Today's Camper" department at Foley Brothers, after which Mama had said she had a grasp of the basic situation and proceeded to shop accordingly. I thought about spaghetti-strapped gingham sundresses, a slinky black sheath, a beaded sweater for evening wear. I thought about white tennis skirts with scalloped hems and white socks that had bunny balls on their heels. White nylon babydoll pajamas. A white dotted-swiss beach cover-up. A white organdy shirtwaist dress. I thought about white.

Should I laugh? Or should I get myself downstairs in under ten minutes and see if the little redheaded fat girl with the pimples could tell me what planet this was?

They'd been right about one thing: you really couldn't see the air here. You couldn't smell it, either. This took getting used to. The job of Junior Hostess turned out to be simple enough: take care of the children of guests. Keep them fed, occupied, happy, safe—and far away from their parents. Simple never was the same as easy; I worked from six in the morning when I got up until ten or so every night, when the last child had been claimed or put to bed by me. I was a slave baby-sitter. *Like a mother.* I was also, like the hotel itself, a victim of history, and of entropy.

Faded beauties tell the saddest stories; my Aunt Alice Rose

from Beeville taught me that, and the Hotel El Dorado confirmed it. I learned that in her youth, the hotel had been both gaudy and popular with Colorado's silver millionaires. They'd come to her debut in June of 1893 in private railroad cars, bringing their new best friends, the European aristocracy, mostly second sons, to bathe in the mineral waters. They'd played polo on the recently landscaped grounds and drunk champagne in the courtyard under the colored lights of the Florentine fountain, with its spray that went up 185 feet to the roof of the hotel. They'd danced under the great crystal chandeliers of the west ballroom. Two months after the hotel opened, the United States had dropped silver as the standard of money; before long the rich had become other people, and they'd gone somewhere else.

The Hotel El Dorado had changed hands and kept on changing hands (during the second World War, she'd been a navy hospital) and the hands had not always been washed; they'd soiled her. Every time she'd been passed from one owner to another she'd lost something of herself. The Spa—pool, bathhouse and all— no longer belonged to the hotel; there was a small, standard suburban-issue pool where the Florentine fountain used to be. The fountain, the landscaped grounds, the ballroom, the chandeliers—gone: torn down, sold off, thrown out. Only one year before, the hotel had been rented to the city to use as a makeshift junior high school after the real one had been condemned. But now there were new owners, with a new plan: they meant to convert the establishment into what was described in their brochure as a "real American family experience." In other words, they decided to turn the Hotel El Dorado into a motel.

The Hotel El Dorado Family Vacation Package! Room and three meals a day, entertainment, sports—trained sports instructors, professional baby-sitting staff—no extra charge! All-inclusive! One week minimum, half on deposit, cash and third-party checks accepted.

I was the professional baby-sitting staff. I was also the trained sports instructors. I taught people, mostly homicidal children who didn't want to learn, to swim. In 1893, the Hotel El Dorado had made a big thing about its employees, "servants" they called them back then, more honestly. They'd been imported for the summer, but could not walk on the grounds nor through the hotel corridors nor speak to guests except when absolutely necessary. Nothing had changed, except that the part of yesterday's servants was played by today's college students.

Oh, there was one change: in 1893, residents of Ironwood Springs had not been employed by the hotel, nor allowed inside it, either. In 1962, *all* the permanent employees lived in Ironwood Springs, and most were Mormons. This was also part of the new owners' plan. Mormons didn't drink, smoke or cheat, they thought, and Mormons smiled at everybody (Jane was, need I say it, a Mormon). They were clean, dependable and they worked cheap—although not as cheap as college students. Mormons were the night managers, desk clerks, bellhops and waiters; they earned a living, not a good one, but some made tips. College students were busboys, pool help, actors and the Junior Hostess. When they hired us, they made us swear not to tell anybody what we made, especially each other. At first, all we knew for sure was that minimum wage did not enter into it, not even in conversation—not until much later, by which time so many things, including race, religion, age, sex and the word "strike," had entered into conversation below stairs at the Hotel El Dorado. In June, there were only the new owners, the Mormons and the Scuz, as the college students called themselves.

And Frank King.

My father's friend. The man had been so sweet in Houston, treating me like an equal, making me think I was a grown-up, and like a child, I'd believed him. Working for him, nothing was as I'd imagined. He was Mr. King, the manager, my boss. He lived on the fifth floor of the hotel in an apartment with his lovely wife, the boring Helen. I saw his sandy hair and square-cut self maybe once or twice a day. He was not mean to me, but he was distant. He treated me like an *employee*, and at the Hotel El Dorado that didn't amount to much.

The ones I envied were the actors. There were five actors, plus the Colonel and his wife, Mrs. Colonel. The Colonel ran the small summer-stock theater; this was something new and everything about it was a little off, including the Colonel himself, who wore white suits, a planter's hat and long black mustaches, and carried an ivory-handled cane. Mrs. Colonel looked like Mrs. Santa Claus. They'd built a small stage in the courtyard and every night at eight, a company of seven performed either *The Melodrama* or the second (and far more appropriate) of their repertory of two, *The Farce.*

We got to know the three guys: Ron from Michigan, Elliot from Oregon and Tommy from Chicago. Tommy was the Negro I'd seen at the desk my first day; he was quick and talented and was studying drama at Northwestern (he usually had to play Othello or a villain, he said). They'd finally given Tommy his room that day.

"This isn't a hotel to refuse service to anyone. It's just that we don't see many people of color around here, in the West, I mean."

Tommy said it was okay, he didn't mind their backward attitude as long as he didn't have to sleep with the kitchen help; Mexicans stank, Tommy said. There was Marsha, the leading lady, who was very very dainty and very, very strong. Marsha's father was a farmer. Marsha had played a geisha in the Iowa State production of *The Teahouse of the August Moon.* She said she'd loved the clothes but hated having to make herself slanty-eyed; it was so unattractive. And there was Betsy Mulhenny, from Baltimore, who had pale white skin and lots of red hair. Betsy was cute and bouncy. Betsy also bubbled. On stage Betsy bounced and bubbled at the same time, particularly during *The Farce,* when all she wore for most of the play was a horse blanket and a smile. Many of the boys among the Scuz wanted to know Betsy better. They said she was Irish, and winked as if I knew what *that* meant, but Betsy wasn't having any of their foolishness; every night after work she went to her room, never once joining the rest of us. She said she needed time to think. Betsy thought a lot.

The actors only had to work a couple of hours a night, counting the group sing before the play, which they led, plus a few hours in the day, rehearsing. As for my own job, about three weeks into June it suddenly hit me that this was what working was like, and that it was very different from being a volunteer Candy Striper at Texas Children's Hospital, my only previous experience with a summer job. You actually had to show up. You had to stay. You had to smile. You had to do what they told you. You had to do things you didn't want to do, when you didn't want to do them. You had to take shit from idiots sometimes. You had to say yes. You had to finish. And you had to come back and do it all over again the next day.

But I was having a wonderful time anyway. There was this busboy.

His name was Alexander Hardwick and he was a communist. Well, almost. He was from Boston and he went to a Quaker college, read books with titles like *Zen Flesh, Zen Bones* and if he hadn't needed the money for college he would have been in Mississippi that summer with the Freedom Riders, he said. His grandmother had already been arrested twice in Jackson; the family was quite proud of her. Alec was a big fan of President Kennedy, and unions. Frank King didn't like Alec one bit. They fought over money from the start. Alec said he'd been promised more, a waiter's job, tips; he wouldn't have anything left for school. Frank King said Alec should be grateful to spend a summer in the Rockies, skinny as he was. Alec called him a Fascist.

Alec had the room just below mine in the stables. We met over an intentionally dropped book, mine, and got to know one another after work, talking. Alec said I was ignorant politically and culturally, but that wasn't true; I was extremely bright, a progressive thinker, an *educated* woman of the world, a constant reader and fan of J. D. Salinger.

"Yeah?" said Alec. "You probably only read *The Catcher in the Rye*."

"Not true. I read *Nine Stories*, too. I didn't like it as much."

" 'A Perfect Day for Bananafish' is the most perfect short story ever written."

"Alec, it's about suicide."

"No, Linda, it's about the price of what you're willing to live without."

Now the clear thin air you couldn't see made my blood bounce. Days seemed fresher, newer, and time with Alec, friend and thorn, increasingly important. Alec pushed, and in the pushing back, automatic when I was uncertain, I began to get better at defending my opinions, and to change some of them. I was a Democrat, or would have been, if old enough to vote. I'd voted for Kennedy in my high-school civics class mock election (the only one to do so; the oil depletion allowance did not make for good Democrats in Texas). I'd read *The Making of the President;* I knew how politics was. What the stakes were. We all did—we were the "bomb" generation, the ones who, when little, got beneath our desks and covered our heads to protect ourselves from the atom bomb every Friday at noon when the sirens practiced. Stories about nuclear holocaust were part of the fabric of our lives; *On the Beach* had affected me far more than *On the Road.* My country was locked in cold, mortal combat with the Russians. In February, we'd listened over the PA system at my high school to John Glenn blast into orbit, but none of us could forget the Russians had done it first, again, and now they'd built this wall in Berlin, as if Cuba weren't enough, with its Bay of Pigs—what an embarrassment to freedom that had been. The President had said we were going to the moon, could you believe it? Nobody did; the man had his hands too full with the communists to worry about the moon, not to mention his problems with the South. There were some, back in Texas, who said Kennedy himself was a communist, but what most of them meant was "nigger-lover." I came from, and was raised around, people who believed in equality, and in equal but separate education. According to my father, Martin Luther King, Jr., was a good man, but had made his point and ought to stop now before he made real trouble. To tell the truth, I'd never thought about these things much. I'd cried over *To Kill a Mockingbird;* I considered myself a just person. "What's fair is fair," I said to Alec.

"Read James Baldwin, not Harper Lee," said Alec.

"Do you know, Alec, that there's just as much prejudice in the North?"

"Do you know, Linda, that the city of New Orleans is right this very minute offering a one-way bus ticket to any Negro who wants to move north?"

"These things take time," I said.

Alec didn't fight on this; he laughed at me as though I were stupid, and his laughter confused me more than his anger would have. Was I missing something?

We read to one another on our afternoons off, sitting cross-legged in high, flowered fields. We waded in the green river. One night, Alec and I crawled over the fence surrounding the big mineral pool that no longer belonged to the Hotel El Dorado. The pool was closed after dark. There was no moon on this night. Steam rose from the water like fog, an invitation to go swimming without our clothes. In the pool we moved through the mist, talking our separate stories, offering our pasts, our preferences. I'd hoped Mickey Mantle would break the Babe's home-run record; he'd rooted for Roger Maris. Mantle, Alec said, was from Oklahoma, a backward, rednecked place. We talked about our particular ideas of justice (I still couldn't imagine anybody wanting to spend the summer in Mississippi, no matter how right the cause, but then I'd been to Mississippi), our bodies drifting together almost but not quite accidentally touching, then moving away. Afterward, we lay on the grassy slope by the pool, facing one another, dressed. Alec reached out and ran his fingertips gently along the curve of my side from shoulder to thigh.

"This," he said, "is the prettiest part of a woman."

These are the days of wine and roses, I told myself. For a girl used to Texas boys, who hadn't noticed anything about me but my tits since the summer I'd grown them three years earlier, this was heady stuff. Maybe Alec and I could join the peace corps as a couple. Maybe they could send us to a deserving Caribbean island, that would be nice. Meanwhile, sex with Alec was always a possibility but not a probability; after my numbingly dull steady boyfriend and I had stumbled our way into bed and it had turned out to be not much to speak of, I'd decided to give up sex. For now.

Talking was the sport of the Scuz (with whom I had formed a natural alliance; even though I wouldn't begin college until September, I certainly was not a townie, nor a Mormon). We went to the movies only once that summer, to see *Lawrence of Arabia;*

we said it was terrible the way the limeys treated the wogs. None of us had a car. We didn't watch television, even though that summer somebody had put up something called a satellite, whatever that was, to bring TV from one side of the Atlantic to the other; we didn't care. Newton Minow had said (and we agreed) that TV was a "vast wasteland." You could drink something called 3.2 beer in Colorado when you were only eighteen. I was only seventeen. When we had beer, we drank and talked. When we didn't have beer, we talked. I began to learn that summer about the different lives of people who'd grown up in houses that were attached to one another, or how it felt to live on a farm, how it felt to wear heavy coats every day of winter and take subways to school, what it was like to live next door to Negroes, how it felt to be one. Once a group of seven of us managed a day off together and went hiking. At some point we came to the town dump, and in the dump was an old school bus. We climbed inside it and, being city kids, most of us, decided to have our picnic on the bus. Having brought with us some food that was neither new nor quite yet spoiled, although stolen from the hotel kitchen, and some 3.2 Coors we'd paid for, we spread out as best we could. I got a cheese sandwich and an orange and began working my way down the aisle. Half of the seats were broken or missing. Most of the rest were taken.

"Come sit by me," said Alec. I loved his bony face and the straight, yellow hair that was fine and fell into his eyes. He had pale, kind eyes. Teacher eyes. Martyr eyes.

"No, I think I'll sit there," I said, pointing.

"In the back? Why?"

Beyond Alec's shoulder in the driver's cracked mirror, I could see a clear if partial reflection of our friends, and Alec and me, picnicking on a dead bus. I turned, made my way to where I was going and sat down. I'd never in my life sat in that particular place and I wanted to know if anything looked different from the back of the bus. It did. Everything looked different from the back of the bus.

Shortly before I'd come to Colorado, my mother and I had had a fight, and in the middle of it she'd yelled at me, "You were a good Christian girl until you took up with those Greeks. I blame them for everything that's wrong with you."

Since we didn't know any Greeks, certainly none lived in our neighborhood, I asked my mother which Greeks she meant.

"You know—Plato, Aristotle, Sophocles. Those Greeks."

In a way, the Greeks were to blame for the trouble Alec started. Alec read too much, more than I did, and had these odd notions of fair play that had come from books and the people who wrote them, not all of whom were Greeks; some of them had names like Jean-Paul Sartre, Albert Camus, Rachel Carson and Karl Marx. And some of his heroes were the people he read *about,* many of whom had plain American names, like Joe Hill.

Late in July, the Scuz finally began to talk to one another about that which we weren't supposed to speak—our salaries. I don't know why it took us so long. Everybody had been complaining since the first day; nobody was getting quite what they'd been promised. Under pressure, I confessed I was making $85 a month. It wasn't much, I knew, and I hadn't wanted to admit I'd accepted a job so low-paying. This caused an uproar. It seemed I was the highest paid person in the room. The busboys said they were being paid $65 a month plus tips, only there were no tips; the waiter didn't share and who tips a busboy?

We had to find out what the actors were getting. Like me, they weren't true Scuz, since they were actors and therefore strange, weird even, but they *were* college students and we'd gotten to know and like most of them. There was no question they had the glamour jobs and the glamour pay. We just wanted to know exactly how much more than us they were making. It had to be a princely sum; look at all the money the hotel was saving on our salaries. The actors were the last to crack, but one night Tommy got drunk enough to tell us, and that's really when the whole business about the strike started: the actors were being paid nothing at all. In fact, they had to pay the Colonel for the experience of performing six shows a week, not to mention the nightly sing-along, plus pay the hotel a little something extra for their room and board, although they were treated no better and had no more privileges than the rest of us. It was not what we had expected. No wonder everyone had been sworn to secrecy. What the Hotel

El Dorado had going was a sweet little scam. What the Hotel El Dorado had going was us. Coming, too.

Alec called for a meeting the next night after work. We met in the damp, moldy basement where the Scuz ate. Alec stood on the table, not entirely necessary, as only twelve people showed up. He gave a speech, reminding us that in April the six biggest steel companies had gotten together to raise the price of steel, and that the next day a furious President Kennedy had given a five-million-dollar defense contract to a small steel company that had *not* raised its prices.

"And you know what happened the day after that?" Alec was really getting worked up. I loved it. "The Big Six backed down! That's what happened!"

Alec said we must organize for the benefit of the worker, which I didn't immediately understand meant us; I mean, I knew I worked but didn't know I was the worker, and I didn't quite get the connection to steel, but it was a fine speech with plenty of fine words like "oppression" and "downtrodden." When he was done, Alec suggested we close by joining hands and singing "Union Maid." Unfortunately, nobody else knew the words so we joined hands while Alec sang: *"Oh, you can't scare me/ I'm stickin' with the union."* The rest of us, unsure what to do, bowed our heads as if in church.

Walking back to the "dorm" after the meeting, Alec was angry. He said we didn't understand about these things, and that was the truth; we didn't. Most of us were children of middle-class parents who did not belong to unions themselves and probably didn't like them very much. Some might even have come from families who were Republicans. I didn't. Both my parents were Democrats (Mama said voting for General Eisenhower hadn't counted), but when you looked in your history book under "organized labor," you did not see the word "Texas" mentioned very often. Like so many other things I knew nothing about, I knew nothing about unions, except they were probably communist, which, of course, was bad; everybody knew that, and in spite of what Frank said, Alec was no communist. I knew that, too. I suggested to Alec we simply go to Frank King and ask for more money. I was sure Frank didn't understand how many of the kids needed this money, were counting on it for college.

"Are *you* going to explain this to him, Linda?" Alec knew my father was paying for my college. Also, I'd made the mistake of telling Alec $85 a month was the most money I'd ever earned. I did not tell him it was the only money I'd ever earned. Alec didn't have to know everything.

"Well, uh . . . sure. Why not? Frank likes me." Even if he hadn't met my train, even if he did ask me to call him "Mr. King" when other people were around, which during the summer was every time I saw him, he was still my father's friend, and mine. Of course he was.

Alec raised one eyebrow, the way he could. "You do that."

In bed that night staring at the mountain two feet outside my window, I thought about unions. They had good songs, I decided.

My opportunity came two days later. Frank called me into his office to tell me the Hotel El Dorado was about to entertain its first family convention. A group of one hundred Mormons from Salt Lake City was coming down to spend the second week of August, bringing their families (which meant, dammit, bringing their children). I knew by now that Mormons had many, many children, and I didn't care what you told me about how pious and good Mormons were—none of that, I'd learned, extended to their children, who were just as rotten as anybody else's kids. Before Colorado, I'd had no truck with Mormons and no one taught Comparative Religion at Mirabeau Beauregard Lamar Senior High School, nor at St. Luke's United Methodist Church. I couldn't begin to tell Frank how happy I was to hear about the hundred Mormons coming to see us.

Frank actually was happy; it meant more money. The hotel, despite all the changes, still wasn't doing well. But obviously the convention was going to mean even more work for everybody.

"There's something I'd like to talk to you about, Frank."

He looked around to see if anybody was close enough to hear me call him Frank, and when he saw there wasn't, shut the door to make sure.

"I talked to your mother yesterday, Linda. She called to find out if you were having a good time and were you taking care of your nice clothes? I told her you were having a ball. You are having a ball, aren't you, Linda?"

"A ball, Frank, a real ball. But Frank, some of the other kids and well, me too, were wondering—and I said I bet you didn't know how bad it was for them, the money, I mean, and when you found out—"

"I don't want to hear about money from you. You stay out of this."

"But it's not right. It's not *fair*."

"I said stay out of it."

"Now wait a minute—"

"He's a communist, that little creep. I don't know why I hired him, he wasn't supposed to—are you sleeping with him? If you are and your mother finds out—we wouldn't want that to happen . . ."

"I'm not sleeping with Alec, Frank."

"No, *we* certainly wouldn't want your mother to find out you were sleeping with someone in Colorado, would *you*?"

"I'm not sleeping with him, Frank."

"Will your mother believe *you*, Linda?"

So that was how blackmail worked. Very efficient, it was. Of course my mother wouldn't believe me. Sex was something nice girls didn't do, and for more than matters of reputation; pregnancy was always there, looming, waiting to ruin a girl. Mothers worried all the time about stuff like this. They thought we'd never be able to control our baser urges, and in a way they had got that pretty much right. Not all nice girls "didn't," but those who *did* didn't talk about it.

I told Alec what had happened, and he said I was lucky King hadn't fired me. He said that's what happened to workers who rose up to test the yokes of their chains, which sounded not right, if you know what I mean, but I didn't say so, Alec being a sophomore. I said I didn't think Frank would fire me; he wouldn't want me telling my father how unfair a hotel Frank ran. Alec said my father already knew, he was a management tool, too. I got mad at that. Just because my father, who had no college, didn't make as much money as the men he trained, who had gone to college, it didn't mean my father was a management tool. Take that back. Alec wouldn't, so we didn't talk for a week, during which he got most of the busboys and four of the five actors who, except for Tommy, could never be depended on to feel passion over anything but themselves for very long, worked into a lather over how much money they weren't getting, how much they were being exploited. After that it was all rumble rumble rumble, mutiny mutiny mutiny. The only one not to join the mumblings or the meetings was Betsy, the Irish actress from Baltimore, Miss Horse Blanket. She was always somewhere else, still thinking, I supposed.

Frank retaliated by extending everybody's hours and telling them that from now on they had to work the morning of their day off, too. People were caught. Summer was half gone; it was too late to get a job anywhere else. Something had to be done, but what? By the end of July the Hotel El Dorado was divided into more camps than a convention of Baptists.

The Jews arrived the first week of August, two days before the Mormons and one day after we heard Marilyn Monroe had died. The Jews were a surprise to the hotel management, a lucky surprise they thought at first. What happened was, a busload of high-school students from Long Island, New York, touring the West, had planned to stay in Aspen where the hotels were much nicer (and much more expensive), but the hotel they'd planned to stay at had turned out not to be kosher, so they'd called around. The Hotel El Dorado had told them sure, come on down—kosher?—we got everything here.

When I heard about this, I smiled. I was cool. At least I knew my part better now; back in June we'd had another group of Jews, three families with twelve small children among them. It was my first week of dining with hotel guests' children. I'd already figured out that little children needed their meat cut up for them—and a lot of little children meant a lot of itty-bitty bites to carve—but nobody needed any help with fried shrimp. I would sit down at the head of the children's table each night and count heads, then announce, "Okay, who wants what?—say, they have fried shrimp tonight! I love fried shrimp, don't you?—of course you do. Let's all have fried shrimp! Oh, waiter," and all was fine until I fed shrimp to twelve Jewish children, not a one of whom said a word. I swear I never saw children take to shrimp that way. Seven of them asked for seconds. Then the little turkeys went running straight to their parents and told them I'd forced fried shrimp down them and, golly, what *didn't* happen after that. Well, how was I to know? There were about as many Jews in our neighborhood as there were Greeks. All I had in mind was feeding them something with handles.

A busload of Jews? At least these were in high school and could be assumed to know how to cut up their own roast beef. Whether the kitchen at the Hotel El Dorado was actually kosher was another matter, and not my matter.

The students turned out to be terrific. They were up for anything. It was funny being in charge; most of them were no more than one or two years younger. I played and called it work. They had such spirit. Several had been to or were going to Israel. All I knew about Israel, and most of what I'd learned about the Holocaust, I'd gotten from *Exodus*. My schooling had had little to say on either subject. I had cried a long time when I read that book. From the Jewish students, I heard two languages that were new to me, one a language of humor, a mocking, streetwise, city sensibility of words; the other, Yiddish. I learned I was a *meshuggeneh shiksa,* some of them said, but they didn't quite explain so I thought it meant "tall." They taught me to dance a hora, which I have danced since then but never has it felt as right as it did around a fire in the woods on a sharp mountain summer night. They were totally different from anyone I'd known. One of them, a seventeen-year-old boy named Bernie Bell (he said his family had shortened it to Bell from something he promised to teach me to pronounce) played guitar and sang. He introduced me to folk music, all those coal miners down where the rain never falls and the sun never shines, all those flowers going God knows where, like the soldiers; and still John Henry was a steel-drivin' man. He taught me a new song, about everything blowing in the wind, something from back east, he said; a Jewish kid had written it. Why, these weren't songs, they were stories—about injustice, most of them. Jews hated injustice, they told me.

When the Mormons got there, all one hundred of them, and their children, the Jewish students saw I was overwhelmed and pitched in, each student taking two or three kids to watch, which was wonderful for me and lasted about two days. Then the Mormon kids' parents found out about the Jews.

"It's not that we have anything against them," the Mormons said.

For people who claimed to want to bring everybody into their church, Mormons sure stuck to themselves. They did not enjoy or appreciate the company of Jews. Or Tommy. The Mormons said outright they didn't mind a Negro on stage, but thought that was probably where he ought to stay, the implication being: "and not walking around the grounds as though he were a guest." And some of the Jewish students agreed with the Mormons about Negroes. They said you couldn't trust them. My family might have agreed with both groups to some extent or another, and they thought Mormons were pretty strange, too.

That was the week I turned eighteen. The night of my birthday, the Scuz threw a party after we got off work. The Jewish students came, too. Bernie brought his guitar. Alec asked him if he knew "Union Maid." He said no, but he knew "Which Side Are You On?" and taught it to us. After that we sang, "There's A Meetin' Here Tonight," and the next thing you knew, there was. Tommy was explaining our work troubles to the Jewish students with grand, sweeping gestures, when Frank King walked in, carrying a quart bottle of 3.2. Coors with a ribbon tied around its neck. He was mad, you could tell, but he went ballistic when he saw the students, who were, after all, guests.

"What has that Negro been telling you?"

"I'm not a Negro, I'm a black," yelled Tommy, and it was news to me. I'd never heard that term before. Frank yelled he would fire Tommy on the spot if he didn't shut up, at which point Alec yelled he would quit if Tommy were fired.

"Communist creep."

"Fascist."

Bernie and the Jewish students, the rest of the Scuz—pretty soon everybody was yelling, but Alec yelled the loudest and what he yelled was one word: strike.

"Strike now!" he yelled.

And we began to chant, "Strike now!" Soon everybody was chanting, even the Jewish students and most of the kitchen help, who had wandered in, though they were Mexicans and no part of our summer so far. Frank stood in the middle of the room for a moment, staring at us, then stalked out of the basement, red-faced, still carrying what I could only assume was my birthday gift.

We had no torches, but with great excitement, most of the help got up, went to their rooms, cleaned out their belongings and moved to a motel down the road. The Jewish students helped us pack. We couldn't afford much at the motel; twenty-odd people would sleep in three rooms, if they slept. But once there, reality began to hit us, especially the ones who really needed the money, meager though it was. Alec was suddenly the most depressed, a little belatedly, I thought. He was not going to be able to go back to college if he didn't get the rest of his pay for the summer, which he most definitely would not get if he were fired. Some of the others faced similar problems. The air seemed to have left our balloon. Except for Tommy, who was not depressed at all. He was flying, he was so angry, and still high on the drama of the moment. Tommy was, after all, an actor. He said this was just like in *A Raisin in the Sun,* and we all agreed, though I thought saying we were doing this to hold the family together was stretching it a bit. Also, Tommy didn't need the money; his father was a lawyer.

It was almost five in the morning but I was restless. I decided to take a walk. I walked slowly, shuffling my feet, feeling chilled and light-headed, worrying all this over in my head. After a while I noticed I was on the road that ran up the other side of the Hotel El Dorado, the side where they picked up the garbage. I stumbled over something and looked down. Lying on the ground next to the Dumpster was an unopened quart bottle of Coors with a red ribbon still tied around the neck. What the hell, I thought, and picked it up, opening the bottle on the steel edge of the Dumpster's top. Some birthday. Some coming of age. Trees arched over both sides of the road; the wind made a sweet noise in their branches, reminding me of the beginning of the summer, when I had thought magic was afoot. That made me sad. I finished about half the quart and decided to sit down in the middle of the road to finish the rest, which I did. It seemed reasonable. Cars rarely came on this road at night; it was only a little service road and, anyway, soon it would be daylight. The middle of the road seemed an appropriate place to talk to yourself.

You're out of work. You may have gone on strike. On *strike*. How can you go on strike—you're going to pledge a sorority, for God's sake. I didn't know what to do about anything. I was sure I ought to call my parents—what if Frank King phoned them and said I was in a motel with boys—many boys? They wouldn't care that other girls were there, too. When they heard some of them were Jewish and, worse, from New York, they'd like it even less. Also, I wasn't quite sure we'd done the right thing. Oh, I knew we'd done *The Right Thing*—but had we done the *right* thing? It was wrong to fire Tommy and still, we weren't communists, were we? On the other hand, we weren't going to lie down for any greedy, bigoted management, were we? Just wait until the hundred Mormons woke up—hungry. But neither could I see Frank King backing down. Joe Heller was right. There was always a catch. Why did everything have to get so complicated? And what happens now? I wondered.

The car was moving too fast or they probably would have seen me; the sky was already light purple going on pink. I didn't move. At first I was too surprised, then it was too late. There was a terrible tearing screech of brakes. So that was the catch, I remember thinking. I die now. I see.

The car skidded to a stop with at least six inches to spare. Two doors slammed and two people rushed to the front of the car and leaned over to see what kind of mess they'd made. I looked up into the concerned, nineteen-year-old Irish face of one Betsy Mulhenny, who for once was not bubbling and bouncing, and into the very pale face of her (clearly) all-night companion, my boss, Mr. Frank King, who got considerably paler when he saw me.

For a minute nobody said anything. They stood back up, staring down at me. Betsy tried to smile, and when she couldn't, turned, went back to the car, reached into the front seat and took out something brown and folded. She walked up the road toward the hotel, hugging her horse blanket close to her chest.

"Uh, Linda . . ." Frank was leaning against a tree, looking at Betsy's receding back, and not at me.

"Yes, Frank?"

"About what you saw, or think you saw . . ."

"About what I saw."

"Yes, well, maybe nobody would believe you."

"My parents might not, you're right."

"That's what I meant."

"But your wife might."

Frank was still looking at Betsy's back. It was much smaller now; she was almost to the hotel door. He didn't say anything, just kept on looking, as if there were answers in that back. I spoke.

"About the strike . . ."

Frank turned and looked at me a long time, as if he were trying to figure out who I was. Or who he was. He looked down the road again, at Betsy, and spoke, this time without looking at me at all.

"I'll raise you all to minimum wage. It's as high as I can go. Hell, I can't really go that high . . . but I will."

"And nobody's fired."

He sighed. "And nobody's fired—except for that little commie bastard creep . . ."

"And *nobody's* fired, Frank."

We watched Betsy disappear into the employee entrance of the hotel. She seemed so tiny. The sun blasted its way over the mountain, slashing us both across the eyes, the way light does when it bounces off a mirror fast.

"Okay, nobody's fired."

"Good night, Frank, or rather, good morning."

"Linda?"

"Yes?"

"I told you never to call me 'Frank' at work."

"Is that what you call this?"

Summer slid to an end, peacefully, if dully. Everybody but one of us went back to work. Alec quit the day after the almost-strike. In triumph. The workers had won in less than twelve hours. Imagine that. He wasn't abandoning us, he said. It was only that he'd gotten a letter from his father, who'd found him a job for the three weeks before he was due back at college as a delivery boy for a Boston print shop. The pay was terrific, he said, even if it wasn't a union shop. I asked him why he thought Frank had given in on *our* pay. Alec said he'd seen the fear in Frank's eyes. I asked him what he thought Frank was afraid of.

"Us," said Alec. "We're something new."

I wondered.

I'd never told Alec or anybody else what happened on the road. That morning, when I'd gotten back to the motel, Alec had been waiting, still depressed about the reality of unemployment. He'd given me my birthday gift then, which he said he'd forgotten about until now, what with, oh, everything. It was a book. All summer Alec had pushed books on me, everything he thought I should have read; after all, he had. I looked at the book. It was his copy; I'd seen him reading it. *Siddhartha*. Alec had said it was all about how wisdom cannot be taught, that it has to come from inside, from some inner struggle.

My train left Ironwood on the day after Labor Day, the day summer dies. Frank King drove me to the station. He said to give his love to my parents. He looked at his feet the way people do when they want to tell you something they don't actually want to say.

"It really wasn't that I was greedy, Linda. Do you understand that? They paid me peanuts, too. But I needed this job, and to keep it, I had to do what I had to do. What they told me to do."

"And now?"

"They've fired me. I found out this morning."

"Why?"

"The hotel's been sold again."

"What this time?"

"There are rumors of a nursing home."

Pulling out of the station, we followed the green river into the tunnel and canyons beyond. I looked into the river's million mirrors, hoping to see something new, but all I saw, to paraphrase another book I'd read that summer, were nothing but a bunch of strangers in a strange land—and I was not the only one who didn't *grok*, I'd learned. White people didn't understand anybody but themselves, and neither did black people, Mexicans, Jews nor Mormons. People from Boston thought people from Oklahoma were dumb. Texans and Coloradans each thought the other obnoxious. Young mistrusted old and the other way around. Management called angry workers communists. Angry workers called management Fascists. Irish girls put out. Actors weren't dependable. Japanese had funny eyes. Everybody misunderstood everybody all the time; everybody refused service to somebody, and nobody liked mirrors worth a damn.

And still, I'd found my magic that summer—the magic of ideas, so many new ones, and so different. Ideas, I saw, came from knowledge, and knowledge, I saw, changed things, most especially *applied* knowledge—as I'd discovered in the middle of a road to a Dumpster early one August morning. It was a good thing I was going to college; if this was how things were, there was a lot more I needed to know about everything, and why.

What I did not and could not know that day was that if no one was what they seemed, neither was anyone entirely unpredictable. Some of what was in us then would be in us always, adapting itself as necessary. I would continue to be confused about love and sex and the power of both for years. Tommy would stay somewhat confused about who he was, and although both he and Alec ended up in Vietnam, only Tommy was drafted, and of the two of them, only Tommy died there, a Green Beret; so dramatic, I remember thinking when I heard. Alec would become an account executive at a Boston advertising agency; his biggest accounts would be a natural cereal and a steel company. Frank would leave the lovely but boring Helen and marry Betsy, who was half his age, but neither they nor the five children they would have and raise before Frank died would care; they would move around a lot over the years, always from one hotel to another. Many years later, I would take my children to spend a weekend with them at a lodge they ran in upstate New York. They were two of the happiest people you could know. I would lose track of Bernie and regret that I had; I'd like to tell him my daughter plays the guitar for a living.

But I knew nothing of these things on the train that day. I knew only that the magic of ideas was a reckless, reckless magic. We were going in and out of canyons again. I picked up Alec's copy of *Siddhartha* and began to read, never noticing exactly when my train and the green river went their separate ways.

WHAT'S LOVE GOT TO DO WITH IT?

February is when it's cold and dark and there's no baseball. The only good thing about February, you might say, is that it's short, but I say you're wrong—we need all the February we can get. My father taught me why. Once I asked him why Valentine's Day was in February, why not at least delay it until March? He said Valentine's Day was not celebrated in March because nothing important could possibly happen in a month where they drank green beer. Okay, but why not April or May? I liked May, swimming pools opened then. He said I didn't understand: Valentine's Day was in February because that's when we needed it. Over the years I've come to think my father was right about this, too. February is the perfect time to be in love. My pal Nadine said she began to fall in love with David when he offered to help her move from one apartment to another in New York City, in February. She said it showed her something. That makes sense to me, not that lovers should make sense; if one means to perform an act of faith in public, a little lunacy is probably helpful. People who are sensible about love aren't always good at it. You've probably noticed.

Besides, love that seems rational today will often seem tomorrow to be the act of one whose elevator doesn't stop at all floors. We find our way to love through different ways at different ages, and how we behave once we get there isn't the same at twenty as it is at forty. Still, the feeling we get inside when we're falling in love (the Yiddish word *zetz* describes it best, I've always thought) never changes, and that it doesn't is one of life's little miracles— or bigger ones.

And if, as has been said, being in love is being in the mood for believing in miracles, what better time for believing in miracles than February? It's no trick being in love in June, when the wind is green and the grass is soft, and the sun is sweet on your face. Any fool can fall in love in June. In fact, June is so distracting that if you don't pay very close attention, you're likely to think you're in love with somebody when what you're really in love with is the set. But in February, chances are, the prettiest sight you're going to see all month is the face of the person sitting right next to you. Concentrate on that face. Kiss its cold nose. See if you can think of something to make its chapped lips smile and its bleary eyes light up. In the coldest February, as in every other month in every other year, the best thing to hold on to in this world is each other.

Many Februarys ago, I married a man on Leap Year's Day. I remember thinking it would make our years together seem longer if we had an anniversary only every four years—I was a lot crazier then than I am now—but I was right, too: our first year together seemed so long we decided to call a cease-fire the following February, on Valentine's Day. But I like being in love, I like having someone be in love with me.

The first time was in Texas in 1950 (falling in love for the first time, like swinging a cat, teaches you something you can learn no other way). I was short, left-footed and almost six and a half. Roy was handsome, talented and thirty-nine, but no man is perfect except in fairy tales, and he was no fairy-tale prince, he was a real king: The King of the Cowboys. We were a perfect match, Roy Rogers and me.

The night we met and fell in love was at what in most places was called a rodeo, pronounced ro'-dee-oh (in most movies, it was called a ro-day'-oh, but that is because they made those movies in California where you get just about what you'd expect when it comes to fancy talking). However, in Houston back then, they called it the Fat Stock Show, and every year Roy Rogers was its star, along of course with Trigger the Wonder Horse, Gabby Hayes, Pat Brady and Nellie Belle (Nellie Belle was Pat's faithful jeep) and The Sons of the Pioneers. Dale Evans was also there.

That February, I had a broken arm due to some bad information concerning human aerodynamics (I did that a lot, you'll have noticed), but a little bitty old piddling thing like a cast wasn't going to keep me from going with my parents to see Roy Rogers at the Houston Fat Stock Show. It was wonderful: first there was the rodeo part and then Roy came out and sang and Trigger counted to three, twice, and Gabby sputtered and Pat did wheelies with Nellie Belle and the Sons sang all the songs. Dale prayed for us.

Next it was time for the big finale, when Roy would ride around the arena and shake hands with all the children, who, when they began to play "Happy Trails to You," would run down to the fence circling the arena in order to be ready for Roy. However, my parents wouldn't let me go down to the fence, which broke my heart, because it wasn't so crowded around that ring, no more, say, than some presidential photo-ops I covered later, but they were scared about my arm and so, my life having come to a premature end in 1950, I sat down. Then this rodeo clown saw me. The clown took me backstage, right into Roy's dressing room, and that's where it happened. It was clear. The King of the Cowboys was in love with me, anyone could see that in his eyes, and I know he would have asked me to marry him if he hadn't met Dale first, or Trigger. Roy did what he could. He signed my cast: *To Linda Jane, Happy Trails, Roy Rogers and Trigger.* The love part was implied.

I and my autographed cast were the biggest thing in kindergarten, even if six weeks later it did take Dr. Andre two hours to cut the old-fashioned, thick plaster cast off without touching

Roy's writing, especially the love part, which was implied. I wrote to Roy of our undying love and where we ought to move after he got rid of Dale. (I thought Dallas might be nice. If we could teach Trigger to count to five, he could run for mayor.) Roy never wrote back. The next year, I went to the Fat Stock Show and took my cast, which I waved at Roy, but he must not have seen it or me. I was not discouraged; I kept that cast and I kept on going to the Fat Stock Show, waving my cast every year until the sixties, when Houston turned all hat and no cows and they began calling it a rodeo instead of the Fat Stock Show and started bringing in television cowboys, like that Hoss person who could not sing or count to three or even pray very well, but that's progress for you.

Roy never came back. And he never left Dale.

I grew up and fell in love with someone else, several someones else; and now, so many years later, I see Roy and Dale sometimes on the cable television show they have, where they show their old movies and, during the breaks, sit on the set, the front porch of a ranch house somewhere in the West of my heart, rocking in their chairs, talking about the old days when they were young and making those movies.

It's a little like a weekly visit with your relatives, the ones who are old and kind and tell you the same old stories every time you go to see them. Every once in a while, Roy seems to nod off in the middle of one of Dale's stories, I give him that much credit. Of course Roy and Dale and especially Trigger the Wonder Horse have gone through some changes, too: I read that when Trigger died, Roy had him stuffed. I understood, although, were I Dale, I'd sure take my vitamins. What Roy wanted was a way to keep Trigger near him forever, the way I keep the cast to remind me of a time I'm never going to see again, a time when cowboys could be kings and clowns could be angels and maybe, just maybe, little girls could fly.

Maybe it's because I forgave Roy for Dale and understood about Trigger that from that day until this, where love is concerned, I've been an enlightened woman, never measuring a man by the weight of his wallet, the width of his shoulders or the size of his tallywhacker. Nor have I discriminated against one, romantically, on the basis of his race, color, creed or his origin. I tell myself I've never had *any* prejudices about men to speak of. In public. However, in my heart, I always knew I couldn't fall in love with a short, bearded, bald or balding or younger man, and, yes, it was wrong of me to feel that way, but that's why they call it prejudice. Then a few years ago I accidentally fell in love with a man seven years younger than I am (I asked him where he was when Kennedy was shot; he said he was at band practice) who was bearded and had a bald spot, and now I'm seven times happier than I was. Somebody should have told me sooner.

The seven-year gap in the times in which we were raised has its downside, though—there's something of the yuppie growing in him, something of the hippie still in me. He does not rage at the world as often or with as much heat as I do, and he is more into machines than I am; he has many and knows how to work them, which usually I do not. He can even program a VCR. His clothes have names; sometimes the names are sewed on the outside of his clothes, sometimes only the symbols of the name: little men on polo ponies. And although I've never heard anyone I'd trust say they saw him eat a kiwifruit, he has been heard to order his fish blackened.

We discuss what to do with the loft we intend building in the bedroom. I say we could put some pillows, a few flowers, a poster or two and some incense holders up there, you know, a place to meditate, but Rolfe wants to fill the loft with exercise machines, which he says are much better for you. He reads The Sharper Image catalog and orders stuff from it, and has a platinum American Express card. I gave him a golden retriever for Christmas, which was a pretty yuppie thing for an ex-hippie to do, but I put my foot down when he wanted to call the dog Amadeus. The dog's name is Bo. Rolfe spells it Beaux. Rolfe gives me interesting gifts, too. That's the trouble; one Christmas he gave me a book about everything you can buy at a hardware store. But he thinks I'm pretty.

Men today are funny about gifts. Sometimes I think they take us too seriously. They give you a briefcase so you'll have something appropriate to take with you every morning to the Supreme Court, or a food processor so you'll have something appropriate to do when you get home from the Supreme Court, or a word processor for your weekends. Once, a man I was in love with gave me a microwave for Christmas, which should have told me something, but didn't—we lasted another six months. In his defense, the Christmas before that one, he gave me diamond earrings and I swept one of them out of the house accidentally, while taking down the Christmas tree. Another Christmas I was going with a news cameraman. This was when I was a news reporter. We worked for the same network and had been carrying on for most of the presidential campaign we were covering—a lot of that goes on during an election year, you can ask Gary Hart. When the campaign was over and Christmas came I received a beautifully wrapped gift from my boyfriend, the cameraman. Now this, I said to myself, has to contain a gift as romantic as these wrappings, as romantic as our time together, and I guess it was, if you consider several hundred miniature bars of soap from all the hotels and motels we'd stayed at during the campaign romantic. When I told my pal Nadine about the microwave and the soap, she said that was nothing; the same Christmas I'd gotten my soap, she'd gotten a smoke detector. I am a modern woman, but between thee and me, it may be we've gone too far.

This is the same sort of thing that was done to my father. We always gave Daddy practical gifts for Christmas, a pen-and-pencil set for his desk, a pair of socks, a tie, a lawn mower. If Daddy were around now, for Christmas I'd buy him a box of crayons, a big box, the one with gold and silver crayons in the top corners or maybe a bound book with blank pages for him to fill with poems, or a Lionel electric train, the one with electric red lights and whistles. The man deserved those things. He gave them to me. If he could have, he would have given me that pony.

I thought about my father when I came across the letter, which I found when I was looking for something else, the only way anybody ever finds anything in my house. I was getting ready to renovate and began by sorting and throwing out the litter of life.

The letter was in my father's desk. After Daddy died, the company he'd worked for sent me his desk, after I'd asked for it. When I was little and Daddy and his desk were so big, I would go to his office and he would let me sit on top of his desk, play under it, crawl over it; I would stand on it to see out the window to watch the parades that marched down Houston's Main Street, celebrating the Fat Stock Show and rodeo, the circus and, naturally, football games. My father was a large, gentle, often confused man. He had some difficulty with certain aspects of ordinary life; he spilled things on himself and was always bumping into things, sideswiping doors when he walked through them, taking off pieces of the house when he backed out of the driveway, reaching over to hand you something then dropping it. It wasn't that he was clumsy. It was just that he seemed genuinely unsure where he stopped and the rest of the world began.

We would go on our private picnics together several times a year and it was always an occasion. Mother never went along, or wanted to: picnics weren't air-conditioned. Daddy and I would go to the woods and hike a bit, then build a fire and burn something for dinner and it tasted just fine to the two of us; in fact I cannot smell meat scorched over charcoal without getting lonesome for my father. Often we would ride horses together. Daddy taught me how to ride, but never appeared comfortable doing so himself. He always looked bigger than the horse. When I was a very little girl, all the very little girls who were my friends loved going places with my father. He took us out Main Street to Playland Park, or to the much smaller amusement park to ride Old Bill, the slowest horse in town, and he always let you ride one more ride. After I was grown and had children of my own, he would take them to Playland Park and to ride Old Bill, or to the circus, grateful for the excuse, because he loved all those things and had been deeply hurt when I outgrew them. Recently, I was in Houston, and one Sunday afternoon I drove out to the end of Main Street. Playland Park was gone, replaced in spirit by Astroworld and in fact by a parking lot, but the little amusement park was still there, and bless me, so was Old Bill, still walking his circle, still carrying the inevitable little girl on his bowed back and, oh, wouldn't I love to ride one more ride today and watch my daddy smile.

My father loved me very much. I was lucky, I knew it. He believed in me and believed, or let me believe he believed, that I could do no wrong. In return I adored him, saw him as my hero and wanted to be like *him*, not my mother, even though he was an alcoholic. Like so many children of alcoholics, I didn't get angry at the one who drank but at the one who didn't. Daddy was only sick, Mama and everyone said so, but Mama was a sober grown-up, and she was supposed to make my world right, that's what grown-ups were for. Daddy was, like most alcoholics from time to time, a mean drunk, mean with words, though, not fists. He wasn't a violent man, except perhaps toward himself and even then his violence took the form of trying to drink himself to death.

He hit me only once that I can remember, but I don't count that, he was not drinking at the time, and anyway it was more out of fear than anger: I was five and, hearing my father call me to dinner, I'd hidden in the bushes instead, where I'd watched my parents get increasingly worried, then scared, until finally I'd jumped out and yelled "Boo." Probably he should have hit me harder. Yes, I wished he were stronger, strong enough not to drink, but he was always there for me when he wasn't drunk and he knew plenty about love; he was generous with his affection, given to great, awkward, engulfing hugs, and I can remember so clearly the smell of his hugs, all starched shirt, tobacco, Old Spice and Cutty Sark. Sometimes I think I've never been properly hugged since.

Daddy was almost always cheerful, but my guess is he was not an especially happy man, nor necessarily an especially unhappy one, although I suppose I'll never know; if I'd asked him such a question, he would have said of course he was happy. But if his life exceeded his parents' expectations, perhaps it did not live up to his own. He went to work every day, he paid his bills on time, fed his family, sheltered them, was good to them, and he was loved by his family and friends, although he was often humored by them, too. He was an undereducated, thinking human being. When he was young, Daddy had loved poetry, that is, until his family had managed to straighten him out in time to go into the insurance business. When I was young, Daddy taught me poems. I was five and could recite the last verse of *Thanatopsis*, although I had trouble saying "Thanatopsis." We both loved words, and like a lot of people who love words but do not hear a great variety of them in ordinary conversation, we mispronounced the words we knew only from books, and sometimes he mispronounced words for no good reason at all. He once told me I could not go to a party without a "chafferone." Mama would laugh at him when he said things like that. So would I. I'm sorry I did that. My father, I think, was ashamed he had so little education and somewhat surprised he was a success financially, and he was not comfortable with it, believing, as alcoholics do, that he did not deserve it. Did he feel that with more education he could have made other choices, been more of himself? More was always what he wanted for me.

We saw every movie Martin & Lewis made. If we could, we saw them twice. Mother hated Martin & Lewis: she said slapstick was vulgar and what's more, she said, it wasn't funny, not a bit. Daddy and I considered pie in the face hilarious. After the movie, we would go out to eat a steak. It was always a steak. Many years later, when I was married and living in Chicago, Daddy would come to visit us, bringing with him a beer cooler filled with steaks he'd hauled from Texas, to make sure, he said, we had something decent to eat. A tall, formerly thin man who still had skinny legs, he loved steaks better than any other food (my mother actually preferred hamburger) and liked telling people that when I was three years old and we were on a train together, the waiter in the dining car asked if I would like a sandwich, and I said, "A sirwoin, please." Mispronunciation is genetic. Those times I got to go with him on his business trips around Texas, we would get up early and walk around the new town and, as Daddy liked to say, "get to see the feel of the place." On our walks Daddy would talk to me about the traveling we would do when I was older. He always meant to travel, he said. Most of all, he wanted to see Paris, France, and he would tell me about how he almost got there the summer I was born.

In the summer of 1944, when so many young American men were going to Paris to march down her avenues in triumph, my father, Lonnie Ray Smith, was a sergeant in the Army Air Corps. He could have been one of those men in Paris, but he was thirty-five years old and he had a wife and a new baby, and was nowhere near France. Nor was he anxious to get shot at. Still, if his age and his obligations had kept him far from battle, they had also kept him far from that great adventure which he, like most men, had been raised to believe was a part of war. And far from Paris, France. If it takes courage to be willing to die for your country in war, there's also some courage needed to have a baby during a war; it's a way of saying you believe there will be a future and you aren't afraid of investing in it. There is a war bond in my house and the name on it is Linda Jane Smith. The date is August 15, 1944, the day she was born. The bond was a gift to a new baby and was itself another form of investment in the future. Daddy said he expected the country to keep its promise, and it did, and I keep the bond to remind me of Daddy. And Paris. It was his secret, this wanting to go to Paris, and later it became our secret, but the trip he always talked about was always postponed because there were always obligations, and he was a man who fulfilled obligations. Daddy said that was okay, there was plenty of time. There wasn't, but four years after he died, when I was thirty-four years old, I made that trip, and once there, this toast: Here's to Paris, France, to the Americans who saw her in 1944 and to the one who never saw her at all. Here's to courage.

When his company sent the desk, they sent a note saying one drawer was locked and they were sorry but they had no key for it. Neither did I. A locksmith opened the drawer. Inside were poems my father had written and kept for . . . for what? Me? Him? Another thing I'll never know. Also inside the drawer were little notes, scraps of paper with descriptions of people in our family, places he'd seen, a story he'd started, the scattered writer-bits I am so familiar with in my own life. The last box inside the drawer contained every letter I'd written to him, from the first "Dear Daddy, I am fine, how are you? Love, Linda" sent while I was at camp—to the last one, written in 1974, the day after my

thirtieth birthday and six months after my third husband, sometime during the third quarter of the Super Bowl, got up from
his chair and went back to Texas. He took the Porsche. He did
not take me. My letter to my father ended with this:

*You and Mother have been married now for almost forty years. Yet
every time I've married, at the very moment I said "I do," a voice
inside my head said "Oh no you don't," and would not shut up until
indeed I hadn't. What do you know that I don't, or the other way
around?*

My father died a week later. I didn't marry anybody for almost
two years.

Marrying four men between your twentieth and thirty-first
years (and never marrying again) is plain tricky to explain, unless
you're a movie star, Hungarian, male, nuts or all of the above,
which I'm not. If I'd merely slept with them instead of legalizing
things, I wouldn't have to explain a damn thing; most of my
women friends have slept with more men than I have. Nobody
snickers at them, nobody assumes there must be something very
wrong with them.

Everybody tells Liz-Taylor jokes. Nobody tells Jessica-Lange
jokes.

Even close friends eventually get around to asking me why my
marriages failed and think I'm joking when I say three out of
four didn't, it's only that they didn't, well, take root. My fault,
probably. Mama used to say to people, "Linda? She's going to
keep on getting married until she gets it right."

Certainly I never got it right with my first husband, not from
the first weekend Arthur took me home to meet his parents.
His mother's name was Ethel. Her husband's name was Al.
Al made no sound when he laughed, none at all. Arthur was
their only son. That weekend Ethel told me her son was a genius
and her family came from Savannah. I did not immediately
understand this meant she was too good for Jackson, Mississippi, and, most of all, me, but I was nineteen, from Texas and
accustomed to not immediately understanding almost every-

thing. She asked if I wanted a highball. I knew this was some kind of drink, because I'd seen the word in books, but I'd never heard anybody say it out loud. In Texas, liquor by the drink was illegal then. People drank anyway, but generally they settled for bourbon or scotch, plain. Some people added ice. Some even added water. My Aunt Alice Rose from Beeville added Coca-Cola to her bourbon until she decided all that Coca-Cola was making her fat. I told Ethel I'd love a highball, thank you.

Ethel gave me a tall glass of brown, which turned out to be just ordinary bourbon and Coca-Cola; she gave Arthur and Al tall glasses of brown, which turned out to be Coca-Cola and no bourbon; then she poured herself a medium-size glass of not-so-brown, which turned out to be bourbon and no Coca-Cola at all. Ethel didn't want to be fat, either.

Highballs weren't exotic, I discovered, but they brought a certain perspective to the rest of the evening; after a while Ethel and I had trouble saying "Savannah" and so she concentrated on Arthur, her son the genius, the one who was about to throw away his future and quite possibly the future of Western civilization and, who knows, maybe even the whole damn South, in order to marry this nobody who came from Texas, but not from oil. A genius deserved more. You didn't see Einstein marrying somebody from Houston, no you didn't. Arthur's mother was much like my father in always wanting more for her child. Trouble was, neither my father nor Ethel saw Arthur or me, respectively, as more. I agreed with her about Einstein, but Arthur? Was he a genius? Our friends at Vanderbilt, where Arthur and I went to college, said he was, but Vanderbilt was in Nashville and genius was not its most important product. I thought it would be swell if Arthur really were a genius; I was flunking every course but one (not going to class can have that effect) and figured nothing short of marrying a genius would cover my undistinguished tracks. Marriage was an honorable and common retreat for confused young ladies then; it was the one job for which no education or experience was required. It paid accordingly.

I hear Arthur is president of a bank somewhere in Georgia. I hope it's a bank in Savannah, that way Arthur won't be the disappointment to his mother that his father was. As for Arthur, I only hope he's forgiven me for Vietnam. Who knew draft boards paid attention to divorce notices? And anyway I heard he wasn't wounded anyplace really and truly important, at least not to a banker.

I will say this for Arthur: he was sane. Ned, another husband of mine, said I shouldn't worry about him being sort of crazy; after all, he was an architect—the implication being that a slight case of craziness went with the territory. I remember Ned's eyes. They were blue, but I don't count blue eyes as remarkable: three of my husbands had blue eyes. The other one, as I said, went into banking. Ned was tall and quite beautiful, with light red curly hair, terrific forearms and just enough freckles to make me forget what the question was. Five minutes after watching me play chess at Prufrock's, a coffee house/bar/chess parlor/hangout that later had the good grace to burn to the ground, Ned introduced himself and announced he knew everything there was to know about me. Five minutes after his announcement, I vowed to marry him at any cost, which pretty much describes what happened.

The night we were married, we went back to Prufrock's, and after Ned beat me at chess he said he loved me more than I knew and would do anything for me. Anything? Name it, said Ned. So I asked him to do what needed to be done to the wall in the women's bathroom. You take care of it, I said. Take care of it now. Ned stood up, borrowed a marker-pen from the bartender and walked straight into the women's bathroom. My hero. Our friends applauded. I glowed.

The thing about the women's bathroom wall was that this wall had hurt my feelings. It was 1973. The walls of women's bathrooms were often covered with graffiti. *A woman needs a man like a fish needs a bicycle.* You may have seen that wall. Feminist fables in full flower. One night I'd walked into the bathroom at Prufrock's and found myself facing something new on the wall. It said: *Linda Veselka is a ball-busting bitch* (Veselka had been Van's last name; Van was who I'd been married to before Ned). What hurt most was the knowledge that a woman must have written it. I wanted it scratched out but was too angry, too proud or too afraid of being caught doing the scratching, but now my husband would show everybody what a lie was there on that wall.

Ned was gone no more than two minutes. He returned, marker-pen held high. Once again everyone applauded. I believe I may have curtsied. More champagne was ordered (highballs make you fat, you know) and enjoyed. Just before we left, I excused myself, claiming champagne went through me like water, a lie, but I had to see the bathroom wall for myself. It wasn't that it was important or anything, but it was, I believed, a symbol of Ned's intention to kiss my sore places as I intended to kiss his. Once inside the women's bathroom, I sat down as if this were an ordinary trip. I looked at the wall. Sure enough, Ned had scratched out *Linda Veselka is a ball-busting bitch*. The graffiti on the wall now read: *Linda Ellerbee is a ball-busting bitch*. I told myself it was progress.

In 1973, five months after we were married, Ned left New York and, as I said, he took the Porsche with him, but not me. My children and I had gone to a friend's house that afternoon so Ned could watch the Super Bowl uninterrupted. When we got back, the game was over and he was gone. Closets cleaned out, nothing, not even a note. Three months later, the telephone rang one night, and when I answered, Ned said hello. I had not heard from or of him until that moment and was, I guess, shell-shocked; I said the first thing that came to mind.

"Who won?"

"What do you mean who won? Who won what?"

"The Super Bowl," I said. "Who won the Super Bowl?"

"That's the kind of thing you say that makes me want to be somewhere else."

Van, a wonderful man and father of my children, was my second and very best husband. Van and I married in 1968 and the first thing I did after that was to have a baby. It also was the second thing I did, due to some inaccurate advice concerning contraceptive foam. The third thing I did was to tie-dye all of Van's underwear. Tie-dyeing, like getting pregnant, proved easier to start than stop, but happily Van didn't mind wearing purple-and-yellow shorts, or else Van never noticed his shorts were purple and yellow. It's possible he didn't; Van's gaze was permanently fixed on the Big Picture. Me and Van, we made babies and promises, watched a calf get born one Easter morning about the same time the sun came up, dreamed of ice-cream cones that would not melt, broke our promises, cried, moved to Alaska to live in the woods, changed our directions and our minds, then one day discovered we had lost our prettiest and most basic illusions about each other. Next we lost our sense of humor. After nearly four years, we lost our way home. Van lives in Virginia now; he's a carpenter. On Friday evenings he makes nachos for happy hour at the local health-food restaurant. If our children don't turn out to be writers, it's not because Van and I didn't give them material.

Sitting in my odd old house, holding the letter I'd written my father, the letter I found in his desk, I wondered, as my friends, my children and surely my husbands had wondered, what was wrong with me; all I ever wanted was what Daddy gave Mama and me the Christmas he wasn't supposed to live until New Year's, and what I saw that day in the hospital corridor when nobody thought my mother would come out of surgery, her heart was so bad. Both my parents suffered serious illnesses of the heart, but in them it was only an affliction of muscle, artery and blood. When my father was thirty-nine, he had a heart attack. The Sisters, even the doctors, said he would die and Mother, believing them, returned the beautiful Victrola in the maple case, a piece of furniture really, and the doll with the white satin dress that Daddy had bought us for Christmas but hadn't given to us yet, because Christmas wasn't for another week and he hadn't known he was going to be in bed dying at the time. Mother said he couldn't afford such gifts, not now, and anyway, after he died she wouldn't want them, because the best part of her life would be over, she said. I would understand when I was older, she said. I was five. I understood vaguely that my daddy was going to die—it had been explained to me by my mother and my grandmother who said Daddy was going to heaven—I was less sure I understood what dying *was;* my father was often gone on business trips. Was heaven one of those? At night I could hear my mother cry in her bed, softly, in gulps, like my broken baby doll, but Daddy, who also believed the nuns, saw it differently. He had one of them call the stores. That Christmas, Mama got her beautiful Victrola and a set of Glenn Miller records and I got my doll with the white satin dress. And the nuns were wrong about Daddy. He lived. You don't get a Christmas gift like *that* very often.

Years later, the doctors were wrong about my mother; her heart was tough enough to survive even them, but we didn't know that in the waiting room that morning. I was twenty-three, and all the way to the hospital I'd been composing what I would say to Mama before they took her to cut into her heart, whose center I supposed myself to be; hadn't she told me all my life I was the most important thing in the world to her? Threading my way through the hospital corridors, I practiced my opening line, which had to strike just the right note. Who but I could give her the strength and confidence she would need? Whose face but mine would she want to be the last one she saw before they cut her open and she died probably? Whose kiss but mine . . . ? I turned a corner and there was my mother lying on a stretcher in the hall, waiting for them to come for her. My father was standing over her. Something about the two of them made me stop and then, as I watched, made me keep my distance, as if there were a wall between us, and around them. It was clear to me at that moment that for them, nothing existed outside them, nothing; there was only the man, the woman. She didn't see me, nor from the looks of it care much whether she did. They weren't talking. He was holding her hand. She was smiling into his eyes; and they were, I swear, speaking a language that at twenty-three I hadn't begun to understand, much less speak myself, but I could see them do it, literally see them, and I moved closer to see more, stunned, fascinated, very very jealous that I had fallen in love with someone, married him, divorced him and never once come close to what I was looking at in that hall. Next time, I said, I will know better. I will love like that. Two weeks later, I met Van at a party of my parents' friends, a party I attended in their place while my mother recuperated from the surgeons.

Downstairs here somewhere I still have Mama's beautiful Victrola; it still works and the Glenn Miller records are still wonderful to hear, even with the scratches of years. The doll with the white satin dress was lost a long time ago, but I'm not surprised. It was a Bride Doll.

When Van and I married, a Methodist preacher did it to us. It was the second time I was married by a Methodist preacher. Once I was married by a justice of the peace and twice I was married by judges, one civil, one criminal. If you're counting, yes, it adds up to five weddings, but that's because I married one of those men twice, an accident both times, I like to think. I never cried at my weddings, although on two different occasions the man I was marrying did. The only time I ever wanted to cry was the second time I married my first husband. I never would have married him a second time if I hadn't married him the first time, but I was caught; nobody knew about the first wedding—we had run off to Ringgold, Georgia—and since we were already married I figured we'd better get married. It seemed easier than explaining. Pretty soon so many people had been invited, so much money had been spent, so many plans had been made—I was too much a coward to stop the process. My father did not know I wanted to cry that day, but I knew he wanted to. He felt what I was about to do was wrong and he didn't like the man I was marrying, hell, maybe he wouldn't have liked any man I was marrying—he was a father and I was his daughter and possession is nine-tenths of the heart. On my wedding day, at the last minute, he offered me a way out, or thought he did. We stood at the back of the church and Daddy, holding my hand, said, "Linda Jane, there are two doors here. One will take us down the aisle and one will take us out the door. We can go either way, and either way you decide to go I'll be with you. Love is too important to be taken too seriously."

The man taught me so much. He taught me or tried to teach me everything he knew about love, which was considerable, and if he and my mother had shown me how dreams could fail sometimes when the people who dreamed them weren't ready to live with their dreams coming true, they'd also shown me what a good marriage was. Now he was ready to save me, if he possibly could, from myself. But Daddy didn't know I was already married. My mother, suspecting the truth, said it was the worst mistake I ever made. She was wrong. It wasn't even close.

I REMEMBER SKY

I remember days, or at least I try.
But as years go by, they're a sort of haze.
And the bluest ink isn't really sky.
And at times I think, I would gladly die
For a day of sky.

—STEPHEN SONDHEIM

Next to that of my parents, the marriage I've known and most envied is Chuck and Beth's. Right now Beth is in the pool floating on a great pink raft, her favorite, the one with the back elevated for reading but she's not reading, not today. James, her nineteen-year-old son, is inside Beth's house with his friends, watching a tape of *Lethal Weapon II;* we can hear them a little bit, hear their laughter. Beth's daughter, Lisa, who is twenty-two, has a summer job in New Braunfels at Water World. Chuck is at work. He's called twice, wanting to know what we should do for dinner. Linda's in town. Should we go out and eat Mexican food or stay home and cook Mexican food?

"If we stay home," I ask, "what exactly shall we cook?"

"Chicken Portuguesa, I think," says Beth.

"How fine," I say. "I haven't tasted your Chicken Portuguesa in twenty years, not since Van and I were married and living in Eagle Pass."

"I make it all the time. People ask where I got the recipe."

"Where did you get the recipe?"

"You taught me," says Beth.

The sky is a typical one for Houston, all clouds, then no clouds and, yes, it's going to rain, no, it's not, well, maybe, oh, who knows? The sky changes its mind so often in Houston in summer. The heat doesn't; it's always there, heavy air you can see and touch, and taste. We float beneath pine trees. Subtropical it may be, but it's also East Texas and that means pine trees. Their cones lie on the ground and hang from the branches, threatening to fall on us. Later the mosquitoes will do their dance with the pines, but by then we'll be inside, safe from bugs and trees and memory, which, for Beth, might be dangerous now, but in time all things get remembered.

We are two old friends floating away our afternoon, and Houston is so different from Eagle Pass, you would never know they're in the same state. One is Gulf Coast, the other Mexican border. One is now, the other then.

"I remember sky," says Beth.

"Sky?"

"Do you recall," says Beth, "a day you and I were driving from Eagle Pass out to the old radar base? We were in that Volkswagen you had and all of a sudden you pulled the car over to the side of the highway and stopped and I said what are you doing and you said look, Beth, did you ever see a more magnificent sky in your life and I looked, and I think about that every time I see a good sky. You said nobody has ever been able to put light like that on canvas, and you were right."

When I read Larry McMurtry's book *Lonesome Dove,* it was easy to fix in my mind a picture of that made-up town. It looked, I imagined, the way Eagle Pass must have looked in 1870, which, except for more buildings and fewer horses, was not too different from how Eagle Pass looked in 1970. On a clear day you could see nothing forever.

What scenery we had was provided us by our sky. If the land didn't change, the sky did. Our mountains were thunderheads, desert clouds, the kind that talk about rain and break their promise. Our rivers were red and purple streaks of sunset. Our trees— well, in Eagle Pass, if you wanted trees, not even the sky could help you there. Beth never thought the land was ugly the way I did, but Beth was from South Texas; to her, barren did not mean ugly. Eventually, I came to see it her way, but it was too late, by then we were moving on, Van and I, headed for Alaska, where in time I would even become tired of trees and rain, tired of deep greens and blues and mountains that blocked the sky, and would long for the yellows and reds and even the browns of Eagle Pass, Texas, down and dry by the Mexican border with all the sky you could ever want to see.

I was out of town when Beth and Chuck first arrived in Eagle Pass and rented the house next door to ours. I had a washing machine and Beth didn't, so she borrowed mine. Van told her to. Beth already knew Van. Her sister had dated him when she was in college. Beth always said she knew my husband and my house before she knew me.

Knowing my house wasn't difficult; it was exactly like hers. All the houses where we lived were alike; one-story, wooden frame houses with linoleum floors and casement windows that always stuck when you tried to open them, or shut them. During World War II, the army had built a radar base twelve miles outside Eagle Pass, six miles east of the river they call the Rio Grande on the Texas side and the Rio Bravo on the Mexican side. The base had a runway, barracks, and fifteen houses for officers. The houses were built in a circle, like a wagon train. When the war ended, the base was closed and the barracks mostly torn down, but the runway and the houses in a circle remained, lost in the monte, that tangled, mesquite-covered scrub brush land that borders the river down there. In 1969, Maverick County decided to rent the houses to people for $100 a month, a lot of money then for us. Van, my husband, earned $9,000 a year. Chuck earned $12,000. Chuck was a lawyer.

Both men worked for Lyndon Johnson. That is, they worked for the Model Cities Program, which had been Lyndon's notion, a part of his War on Poverty. The idea was that local communities would tell the federal government how to spend its money to improve living conditions in their area. The purpose was to help the poor. A number of small towns were selected to be "model cities," the ones that would show the rest of the country how this clever new program worked. When Eagle Pass was chosen to be a model city, the merchants there decided that what the federal government ought to spend its money on, what would really help the poor most, was an air-conditioned mall over the stores along Main Street. Van and Chuck were sent to Eagle Pass to adjust their aim.

For Chuck and Beth, it had not been such a long trip; they came from Hidalgo County, also in South Texas. Chuck's father was a farmer, Beth's ran a cotton gin. Chuck worked for Beth's father the summer he graduated from high school. That's when he and Beth began to date. Beth was a year older than Chuck. I asked her once if that hadn't been odd. Dating a younger man was something different then. Beth said no, it didn't matter, it was such a small community, there weren't enough people to allow them to make silly distinctions like that. She and Chuck had a lot of common interests, shared common goals—they laughed together and thought the same about so many things and, said Beth, there was sex. They had discovered they liked it.

Beth said that, deep down, she never thought they would get married. She was in awe of Chuck, he was so smart. She said it made her feel inferior, his brain was so big. Chuck went away to Tulane in New Orleans, and when he came back home for vacations he began to press Beth to get married. Although she loved him very much, Beth was unsure, but during his last year, when he came home for Christmas, Beth became pregnant. On Easter, 1967, they were married.

"I worked for the welfare department, Chuck went to law school and we had a baby. And we all grew up together."

I have seen the wedding picture many times. That picture is on the bookshelf in the room where I am staying now, in their house in Houston. I look at it at night. There is Chuck, pale and blond, studious-looking, and there is Beth, dark-haired, dark-eyed and so beautiful, so vibrant, so strong.

I push my float to the side of the pool to get a cigarette, which I've sworn to give up this summer but so far I haven't. Lighting the cigarette, I flutter kick my way back to Beth, who is kind enough not to mention my cough. Beth never smoked, not even back when it seemed everyone did and it didn't matter because we were all going to live forever. Not smoking was just one of the many things I envied about her.

"Beth, you knew so much more than I did about some things. I couldn't sew. I couldn't iron. I didn't know what you used to clean what, when to use bleach or how often plants needed watering. I was only learning to cook. I was jealous of you." It was my second marriage and I had been determined to get it right—determined to learn to be a wife.

"That's funny," says Beth, "I wanted to be like you, and I wanted to because I felt that I was weak. I felt you had a direction and a purpose. I was still struggling. I even struggled with the way I felt about that. As for the other stuff—I had four younger sisters, and I don't know whether it was by choice or whether it was just expected of me, but I knew a lot about cooking and home economics, that was my field. I really thought that's what I wanted to do. I saw myself as a dietitian at one time. I was going to help people eat better. I always had a desire, silly as it sounds, to, oh, you know—save the world. Cooking was going to be my way of doing it." Beth blushes. "Maybe it has to do with youth. Maybe when you're that age—in your twenties—you think you can do good. Fix things. Things seemed fixable then."

James comes outside to tell us Chuck has called again. We say to tell Chuck it will be Mexican food at home. Just like the old days.

"Do you remember, Beth? Do you remember how we'd share our meals? You'd say, 'I've got some hamburger, have you got any onions?'"

"Hamburger stroganoff. Pounds and pounds of hamburger stroganoff. And cheese and weenies."

"And tacos, Beth. Tacos."

"Tacos we bought across the river in Mexico. A sack of five for a dollar. The greasiest, best tacos ever. Do you remember that goopy stuff we used to buy to take with us to the movies?"

"Chiliquiles?"

"Chiliquiles. What were they, tortilla strips covered with cheese and tomatoes? Too goopy to eat in the movies, but we did. We ate chiliquiles and watched *Butch Cassidy and the Sundance Kid,* all four of us dripping tomatoes and laughing at Paul Newman. You bought a poster from that movie and hung it in your bedroom. Tell me which one you had the crush on, Butch or Sundance?"

"Both, I think. Sundance for sex. Butch for fun. But I didn't want to be Etta Place. She had no fun. She didn't get to die with them."

A small hot breeze touches my face. The sky is ragged. There are more clouds now.

"We didn't have much, did we, except fun? We'd go to the grocery store, take the kids to the doctor, talk, cook. We didn't go shopping, though, not like women go shopping today."

"Linda, there was nothing to buy."

I must be careful about nostalgia. Beth is right. There was nothing to buy. And no money to buy it. Neither of us worked outside our homes. Mainly we had babies. First Beth, then me, then me again, then Beth. Her babies bracketed mine, her James being the last of the lot. Sweet Baby James, we called him, after the James Taylor song. *Deep greens and blues are the colors I choose/ Won't you let me go down in my dreams/And rockabye my sweet baby James.* Our lives were rich, if not full. We owned much—our time, our dreams and all our tomorrows.

Mornings, after our husbands took one car to work, leaving the other car for the two of us, we would do our housework; I taught Beth to listen to rock 'n' roll on the radio while she cleaned. The local radio station played rock 'n' roll until noon. From then on, all the programming was in Spanish. After our houses were more or less clean, sometimes we'd go to Mexico to buy staples. A 100-pound sack of dried pinto beans cost $11. We liked going to Mexico. Eagle Pass wasn't like most border towns, where you have a big town on the American side and a small, quaint town on the Mexican side. Eagle Pass was across the river from Piedras Negras, Mexico, a large industrial city of about 250,000 people. Piedras Negras dwarfed Eagle Pass, dominated it, provided its reason for being; you saw more pesos in the stores of Eagle Pass than dollars, and if you wanted to ask the butcher for a particular cut of meat, you'd better know how to ask for it in Spanish. We learned. Chuck already spoke fluent Spanish. The rest of us studied and practiced constantly. We had to. We wanted to.

Not everyone who lived in Eagle Pass felt that way. Some pretended as much as was possible that this giant of a country no more than 200 yards from Main Street simply did not exist. The worst offenders were those who were brought from other places to work for the U.S. Border Patrol. Several of these families lived out at the radar base with us and were aghast that we would buy our food in Mexico, take our children to the doctors there and, when we could afford a night out, play there. It would make Beth so angry. Here they are, she'd say, in jobs that force them into daily contact with Mexican people and yet they hate them, they hate them so much—and they hate being here. Beth could not believe how unhappy these people made themselves nor how they kept themselves strangers to a remarkable, ancient culture so close to them, so available. Beth said they were just plain ignorant. I said they were stupid because they didn't try to correct their ignorance—about anything.

One time, a Border Patrol family who lived a few houses down from us decided they wanted a tree. We had yards with a little grass here and there—some of it was even green once in a while—but no trees. And this Border Patrolman went out into the monte and dug up a mesquite, which had to be difficult—they have taproots that go to Egypt—and there he was with this big mesquite he was going to plant in his front yard, not understanding that mesquite weren't trees, they were weeds; ranchers and farmers fought them back constantly. Mesquite took all the water in the ground, crowding out and eventually killing everything else that grew near them. People from that part of the country were about as fond of mesquite as they were of rattlesnakes. Anyway, he planted his, or tried, but it didn't take to the land any more than he did.

Afternoons, Beth and I would gather whatever babies were around at that time and our puppies and kittens, which seemed to be around all the time, and sit outside on aluminum lawn chairs with green-and-white plastic webbing that was mostly worn through and risky, or in one of the raffia rocking chairs I'd bought in Mexico, which came unpeeled if you weren't careful and weren't built right to begin with. When you rocked you had about a fifty-fifty chance of going over backwards. We'd sit in the driveway of my house under the shade of the carport, the only shade there was, watching our children play in the dirt, keeping an eye out for snakes and scorpions and tarantulas, and we'd talk about, oh, yellow waxy buildup and what we were going to fix for dinner that night, if we should play cards at their house or our house— the important things in our lives. We didn't talk about what we would do in the future. We thought we were doing what we would do in the future.

Sometimes we'd just watch the sky, and rock.

Beth was my first woman friend. I'd had girlfriends but this was different. This, I thought, was what it was like to be a woman, laughing women's laughter, making gentle fun of the men we loved, the life we lived, the way things were, ourselves. The rest of the world seemed far, far away. And it was. The closest city was San Antonio, more than 150 miles from Eagle Pass. The local newspaper was a weekly and not partial to news anyway, which didn't matter; there wasn't any in Eagle Pass. We had no televisions, because there was no television to watch: there was no cable, there were no satellites. There were two movie theaters, one showed movies in English, the other showed movies in Spanish. Neither changed features more than once a week. At night we often went into the monte and built a campfire. I'd take my guitar, an old Goya I'd bought during the great folk music scare of the early sixties, and we'd sit around the fire, drink tequila and sing. How we sang. In English. In Spanish. We sang the folk songs I'd learned in my college days. *There is a house in New Orleans/ They call the rising sun . . .* We sang songs from the Mexican revolution. *La-da-da, la Valentina . . .* and the birthday song, never mind it was no one's birthday, the song was too beautiful. *Estas son las mañanitas/que cantaba el rey David.* "These are the little mornings the King David sang about." How pretty is that song in my memory. We sang the cowboy songs, of course. *From this valley they say you are leaving/Do not hasten to bid me adieu,* our voices, particularly Beth's, sweet and true, rising with the sparks from the fire to mingle with the stars of the clear night sky above the Rio Grande. It was a safe place, a safe time, and like dogs when you pet them, we thought it would go on forever.

Nothing you think at twenty-five is so. Van was getting more political by the day. Me, too. The poverty we saw and the indifference of most of the people who lived in Eagle Pass to that poverty, not to mention the racial bigotry of most of the Anglos, angered us. In the big world outside, the real world, cities were burning, students were rioting, women were finding their voices, there was a confusing war and young men our age were dying in it—Van's brother was in Vietnam; the old order seemed precariously balanced, something was blowing in every wind. We couldn't see it, but we could feel it. Feel *it*—something—coming. Van got a job offer from the Model Cities Program in Juneau, Alaska. After thinking it over for close to thirty seconds, we said yes; we'd never seen Alaska. It seemed closer to that real world than Eagle Pass. (And it would be. Too close. That time in Alaska would raise questions I wouldn't try to answer until years later in my life and six chapters later in this book.)

Not too long after we left Eagle Pass, Chuck's father was killed, electrocuted in one of those horrible farm accidents. Beth and Chuck went home to the little town of Edcouch in South Texas to help, to be near Chuck's mother. Chuck went to work for the district attorney of Hidalgo County and Beth went back to work for the state; they needed the money and Beth was, well, bored. And lonely. Soon Chuck realized he hated his job. He was assistant D.A. which meant that he was prosecuting people, some of whom he knew, some of whom were his friends, for felonies like possession of one joint, for which the state of Texas would put you away for life.

Chuck decided if he were going to stay there, he would have to join a law firm and start defending those people instead, but the truth was he didn't like trial work. He wasn't flamboyant, he was a scholar, a student of the law and—in his heart—a student of justice. Too bad there were no jobs for a student of justice.

When the oil company asked him to go to work for them in New Orleans, they went. The boy from the dry country became an expert in riparian law, the law of rivers, and of off-shore oil leases. Beth became the lawyer's wife and the community volunteer. She gave guided tours at the museum, directed the children's choir at church, taught Sunday school—she was president of the church's women's club—baked cookies for the PTA, chauffeured her and her friends' children, helped organize neighborhood charities, sewed costumes for school plays and Mardi Gras parades. She worked for everybody; she just didn't get paid for it.

Chuck is home from work now. We can hear him inside the house talking to James and his friends. He comes to the pool wanting to know what we've been doing, what we're talking about, what's going on, meaning what did he miss? Chuck is a cuddly man, his eyes twinkle, he's happy in the company of women and he doesn't like to miss out on any gossip we might have. He walks slowly around the pool, tentative these days. He goes inside to change clothes, then comes back out, muttering and mumbling. Chuck has always muttered and mumbled.

"Meserkle—*¿qué pasa?*" he mumbles at me. He calls me "Meserkle" because in Eagle Pass my last name was Veselka and Lisa, their daughter, couldn't say it right, she called me Mrs. Meserkle. She got over it. Chuck didn't. He goes off to his potting shed to putter with his bromeliads, flowers for the boy from the dry country. Beth smiles at his back, but her eyes are dark and her smile is fragile. She is worried, I can tell. "Beth, when you and Chuck were living in New Orleans, what did you think the rest of your life would be like?"

She turns those dark eyes on me and says nothing. She chuckles and the dark goes away. "Jeez, Linda. I really thought Chuck was going to move up the corporate ladder, you know, way up and I would go on being the lawyer's wife, but there was the oil bust and then . . ." Beth looks up. We hear thunder. It's low at first, just a rumble, then large drops start falling on the pines, on the pool and in between, on us.

"Hey," I say, "it's raining. Do we have to go inside?"

Beth scowls at the sky, black above us but blue over there, across town. "We'll outlast it. It's Houston. Unless the lightning starts, then . . . we'll see." Beth does not want the sky to feel it can threaten her, not even with its lightning. She has been threatened by much more.

Our lives took separate directions over the years, but our friendship lasted through living in different towns, different states. Chuck and Beth were always there, and always there for me. It was in New Orleans that Chuck began to strain against his life. All he could talk about was wanting to leave and go back to Texas. He wasn't happy. It wasn't the oil company, it wasn't his job—he just wasn't happy. For a time he decided he didn't want to be married, and for a while he moved out. Beth was scared for Chuck, for herself, for the "them" they had built with such care, such work, such love.

Beth came to the conclusion she did not want to depend on somebody else for her livelihood, or her happiness. She went to work for a travel agency, teaching herself to use the computer, to deal with large companies, talk business talk—to be a travel agent. She felt she had to take some responsibility for herself, but she also felt she couldn't tell anybody how she was feeling or how things were, because she'd been raised to hold her feelings in and had convinced herself this was what she ought to do to be happy.

Chuck moved back home, but things were still not right with him. He had feelings of people following him in the halls, strange sensations of smells, too many instances of déjà vu. There were small blackouts, little losses of memory. He thought maybe it was a mid-life crisis. So did Beth. But the strange feelings and occurrences didn't stop, they got worse, and it wasn't a mid-life crisis.

I was in Florida with my daughter; we were on our way to the Keys that day in 1986 when I got word Beth was trying to find me and it was an emergency. On the telephone, she was so calm, so quiet. I could hardly hear her.

"Chuck has something very wrong with him. They're going to operate tomorrow morning."

I made it to New Orleans that night. At the hospital, I visited with Chuck, who was scared but being funny because he was.

There was a lot of nervous laughter, more bad jokes. At their house that night, Beth and I didn't talk much. Her family was there, and Chuck's. Beth was playing Earth Mother to them all and was snappish at anyone who wouldn't play their part. The next morning when they cut him open, they found a tumor in Chuck's brain the size of a softball.

In the waiting room, I held sweet baby James, who was fifteen and crying his eyes out for his father. People were saying to Beth, "You can't cry. You have to be strong for Chuck, and the children. You have to be strong."

There is more thunder now, more rain, but no lightning yet. A thousand small circles form in the pool where the big drops hit. The circles grow, overlap, touching each other, touching us. Above us, more of the sky is darker, a flat gray with purple edges, like a bruise. Still we stay in the pool.

After the operation, everything in their lives was changed, forever. The tumor was, of course, malignant. Chuck being so sick was like having a baby again, Beth said. He needed so much care, for his heart as well as his head. Beth would work all day, come home and take care of Chuck, then go to bed only to wake up terrified Chuck wasn't going to live through the night. Every night. She always said her monsters came out at three in the morning. She couldn't imagine a life without him, wasn't sure, at some point, that she wanted one. She didn't think she was strong. She was always so tired. She wanted to please everyone, fix everything, mostly those things that could not be fixed. They said they got all the cancer, but who knew? Thay always said that, didn't they?

Chuck still wanted to move back to Texas and the oil company was willing, so they did, but the move tore at Beth; her daughter was away at college and her son had been pulled from the love and support of his friends he'd left behind in New Orleans, his school, his church and the only home he could remember. Caught between Chuck's needs and James's needs, Beth felt pulled apart, a nonperson herself. New Orleans looked so good to Beth now. Seeing it through the rearview mirror, it was easy to forget the tough times they'd gone through there. All Beth could remember was that in New Orleans, life for a very long time had been— normal.

Gradually though, Chuck got better and Beth came to see her night monsters as fantasies. Her faith gave her someplace to turn in the dark, made her feel that someone was listening and caring how and what she felt. She prayed for the strength to put the monsters out of her mind and come back to reality. She would say to herself, "Chuck is fine. He's lying here next to me, breathing—and I have to be grateful for this moment. Now go back to sleep." She found a job as a travel agent. James began to make new friends. Chuck went to work every day. Radiation treatments were working. Life began to to look as though it included a tomorrow. "We're going to beat this," they said to one another. "The cancer is not going to come back." In 1989, the cancer came back.

Chemotherapy was now Beth's new friend, and worst enemy. Every seven weeks, Chuck took pills, then went into the hospital to lie there for four hours while they pumped poison into him, hoping it would be strong enough to kill the poison already in him. Beth became Chuck's patient advocate, the one to talk to the doctors and take up for Chuck, holler and scream about things when he wasn't able to, when he was—just the patient. But try as she might, she could not come to think of chemotherapy as something good. She could hardly bear to sit and watch him throw up for hours and not be able to do anything about it. The doctors got angry at her and she didn't care, but she had to accept it, the chemotherapy, that was all she could do. Sometimes it was too much.

"Betheeee!"

Chuck is yelling at us from the potting shed. "Bethy, your book's getting all wet." Beth picks up her book from the side of the pool and tosses it onto the patio, which is covered.

"What are you reading?" I ask.

"This Present Darkness."

"What is that?"

"It's not *The Hunt for Red October.*"

"What is it?"

"Religious fiction."

"This is a genre with which I am unfamiliar," I say, laughing.

"Yeah. You would be," says Beth, laughing back at me. "But I, well, I guess I got tired somewhere along the way of reading surging manhood and up-turned breast kinds of books."

Chuck comes to stand over us. "What are you talking about now?"

We both giggle like the girls we aren't anymore. "Nothing, Chuck. Just girlstuff. You know, our periods 'n' stuff."

"Don't forget yellow waxy buildup," I say, ducking underwater to blow some bubbles for the hell of it. This rain has made me giddy. Or something. Underwater the sky looks green.

"You two are crazy to stay in the water in this rain. Two crazy women. *Las dos mujeres locas. Hijole,*" Chuck mutters, going into the house. Chuck mutters best in Spanish. Beth and I look at each other, smiling in the rain. There has been so much. And now?

"I have a hard time thinking about tomorrow," says Beth, not smiling anymore, not looking at me either. "I have—I can—deal realistically with—with the idea of losing Chuck. Cancer teaches you that. I've had to come to terms with my husband's mortality. And my own. What I have too much trouble thinking about is me, what there is for me after Chuck's gone. The possibility of other relationships—how will I feel about being alone, my husband gone, my children grown and no longer needing me? All of a sudden I will not be a mother, a wife. I'll just be Beth again. Starting over. Empty."

"Empty? Never. You've torn your very own self a big hole in this universe. You won't disappear."

"You know, you may be right. I hope you are." She sort of snorts. "Hope hasn't had much of a place in my life lately." The rain is stopping, slowly, the way it started, like tears.

"Beth?"

"Yes?"

"Do you ever picture your life twenty years from now?"

"Yes."

"Is Chuck in that picture?"

"No."

Now it's my turn to look away. I'm crying, but I don't want her to know, not my beautiful, strong Beth, my friend. I look at the sky instead. There are small pale blue patches, little rips in the clouds. The thunderstorm is passing. It's late.

"I picture myself . . . alone," says Beth, softly, ". . . in a little house somewhere in the country. Somewhere along the way I remember reading a book and I don't remember the book or the story, but it was about a woman who lived by herself in this little cabin and when I can't see beyond—beyond Chuck dying—I try to think about that woman and that cabin. She was happy, Linda."

"Tell me about your cabin. That cabin."

"Well, it's not really a cabin, just a small house. Outside there are hills, not mountains, but rolling, soft hills, all green, with lots of trees and cows grazing. There's a dog in the yard and a cat in the house, quilts on the bed—and—a blue granite teapot. When I get up in the morning I make hot tea and toast and go sit in the yard at a little table under a tree with the birds for company. I've always liked classical music, but you remember it wasn't cool to listen to classical music when we were young, and I was young enough not to want to admit I liked it. But as with so many other things, you finally reach a time when you don't care what others think, don't give a damn, really. Classical music makes me feel at peace. These days I search for things that give me peace. So I picture music at night and photographs on the mantel and . . . and . . . me, peaceful."

The rain is all gone. The pool is quiet. "It's not what we expected, is it?"

"No, Linda. It's not."

"If you could go back . . ."

"Go back?"

"If you could go back, what would you change?"

"You mean other than Chuck's illness?"

"Yes. Of course."

"I would have worked hard—harder—at being me. I would have insisted on Beth returning to school. I would have cared less what people wanted for me and wanted me to do for them.

People ask me, 'How do you cope? How do you manage?' I tell them I haven't managed, that I just did what I had to do. You know—somehow I just got through it, all of it. I never felt I was doing it well. I just kept going. I still do. But if I could do it over, I'd make a place for me. And I'd fit in it this time."

"Beth, you have. You do."

"Have I? Did you ever think, Linda, twenty years ago, that we'd be here? I mean, if we'd asked ourselves then where we would be when we're forty-six, it wouldn't have been where we are, would it?"

"No, Beth. We were just worried then about where we were that day. And what we had that we could fix for dinner that night."

"We were on to something, weren't we? I mean that's really all there is to worry about, isn't there? Maybe we should have stayed in Eagle Pass."

I remember sky, too.

"No, Beth. We shouldn't have stayed in Eagle Pass. But I'll tell you what we should have done."

"What?"

"We should have gone inside ten minutes ago and checked to see if we have the right cheese to make Chicken Portuguesa. What is the right cheese for Chicken Portuguesa? I forget."

Beth smiles. Beth has smiles that go on forever. "Whatever cheese you've got, Linda. Whatever cheese you've got."

I can hear music playing inside the house. Classical music. Chuck is humming along to Mozart. He sounds a little bit like a kazoo. We climb out of the pool and, wrapping our towels around us, walk toward that sound, Beth leading, pushing her thick black hair, now graying, away from her face to look up one more time. The sun is setting but there are no purple streaks here, no red rivers to see. There is only sky, the most beautiful sky, as blue as—as a blue granite teapot. Beth begins to hum, too. Soon it will be dark and we will sit down to eat, old friends, all of us, still hungry for more.

WE BUILT THIS CITY
ON ROCK 'N' ROLL

As I've said, I'm a war baby. Born in 1944. What this means is that I am not a baby boomer and therefore do not count. Products are not designed, neighborhoods are not gentrified and fish are not blackened for my benefit. Presidential candidates do not choose running mates with me in mind. *Time* magazine does not care what I think and there's no television show called *fortysomething*. You may call it a monumental case of bad timing, but I don't care. If the baby boomers grew up and threw a cultural revolution for the nation, we war babies set the table and brought the records. In our house, it began in the summer of 1956, when my parents lost their only child, a twelve-year-old girl with Mamie Eisenhower bangs who liked to listen to Mitch Miller records. She was taken from them by forces beyond their control, and although they were warned about puberty, there was no way they could have anticipated rock 'n' roll.

It was the summer Elvis Presley came to Houston. Carol's mother took Carol and me to the concert, although back then it was not called a concert, and it did not matter that I said I would not scream like those foolish girls I'd seen on television, I did scream, then went home and threw away my copy of "The Yellow Rose of Texas." Naturally, our parents did not like our music. They couldn't decide if rock 'n' roll was another one of those ill-advised, later-to-be-regretted pranks of youth (something between swallowing goldfish and stealing hubcaps) or The Devil's Final Solution. Their only comfort was that everybody who knew anything about music assured them it would not last.

Rock 'n' roll would not last.

Praise Jesus.

Look at the past, said our parents. Their own music hadn't lasted, and it was good. That was how the world worked: if our great-great grandparents waltzed, their children would cakewalk and their children's children would Charleston and their children's children's children, our parents, would jitterbug. Each generation would hate the next generation's music and vice versa. Now there was no music at all, just this awful noise. How wonderful it would be only a matter of time before it disappeared.

Meanwhile, after going through high school to the music of Chuck Berry, Buddy Holly and Bo Diddley, I went to college and discovered Ray Charles who, along with the Girl Groups, sang backup to my first broken heart, and when I stumbled into the beginnings of a social conscience, it was Bob Dylan who pointed which way the wind blew. The next thing you knew, everything in America seemed turned upside down, but nobody explained 1968 plainer than Crosby, Stills & Nash, nobody spelled Vietnam clearer than Country Joe McDonald, and nobody sang rage, our rage, like Janis. Nobody.

When The Age of Aquarius was dawning, I was changing diapers (all you really ever need to know about bad timing is that I had two babies two years before Pampers). The first time I saw Woodstock was when I saw the movie. My son was born in April of 1970, during that period of our history we loosely call (and I shall loosely refer to as) the sixties, though we usually mean anywhere from about 1965 to 1975. My son's name is Joshua. He does not know why I named him that. I was saving the story for his twenty-first birthday. It's time.

Alvin Toffler, whose book *Future Shock* was published the spring my son was born, looked at the frazzled, frantic, manic pace of American life in 1970 and predicted it would only become worse, constantly accelerating, and that as a result we would become susceptible to a whole catalog of physical and psychological traumas. But for most of us who were there at the time, that future seemed already too much with us. There was revolution in the air that spring. Three revolutions. One would actually happen. One wouldn't. The third is still happening. I was, I am, some part of them all.

The first revolution, the one that got the most press, made the most noise, had the most supporters and seemed, perhaps, the most imminent, was simple enough in intent. Change the world. Right the wrong. Fix the hurt.

Stop the war.

We'd been to the moon and back, but it wasn't enough. Rocket ships had done nothing to stop the war in Vietnam, save the environment or right the injustices of prejudice; neither did rocket ships feed people. We wanted to remake the world, make it fit for humans. We wanted to get back to the garden. So we said. Revolution generally comes from poverty, but this one was coming from a generation that was mostly well-fed and mostly white, a generation which now appeared to be turning from all-American to angry to violent. At the time, the thought of violence didn't scare me as much as it should have, as much as it would now—hadn't Stokely Carmichael told us violence was as American as cherry pie? Hadn't so respected a man as Supreme Court Justice William O. Douglas written a book, *Points of Rebellion*, in which he said the young were absolutely right to rise up against poverty, injustice, poor education and pollution? Dissent, he said, is an American right and while violence is not protected by the Constitution, protest often boiled over into violence because people were emotional, not rational. He was right, and besides, I was twenty-five years old, not an age that scares easily.

As a nation, we didn't like one another very much that spring; certainly the government didn't like those radicals they thought had declared a private war on the United States. Protests and marches don't do it, said Bernadine Dohrn. Revolutionary violence is the only way (in April, Dohrn, a survivor of the Weatherman Underground, a somewhat decimated group after the New York town house they were making explosives in blew up and killed three Weathermen, declared a state of war), and there *was* violence, but there were many more people who didn't like— and were frightened by—the government's response to those so- called radicals (some were, some weren't). Led by the FBI, city and state police all over the country had struck back. They heard the voices of the many, then looked at the violence of the few and concluded the American way of life was in jeopardy, and then jeopardized it further by launching the broadest program of domestic spying, infiltration and slander that this country has ever seen. In May of 1970, at Kent State University, government tactics against the young would expand to include homicide.

Most of the anger of the young was directed at the war, not at the nearly half a million young Americans who were fighting in Vietnam, certainly not at the more than 40,000 who had already died there. It was, we said, a dirty little war and America was playing the part of the bully. The President, Richard Nixon, took a radically different view; he called student protesters "bums" as, on the last day of April, he ordered American troops into what he called an "incursion" into Cambodia, with terrible consequences. The day after National Guardsmen killed four students at Kent State during a campus protest against the invasion of Cambodia, there would be a nationwide strike by students, the first one in the history of our country.

It was the spring Hollywood released both *Patton* and *M*A*S*H*, two movies that, taken together, pretty much illustrated our national schizophrenia about war. It was the spring the Chicago Seven were convicted of conspiracy to cross state lines and instigate a riot at the Democratic convention in Chicago in 1968. It was the spring our government decided to use taxpayer dollars to prevent the election and inauguration of Salvador Allende, a Marxist, as president of Chile. Said Henry Kissinger: I don't see why we need to stand by and watch a country go communist due to the irresponsibility of its own people. Allende was assassinated. An angry, angry spring, it was.

The Beatles had a song out. "Let It Be." The Carpenters had another. "Close to You." Those songs may have expressed what America was yearning for. They did not express what was happening, or who we were. There was another Beatles song. "Nothing's gonna change my world," sang the Fab Four that spring, when in fact almost everything was changing our world, and the thing that was changing it the most for the worst was man, we'd noticed. Saving the earth from environmental corruption by man suddenly seemed a fine and brave (if a little grandiose and a lot chancy) notion, and so a war on pollution was declared, too. April 22, 1970, was proclaimed Earth Day. It turned out to be the largest demonstration in the history of the world (until the anniversary of Earth Day twenty years later on April 22, 1990). If nothing else, it was a public statement of our good intentions. What a well-intentioned group of campers we were; even when we did drugs we meant well, we said, or at least we meant no harm; if nature was good, then all nature's gifts were good, right? Marijuana was the hip escape of choice that year. Twenty-two states had reduced first-time possession of less than an ounce of marijuana from a felony to a misdemeanor. Oregon was about to make it legal. It seemed like a good idea at the time.

The second revolution afoot in the spring of 1970 was the one that has succeeded more than either of the other two so far, and without firing a shot or rallying a rally. It was, of course, a revolution in technology. In general, technological change was outdoing itself that April, often lagging far behind thought, as is its wont, but most of the changes were small, comparatively. The 747, for example. They were brand-new and huge, twice the size of other airplanes; they could carry 400 passengers at a time, in one airplane. To a passenger who could remember when the Wright boys barely got it off the ground, and in 1970 some could, a 747 was big medicine. But it wasn't a revolution. Neither was the fact that the Soviets had an unmanned spacecraft on the moon and China had launched its first satellite, nor the fact that we were still acting out our glorious dream of putting people on the moon, then bringing them back, most of them looking about the same as when they had left, nor even the fact that the French had invented a nuclear-powered pacemaker. No, the second revolution of the spring of 1970 was so tiny to begin with that, when it was begun, it went almost unnoticed. It had to do with computers. Computers weren't new, but most people had never actually seen one. I certainly had not. They seemed to keep getting bigger and bigger. They cost millions of dollars, did mysterious things and were attended by a kind of technological priesthood. They were going to take over the world if we weren't careful. And they did.

But they did it by getting smaller, cheaper and friendlier. Ted Hoff, the man who dreamed up the microprocessor, the first "chip," did not in 1970 think of himself or his team as revolutionaries, yet they were; essentially they took the computer out of its ivory tower, out of its walled-in, glassed-in, air-conditioned cage and put it, you might say, everywhere. The microchip revolution would bring computer technology into everyday life, and the lives of everyday Americans. We might not understand them, we might not like them, but we would learn to use them and we would get used to them because we could no longer escape them.

The third revolution, the one that's still going on and may yet be the revolution of most consequence, was feminine. At the time it was never referred to as a revolution or even a revolt. It was called a movement. The women's movement. Presumably a movement is more polite than a revolution, and a lot slower. There were marches, rallies, battle cries and battle hymns. There were heroines. Villains. There were connections. Cliques. We'd begun to talk to one another, really talk, and to listen, hearing ourselves in each other every time; suddenly a significant number of American women seemed to be standing up and, like the man in the movie *Network*, hollering (whispering, in many cases) that they were mad as hell and weren't going to take it anymore. I was one of those women, one of the whispering ones. Many things in my mind, in my memory, seemed to fall into place. The message I was getting was that maybe I wasn't crazy. And maybe I wasn't alone.

Impossible dreams die hard. Like Toons, they can be pulverized, poisoned, punctured, stomped flat, blown up, gut shot, cut into little pieces, dropped from high places, bludgeoned with a blunt instrument, fried to a crisp and buried at sea; and still they come back, alive, whole and grinning like homemade sin. I was seven years old when I decided to play third base for the New York Yankees. After nearly wearing my brain out worrying about whether to become a trapeze artist, a rocket scientist, a barrel racer or a blonde, how fine it felt finally to know my true destiny. Grown-ups were always pressing you for answers about these things; you had to want to be something. You had to have a dream. Don't get me wrong, I was no fool, I knew the difference between wanting and getting. When they told me you had to be very good to play third base for the New York Yankees, I said I could practice; when they told me you had to be a grown-up, I said I could wait; when they told me you had to chew tobacco, I said I could learn; when they told me you had to live in New York City, New York, I said I could compromise; but when they told me you had to be a boy, there was nothing I could say and nothing I could do.

Hey? Wasn't America the land of the free? Wasn't I an American? Yes, they explained, of course I was, but there were certain facts of life I must understand when it came to freedom and, uh, stuff—one of which was that girls did not play major-league baseball.

Why not? Was there a law against it?

Not exactly, but there wasn't a law against a girl being the President of the United States either, they said, it was just there were certain things girls didn't do. Unwritten rules, they called them. Surely I could understand. Surely I could not. Besides, who said anything about wanting to be President? The President didn't get to wear those neat shoes with spikes on the bottom or travel on a bus with all his pals or slide into first or yell at the ump or steal home. The President probably didn't even know how to spit.

I did.

I knew how to spit just fine, better than some ten-year-olds, but it didn't matter now; I was never going to play third base for the New York Yankees. They'd taken my wonderful dream and driven a stake through its heart. I hung up my glove (a practically new Spaulding), gave away my bat (a practically magic Louisville Slugger) and made up my mind to be a cocker spaniel instead.

But that's just it. *The wonderful thing about impossible dreams is they don't know they're impossible!* Which is another way of saying fools rush in where fools belong, and so, although I grew up and forgot about wanting to bark at the moon, bite people on the ankle and have ten puppies every year, I never forgot about wanting to play big-league baseball. One day, I said, the world would change its mind about what women could and could not do.

Now, in 1970, watching the women's movement explode across the country, I was ready to do something about the situation myself. Only, Eagle Pass, Texas, was a long march from the barricades, particularly for a practically penniless woman with a one-year-old baby girl and a husband. In those days I didn't march, I mopped—to a different drummer perhaps, but I mopped. I was also pregnant again.

What could I do for the women's movement? How could I make a difference? Oh, sure, I would make a difference in my own life and in my daughter's life: my mother had bumped up against walls, I would poke through them, my daughter would knock them down. I had named my daughter Vanessa Ray, "Vanessa" for Van, her father, and "Ray" for my father. It had never once occurred to me to name the girl for either my mother or me, although we both had names I liked as much as I liked either Vanessa or Ray. Had I done it because I wanted to endow my daughter from birth with as many of the trappings of power as possible, even to giving her names that came from men? I thought about that. I decided I didn't want to think about that. Women, I figured, were going to be fast to change their own ideas about what they could and could not do, fast to demand equality—now that they'd been enlightened. Walls must surely come tumbling down now. Except in my heart I didn't believe it would work out that way; I believed that no matter what women demanded, or got by demanding, we would never enjoy true equality with men until men enjoyed and demanded women who were their equal. And there weren't many men who felt that way. Without affixing blame or getting into a variety of complex socio-anthropological reasons why, there just weren't many men like that around.

I decided to grow my own.

It wouldn't be quick, but it was, at least, something I could do, even in Eagle Pass. The absence of those damn walls sure would make life easier for the next generation of women, I decided, and if the walls would not come tumbling down until those on both sides wanted them down and began pushing from both directions at once, then I would raise me a wall-pusher. A wall man. On April 16, 1970, my son was born.

I named him Joshua.

Wall man.

Let it be, I said.

The Beatles that spring said the same thing. Let it be. The Beatles sang a good song, but they were not really revolutionaries. They were, like so many of us, rebels and, therefore, were unable finally to get along with one another. The band broke apart. Our band. The music stopped. A generation, many of whom (me among them) claimed to believe in radical change, began to be faced with its own version of counterculture shock; the very music that had seemed to score an entire political and cultural movement in this country had stopped. It should have been an omen to us because, as was pointed out a long time ago, once the music stops, the revolution's over.

We didn't know then. We thought it was still the sixties. And it was. But it was the beginning of the end. The circus came to town. The circus left town. And when it was gone, what was waiting to replace the passion, the colored lights, the highwire artists, lion tamers and clowns was a national triviality of spirit. A crooked sideshow. At least it got the music it deserved. God, I hated Disco.

Time has a whoopee cushion for every occasion, doesn't it? I am aware, calm even, knowing that in 1990 my daughter turned twenty-one. My son turned twenty. So what? I turned forty-six.

I'm a war baby, not a baby boomer; I'm not hung up about getting older. These things happen. So what? So why do I find it obscene, unnecessary and probably impossible that in 1990 Grace Slick turned fifty-one years old? It wasn't just Grace. Chuck Berry turned sixty-nine. Pete Seeger turned seventy-one. Che Guevara would have turned sixty-two, if he weren't already dead. I could go on. Lord, how did we get this old so fast? No worries, says my daughter. It's sooner than you think. Remember, no rock 'n' roller has died of old age yet. Drugs, airplane crashes and the occasional bullet to the brain, yes, *but not old age.*

Thank you, Vanessa.

The beat, we like to say, goes on. But sometimes the beat seems so different, so changed, I'm not sure how to move to it anymore, even in memory. Maybe especially in memory. If life imitates art, what does television imitate? In 1987 I was asked to write and anchor, as an episode of a television series called *Our World,* a program about—ta-da—*the spring of 1970.*

Well, now.

Did I remember the spring of 1970? Did I remember Joshua's birth? Joshua's name. Earth Mothers. Earth Day. Earth *shoes.* Moonshots. Marijuana. Microchips. The New Morality. The Immoral War. Cambodia. Kent State. Where *did* all those flowers go? What had become of the revolutions that stirred the stew in the spring of 1970? Well, to begin with, I'm writing this on my Macintosh.

As for the rest—we'd long since stopped going to the moon but it seemed to me we still hadn't learned that it's bureaucracies, not dreams, that build spaceships; when the Challenger went down with all aboard in 1986, she did so with the help of parts put together by the lowest bidder. The New Morality? Replaced by the old morality when the children of Bob and Carol and Ted and Alice reached puberty about the same time herpes and AIDS reached epidemic proportions. Marijuana? An idea whose time had come, and gone, replaced by a widespread and quite correct alarm about marijuana, cocaine, crack and the consequences of drug and alcohol abuse in general. Earth Day? An idea whose time had come and gone and would, in 1990, come again. What had been accomplished was nothing measured against what still needed doing.

Student protests had seemed to vanish with the Vietnam War, but I began to notice young people finding their voices again. Tentatively. Every now and then. By the late eighties, they were fueled by a trickle-down economic policy that didn't trickle down to them, or to many other people, a Supreme Court threat to wipe out reproductive and other hard-won civil rights of the individual, and civil wars in El Salvador and Nicaragua in which the United States appeared, in both instances, to back the wrong side, again. There were days when the only effective way to drown out the sound made by the Reagan years was to keep turning up Bruce Springsteen, philosopher-poet of the workingman, who put it so eloquently when he said, "Blind faith in your leaders will get you killed." Now that was a beat I could still dance to. And always, always, there were the Grateful Dead to describe the trip and Jagger to laugh at it, and by this time my own children were listening to these people and this music.

Our music.

I felt sorry for our kids, they weren't as lucky as we were. For the first time, one generation was embracing the popular music of the generation that went before. Adolescence is tough enough without the handicap of agreeing with your parents about anything. Sure, my kids and I can pick a puny fight over Talking Heads versus Joe Cocker, but piddling is all it is, because the genre, if you will, is the same. It's all rock 'n' roll. And it lasted.

For our 1987 television program about 1970, I'd written an essay about the fact that in April of that year, one month before Kent State, CBS News had conducted a poll to see if people still cared about the Bill of Rights. Questions were framed in terms of contemporary events. One of the questions they'd asked people was: As long as there appears to be *no clear danger of violence*, do you think any group, no matter how extreme, should be allowed to organize protests against the government? Seventy-six percent said no. In fact, the majority of Americans they polled refused to support five out of ten of the protections guaranteed by the Bill of Rights, including the First Amendment, another good reason we need a Bill of Rights. Among other things, it protects the minority from the majority who, by definition, need no protection. I was sure that had those people been asked the question "Do you support the Bill of Rights?" those people would have answered yes. All of them. Trouble was, without the Bill, people didn't recognize the Rights.

I'd just finished taping this essay when I was called to the telephone. The man on the other end of the line identified himself as an officer of the law in Washington, D.C. He said he had a young woman in custody who claimed to be my daughter. I said the right thing.

"It depends. What did she do?"

He said did I know there had been this demonstration down in Washington, that it was Spring Break, and did I know all these college kids had come to Washington to protest that "Star Wars Defense thing" Mr. Reagan wanted? Did I know about that?

I said I did, and added that those students had a perfect right to protest the arming of the very heavens above us, and was that why he had arrested this young woman?

He didn't answer the question. He said they had this demonstration and, well, some of the students had gone through police lines.

"*They did?* You mean they knocked down the barricades?" I hoped I didn't sound too happy.

"Oh, no, no. Nothing like that. They just went around the barricades. Went where they weren't told to go."

I asked if that was why he'd arrested this young woman.

He still didn't answer my question. He said twenty-seven of the students had sat down in the street.

Impatient now, I yelled.

"So is *that* why you arrested this young woman?"

There was a pause.

"Three of them," he said, almost whispering, "turned a hundred live chickens loose in the Washington, D.C., rush hour."

"Oh," I said. "May I please speak to my daughter?"

Chickens notwithstanding, I celebrate my daughter's basic instinct and the instincts of all other young people who continue to think that questioning authority is not only okay but necessary.

When I think now about that spring of 1970, it seems so far away and I seem so young then. But we were: young and self-centered and very, very loud, not to mention mostly right. Is this looking back bitter or sweet?

Yes.

The emotions that rocked us then are in some way or another with us still, buried a little, maybe, but there; when it comes to Vietnam, the aftershocks of the heart continue. If you don't believe me, consider the divergence of American opinion over the movie *Born on the Fourth of July*. Perhaps it's true that after a lost war, one should write only comedies. All I know is that twenty years later I still don't understand Vietnam. I can't explain it to my own children. Maybe after forty years, I'll understand. Or maybe when they write the history books, the so-called Dark Ages will include our own.

The third revolution that was begun in the spring of 1970? The women thing? Women have made some changes. So far, most men have found no compelling reason to work to change inequities toward women. Perhaps it's not so much that they want to keep us down, but that they like being up. A natural reaction to power. Where you stand, still depends on where you sit. Unfortunately, the older I get, the less patience I have for this tomfoolery.

I've yet to see a female major-league baseball player. Or a female President. The world hasn't changed as much as I expected. Or is it that I just don't understand men and women? In 1989, *Esquire* magazine began producing a television program for cable, the Lifetime channel. The Lifetime channel is aimed at women. *Esquire* magazine is aimed at men. The magazine and the television channel's somewhat patronizing and completely convoluted solution was to call the program *Esquire—About Men for Women*. Patronizing, because it implied *Esquire* magazine was about men for men, something that confused me, a reader of their magazine for twenty years or so and, I hasten to add, a woman. Convoluted, because they then asked me (still a woman) to appear on the program regularly to explain men to women.

I said I couldn't. I wasn't a man. I said I was still waiting for a few explanations myself. So they asked me to come on the program and talk about what women wanted to know about men.

I said I didn't know what women wanted to know about men. I was not women. I was woman. So they asked me what I wanted to know about men.

Not a damn thing, I said. Having married several and raised one, I already knew more than I wanted to, which was only half true; there are many things I want to know about men. For instance, I want to know why, if men rule the world, they don't stop wearing neckties? I mean how intelligent is it to start the day by tying a little noose around your neck? (For women: I want to know why women have started to wear nooses around their necks. So people will think they're men?)

I have more questions.

Why don't men, when they get really angry, cry? I wish they would tell me, so I could stop crying when I get really angry. Why do men, when they go to the bathroom, stand up and take aim when they could sit down and take five? Why do men have breasts?—a perfectly legitimate question, if you ask me. And finally, I asked the people at *Esquire,* why was a program "about men for women" produced by men? Wouldn't it make more sense if . . .

The answer to all of the above is that this is not a logical world. If it were, many things would be different in matters concerning men and women, and not always to our benefit. For one thing, if this were a logical world, men wouldn't give women the vote in any country where majority rules.

If this were a logical world, eighteen-year-old men and thirty-eight-year-old women would pair off and party while they peaked, statistically speaking. Men wouldn't have breasts they don't need and women wouldn't have babies they don't want. Men would be monogamous, women would be polygamous and eunuchs would be superfluous. Getting a divorce would be simple, inexpensive and quick. Getting married wouldn't be. Women wouldn't wash dishes, mop floors, fix toilets or change diapers. Neither would men. Women would rock as easily as they roll, and men would reach out as easily as they run away. If this were a logical world, men would listen more, women would talk less and vice versa. If this were a logical world, women would be drafted. And men wouldn't be. Men are confused by war. Women aren't. Men fight battles. Women fight dirty. Men take prisoners. Women take scalps. Men tell stories, sing songs, make movies, write books, recite poems, preach sermons, pass laws, hold meetings, have nightmares, howl obscenities, ask questions, offer answers, turn silent, take notes, teach courses, collect toys, keep clippings, call home, give speeches, grow morose, get excited, gather together, part company, pair off and go on and on and on—about war. Women understand scorched earth. They take things very personally.

Finally, in a logical world, *men* would ride sidesaddle. (Think about it.)

But it's not a logical world and as I said before, it hasn't changed as much as I expected it would or, possibly more accurately, *we* haven't changed it as much as I expected we would. By "we," I mean we, the people. Certainly not governments; governments don't change. Only people do.

These days, when so few things including our families work right or, more to the point, work the way we thought they would, it's hard to look at the world we live in and not want to blame someone. Once upon a time, a long time ago, they would bring two goats to the altar of the tabernacle on Yom Kippur, the Day of Atonement. One goat would be sacrificed to the Lord, the other, after the high priest had symbolically laid the sins of the people on its head, was led into the wilderness and let loose to die. That goat was called the scapegoat. You might think this isn't done anymore. You would be wrong. We do it to women all the time. I went to Salt Lake City, invited by the University of Utah to speak at a symposium on women in the marketplace. The other speaker was Gordon B. Hinckley. Mr. Hinckley is a Mormon leader, the first counselor in the First Presidency of the Church of Jesus Christ of Latter-Day Saints. Mr. Hinckley spoke about child abuse, neglect, abuse and abandonment of wives and rising crime among women. Mr. Hinckley said, "Certainly the most obvious contributing factor to this alarming situation is a tragic and widespread breakdown in family life."

Then Mr. Hinckley said, "It is my opinion that the very situation of an ever-increasing number of *mothers out of the home and in the workplace* is a root cause of many of the problems of delinquency, drugs and gangs, both male and female."

Excuse me, but is this the nineties or what?

It's pretty to think that if only women could be made to stay home, the family would function properly and then everything else that's wrong with society would go away. It's pretty. It's also over-simplistic, immoral and, most of all, inaccurate; changes in the family are a *result* of other changes in society, not the cause. This nation has undergone profound economic changes in the last twenty-five years. For example, people who spent 14 percent of their income on housing in 1963 now have to spend an average of 44 percent of their dollars on a place to live. Without the work of wives, 60 percent of the households in the United States would be below the poverty line. Research also shows that most social problems, including teen pregnancy and substance abuse, occur at all socioeconomic levels—and in every type of family constellation!

Fancy figures. Where did I get them? From the University of Utah. Why was that university so interested in this subject? Because more than 60 percent of women in Utah work, more than in any other state and yet, while women earn 65 cents for every dollar earned by men, nationally, the women of Utah still earn a whopping 54 cents; in other words they have a situation in Utah. Is there a connection between those sorry figures and the attitude expressed by Mr. Hinckley? What do you think? Trouble is, this attitude isn't limited to one man or one religion or one state—*or one sex*. This attitude infects all of us. Everybody goes around wanting to believe someone else is to blame for whatever's wrong. If it's someone else's fault then we don't have to change our own ways.

If poor mothering causes teenage delinquency, then poor fathering is okay? If it's government greed that causes a deficit, then personal greed is okay? If black people cause crime, then white people are okay? As has always been the case, if we believe in absurdities, we shall commit atrocities.

There are two things to remember about scapegoats: one is that they don't work, they never have—laying all the sins on one goat never stopped the sins. The other thing to remember about scapegoats is what happened to the other goat. It got killed, too.

Do I sound riled up? Women care about attitudes concerning their working because they have to. When they asked him what he looked for in a script, Spencer Tracy said, "Days off." I consider Spencer Tracy the patron saint of the working mother. Today, although women comprise half the work force in America, women with children are away from their jobs more than any other group of workers. As I'm sure you've read, the absentee rate for women with children is more than twice that for men with children, which has nothing to do with the fact there are about as many female CEOs as there are male secretaries in corporate America, or the fact that "working father" is not a part of our working language. Does it?

Obviously, the average working mother will use the slightest excuse to avoid work: your baby-sitter didn't show up because her baby-sitter didn't show up. Your son is playing Balboa in the third-grade play and you've got to be there when he discovers the Pacific. Your child's dentist refuses to fill anything but his wineglass after 5 P.M. The school nurse says she's sorry to bother you at the office but head wounds confuse her so. Or your four-year-old stands there, smiling, with one giant tear rolling down a cheek, and says, "It's okay, Mommy, I understand. And I'll have another birthday—someday. Don't be sad because you have to go to work. You're the best Mommy in the whole wide world."

Oh, of course you are. Would Superwoman be anything else?

I attended a conference of the American Association of University Women. In the brochure detailing the various workshops, I noticed one called "Having It All: How You Can Juggle Career, Children, Love Life and Leisure Activities and Keep Your Sanity." I went to the president of the association. "What's this? Why are we lying to these young women? You and I know you can't juggle career, children, love life and leisure activities—*and keep your sanity!*"

She said I should relax because they'd cancelled that particular workshop.

"Oh, really?" I said. "And why did you do that?"

She grinned. "We couldn't fit it in."

That's all you need to know about having it all, that and one other thing: in a recent study by *Seventeen* magazine, most young women said they plan to work while their children are young, yet only 3.4 percent said "a most important issue" was providing child care for those who need it. Too bad, because your government agrees with you. Too bad, because we're not Superwomen and you're not Supergirl. (The spell-checker inside the computer I'm writing this on refuses to recognize the word "superwoman." It does, however, recognize "superman.") You better know that now. You better understand that being a working mother means you have to make choices, really painful ones, again and again, knowing every time that no matter which way you choose, you lose—at home, at work (as a consolation prize you get a long guilt trip to nowhere).

Where will men be while you're trying to be Superwoman? The Bureau of National Affairs, a private research organization, released a study called "The 1990s Father: Balancing Work & Family Concerns." It says fathers are increasingly finding themselves torn between work and family because, while fathers "continue facing traditional pressure to be good workers, they also want to spend more time with their children, to be more intimately involved in raising them, but," says one of the experts, "it's not altogether socially acceptable for men to stay home when their kids are sick and such." This, according to the study, "sets up conflicts for the father as he moves through his career."

Well, welcome to the real world.

Sit down and let's talk about this. So it's not socially acceptable to stay home with a sick child, is it? Not socially acceptable to whom? Your child? Your child's mother? *Your* mother? Give me a break. We're not talking about social acceptance here; we're talking about career advancement—success, ambition, power and image. We're talking about the possibility that if you start taking off work for child-related obligations, they might think you're not serious about your job.

Yep. That's what they might think, all right.

"You either have to be in a very senior position where you can call your own shots, or be a specialist," says the study.

Oh, no, you don't. It's not a matter of waiting for the rules to change. I don't mean to sound snotty, and I can't tell you how much I admire a working man wanting to be a working father, but in order to raise a child, you have to stop being one. I was a "specialist." I was able to call more shots than most working mothers, yet with all those advantages, I fell into the same trap you're in, and I tell you, and mean it with all my heart, that if I could do it over, I'd be there for my children far more than I was. Nobody ever lay on her (his) deathbed and said, "Gee, I sure wish I'd spent more time at the office."

So let's all tell our bosses we're not going to Cleveland on Friday, because that's the day Balboa is going to discover the Pacific Ocean, and we want to be there when he plants that flag. Maybe if working fathers and working mothers work together, we can make some new rules around this place.

For Balboa's sake.

In the late eighties, I returned to the college I attended in the early sixties. I was there to speak to the students as part of "Women's Week" at Vanderbilt. Two young women, students, met me at the airport. I asked the one who'd organized the activities how everything was going.

"We had some problems," she said. "We had trouble getting women students involved. Most of them said feminism was so *unattractive*. You know—feminists are strident. Bra-burners and all that. You know?"

I know. (For the record: about as many women burned their bras as men burned flags, which is not many.)

I asked them were they discouraged?

"Oh, no. Not really, after all, things are good for women now. Equal. In the marketplace. Everywhere. You know—look how far we've come."

I asked her what she meant.

"Well, let's see . . . we have a woman on the Supreme Court now. We have twenty-eight women in the Congress. We have minority hire." She stopped, thought a moment and smiled. "We have 'Women's Week' at Vanderbilt. It's very different from when you were here and women couldn't even wear slacks on campus and had curfews and all."

"Anything else?"

"Uh . . . we have Cagney and Lacey now?"

Ah, yes. Cagney and Lacey. That night I talked to several hundred young women about the differences at Vanderbilt between the time I was there and now. And then I talked about reality. There are, I reminded them, *nine* people on the Supreme Court. There are *535* people in the Congress. Cagney and Lacey are not big-city police detectives. They are roles, played by actresses, who also aren't big-city police detectives. And at 51 percent of the population, *women are not minor.*

And, I asked, if you have "Women's Week" at Vanderbilt, who gets the other fifty-one weeks?

They weren't worried, but they should have been. According to the federal government, women are head of household in more than half the households in this country—and more than half the men ordered to pay child support *don't.* (You think feminism is unattractive? Think how attractive welfare will be.) I told those young ladies to go home and practice saying these words: I am a feminist. Of course being a feminist is more than saying you are one, but it's a good place to start; it's no good saying, "I believe in equal rights . . . but I'm not a feminist." If you believe in equal rights you *are* a feminist: feminism means you believe in equality between men and women. Equal justice for all. *And that's all it means.* It doesn't mean turning the tables on men, it means throwing out all the tables except the round ones. It means treating men as if they had good sense instead of manipulating them. That way nobody has to dance backward all her (or his) life. It means not climbing over the backs of other women at work or at home just because that's what you've seen done. Being a feminist means giving back better than we got, when it comes to respect, and it means respecting the work—and the choices—of women.

There was a time, not very long ago, when taking care of a

home and raising children weren't considered anything special, mainly because back then men did most of the considering and almost none of the home-taking-care-of and child-raising. We wanted to change that. For starters, we wanted it understood that being a wife and mother *is* important work—worth ten times the recognition it gets and twenty times the respect—not to mention thirty times the pay. Being a wife and mother, I said to those Vanderbilt women, is the hardest work you'll ever do. Being a wife and mother is honorable. Being a wife and mother *counts!*

And so does being a husband and father.

Read *my* lips. Women and women's work—*all* women's work, especially that of being a wife and mother—will never be taken seriously unless women take it seriously. This is called having good sense.

To me, being a feminist means being equal.

Being equal.

And never, ever settling for less. It's no good putting up with, or worse, saying words like, "These things take time. We must be patient. Wait until tomorrow." It's no good telling yourself, "We've come a long way, baby." *We haven't come a long way and we're not babies.* As for tomorrow, you've read *Gone With the Wind?* I asked them. Or seen it? Then you know what tomorrow is. Tomorrow is another damned day. This is not the dress rehearsal. This is your life we're talking about. *Your* fight. Maybe it will help if you younger women think of progress for women as a road. We graded it.

Now you get out there and pave it.

They say you learn by your mistakes. As a woman I've been lucky. I've made many, which I hope means I've learned something. One thing I've learned is that, even in the nineties, there's no easy way down in this matter. Too many men continue to confuse equality with supremacy—"if you're coming up, we must be going down." Too many women are still afraid of being thought "unattractive." But I still believe in opportunities; I believe that for women, change can only help us in the long run. At the beginning of this chapter, I said that when I was small, I wanted to play major-league baseball. There's another way a woman can make it to the majors and in my lifetime one will, probably. The only trouble is, I still don't want to be President of the United States.

Still, you do get to toss out the first baseball every April. I know it isn't as good as playing third base for the New York Yankees, but I guarantee you this much: my arm's as good as George's. I watched him on television when he threw out the first ball this year. The man throws like a girl.

So much for the nation and me. What about the personal revolution I started back in 1970? What about my other wall-pusher, the one I called Joshua?

He grew up and did the right thing, too. Usually. The same cannot be said of me. The night my son went dancing I learned from him what it was I'd forgotten about revolution. It was his first dance. Watching him get ready that evening made me feel younger than flowers. And older than trees. Finally, after much futzing around, he was dressed and we were sitting in my bedroom. No, I was sitting. Josh was pacing, but that was okay because I had things to say, things I wanted him to remember: all his life there had been so many things I wanted him to remember, important stuff, like how you should never write for any reason but money or subscribe to anything that publishes quarterly, and of course there were things he should remember about girls. I told him don't be concerned about anything, because everything will be fine as long as you understand that while girls are different, they aren't really different. Girls, I reminded him, were the same people who'd been his friends for years, only bumpier now.

"Bumpier. Fine," said Josh, "but there's something else I need to know." Now he was fidgeting. If he'd had a stone, he'd have kicked it for poise.

"Of course there is," I said, as if from a great height. "Social intercourse is confusing in a society that says it believes in the equality of women, but does not believe in the equality of women enough to say so in its Constitution."

"Right, Mom, right. That's just it. Don't you see . . ."

"Stop interrupting me. You're the feminist son of a feminist mother who merely wants to make sure her feminist son doesn't go out there tonight and, despite everything, behave like some junior chauvinist piglet."

Josh was starting to sweat through his new shirt.

"Mom, about girls . . ."

"The girls will be nervous, too, Josh. Some of them have been taught that being nervous is cute and some of them have been taught it's useful, but you, my son, have been taught to treat all humans alike. Right?"

"Right, Mom, I know that. What I'm nervous about is something I *don't* know. Something you never taught me and that's . . ."

"You're wondering if you should open the door for her or pay her way and all that? That's understandable. These are valid questions. There's still a lot of silliness about and between men and women. The answer is, just do the kind thing. You can't go wrong doing the kind thing."

"No, Mom, that's not it."

"Then what? What are you scared of? Not Jenny? You're taking Jenny to the dance, aren't you? You've known Jenny since the third grade, played ball with her, eaten at her house, traded comics with her, been punched out by her [it was the third or fourth grade and as I recall there was some misunderstanding about how babies get made] and you're still friends and she's still Jenny!"

"Mom, calm down. [Why is my son always telling me to calm down?] I have to go now. I'll be late. And, yes, you taught me to treat girls like people. You taught me to be fair. You taught me to be kind. You taught me to enjoy and demand equality in a woman. You taught me all those things, but there's one thing you never taught me. One simple thing. And I need to know. *Now.*"

"Now? You need to know what now? What's left?"

"Mom."

My son is looking at his feet. He raises his head and looks me straight in the eye.

"You never taught me how to dance."

Why is it that more often than not we don't grow up so much as we just grow older? In that respect, women and men are truly equal. I'd forgotten the first rule of revolution. I'd forgotten the music. Had mine stopped?

In the spring of 1990, Paul McCartney said that the Beatles, what was left of them, both as a group and individually, might get together again. Imagine. There was a time I might have. The Beatles, we said—hell, for a while, everybody said—were important. Was it just because John Lennon was dead that I found myself totally unimpressed by thoughts of a Beatles "reunion?" Partly. But I think I might have felt the same if Lennon hadn't died. In the summer of 1989, we had a whole slew of dinosaurs on tour—the Who, the Rolling Stones, Jefferson Airplane and that oldest-establishment-permanent-floating-rock band in America, the Grateful Dead. Some were comebacks. Some had never quit. Some I enjoyed then and enjoy now. Some I didn't and don't. But they were all mostly about the music, the beat, rock 'n' roll, whereas the Beatles were in memory, if not in fact, about something else, something more—and because they stopped making their music in 1970, the Beatles have stayed lost in time. In the late eighties, we had a fine old time remembering the sixties, wallowing in it, asking ourselves what it all meant, some people wondering how we could bring it all back. But it didn't work. The Woodstock Nation wouldn't be revived: not altogether a bad thing. Love is, in fact, not all we need. Nothing's that easy anymore. It wasn't easy then. It was only simple. I ask my son, born the year John, Paul, George and Ringo broke up, if he would like to see Paul, George and Ringo play it again. No, he says. Well, maybe. "If they got Julian Lennon to sit in as a fourth. The other three could learn a lot from him about the sixties."

You know, he's right. If we ever do find out what the sixties meant, it won't be by examining that time but by examining this time, by asking our children, by looking at our children, the children of the sixties, the children of the dream. The way to finally know who we *were* is to find out who they *are*. And to hear the music made by their lives. Their times. Who knows? Different drummers have been right before.

Like the war babies. I suppose I want to think of us as different drummers and, no, I guess I don't mind really, not being a baby boomer, but, Lordy, it would be nice just once to be *what* everybody else is *when* everybody else is, so I could read *Time* magazine and find out *who I am*. Maybe I'll ask my daughter who I am. She knows who she is. She's known since she was nine years old. That's when she wrote her first autobiography.

It began with this sentence: I was a war baby. Born in 1969. *Yeah.*

MOTHER AND CHILD REUNION

. . . is only a motion away.

—*PAUL SIMON*

To find out who someone else is presumes you know who they're not. It was New Year's Eve, 1982, and in New York City, Hallie, Linda and Vanessa sat watching the ball fall. On television. Each of the three women wished she were someplace else. Hallie wished she were back home in Houston, in her house, sitting in her chair, watching her television. Ray, her husband, would be three feet away, sitting in his chair, sound asleep. She would wake him when the ball started its fall, they would count backward out loud, and when the ball landed they would kiss, then for a little while would watch the crazy people on television. Hallie knew they were crazy; only a crazy person would be in Times Square, in New York City, on New Year's Eve. She would shake her head and say, as she always did, that you could keep New York City, thank you; she wouldn't live in such a place if you paid her. Then they would go to bed and Hallie would go to sleep, feeling safe, knowing that when she got up in the morning her world would be right where she left it and the new year would be pretty much like the old year, which was just fine with her. Hallie never liked surprises of any kind.

But it was too late for Hallie to wake Ray. Ray was dead. Hallie was seventy years old—too old to live alone. That's what they told her; that's why she had to sell her house and move in with Linda, her daughter. Linda lived in New York City. With the crazy people. Linda was one of the crazy people. Hallie knew tonight she would fall asleep wanting the new year to be an old year, lonely for the past and angry, so angry, because never again could she count on anything staying where she put it.

Her daughter didn't understand, but then Linda had never understood her.

Never.

Vanessa wished she were in Paris or maybe Hong Kong or Alaska, wearing a green chiffon ball gown she'd designed herself or a red silk kimono her lover had given her or a tie-dyed T-shirt she'd found on top of a mountain with no name. She wished she were in a round bed, naked, drinking expensive champagne from a silver goblet. With Mick Jagger. She wished she were walking down a dark street in a strange city, her guitar slung over her back, no money in her pocket, coming from one adventure, going to another. She wanted every year—no, every day—to be different from the one before. Vanessa loved surprises of all kinds.

But Vanessa couldn't go up a mountain with no name, down a street in a strange city, or into a ballroom anywhere. What's more, she had never even seen a round bed except on television, and while it was true there were silver goblets in the closet upstairs, Vanessa couldn't drink champagne from one because she was thirteen years old, and Linda, her mother, didn't think thirteen-year-old girls ought to be so damned fond of champagne.

Vanessa guessed she would wait for the ball to finish its fall, then help put her grandmother to bed, and after that she'd probably fight with her mother about one thing or another before going to her own bed, where she would lie awake dreaming of the future, when she could leave this house and her mother, who did not and never would understand her.

Never.

The ball was nearly done falling.

Linda didn't know where she wished she were, right then, and wasn't at all sure how she felt about surprises anymore. She thought it would be nice if the ball came to a full stop before it reached bottom and hung there, frozen, the ball and time itself, until she gave them both permission to move. Linda was thirty-nine years old and could use the rest—not that her daughter or her mother would understand that. Neither one of them so much as tried to understand her, and God knows she couldn't figure them out, either.

Ever.

The ball landed.

They toasted the New Year with glasses of Dr Pepper, hugged, wished one another happiness and, having nothing else to say, said they guessed it was late.

Vanessa and Linda helped Hallie down to the basement bedroom Hallie used because she would not climb the two flights of stairs separating the living room from the real bedrooms, and liked because it had no windows, which meant she didn't have to look at New York City and New York City didn't get to look at her.

How was it possible for three women to be so closely related and so unlike? How could they love each other and end up being strangers?

It was ten minutes after midnight.

(VANESSA REMEMBERS)

Mom and I were not close. She was suspicious of everything. If I went to the store for her and on the way home stopped to watch the jugglers in the park, I was grilled about where I'd been and what I'd done. If I said I stopped to watch the jugglers in the park, she wouldn't believe me, so I lied and if I was caught, that made me a liar—and no good.

She said I never let her into my life.

Why should I? For years she had been gone, preoccupied either by the business of writing or by the business of marriage, playing Mommy when she was in the mood. She thought she was fascinating. Anybody who held a normal job or lived a normal life she put down as "uninteresting" and, therefore, unimportant. She was so arrogant. Her ideas seemed to change with every husband—she'd had four—and I had no interest in keeping up.

If I daydreamed out loud, she would get this look of disapproval in her eyes and tell me to pay attention to the present. If I said I wanted to see Bombay, she wanted to know what was wrong with New York. I couldn't win. I couldn't be honest and get her approval. I knew I wasn't supposed to think of adventure all the time, but I did because I saw no reason to spend my childhood daydreaming about practical things. What thirteen-year-old wants to grow up to be practical? Besides, if she couldn't accept my dreams, why should I accept her reality?

Nana, my grandmother, was a stern woman, but not to me. She accepted my dreams, even if it meant—and she said it did—that I would never find a husband. Nana was an old woman who never saw her dreams come true; she had let reality get in the way. Mom judged Nana on what appeared to be there and saw only an old woman. I knew Nana best, I think. We were bound by a common enemy: my mother.

Nana and I would stay up nights, the two of us talking, even though we rarely agreed on anything and I enjoyed shocking her. She would look at me, and, grinning in false disapproval, she would say, "Vanessa Ray, you shouldn't talk like that. It's not nice." It was easy to shock her. She could be pretty backward. Take things. Things were important to her, like the piano she owned but could not play and the country club she used to belong to but seldom visited. We didn't belong to a country club in New York, but we still had the piano Nana couldn't play. Mother couldn't play it, either. Once, when I was in the second grade, I took piano lessons, but the lessons didn't take. Nobody played the piano in our family.

I don't remember how the three of us ended up spending New Year's Eve downstairs in the basement, but all of a sudden it was the middle of the night and we were still there. The conversation, like always, had consisted of small talk. I asked my grandmother a question.

"Nana, what did you want to be when you grew up?"

"Well," she said, and then she stopped, and something happened in her face that made her look younger. "I wanted to be a politician. Of course, that was not possible, so I decided to be Jeanette MacDonald."

Nana laughed at herself and then her eyes filled with tears, the way they always did when she thought about Jeanette MacDonald and Nelson Eddy.

"I wanted to kiss Nelson Eddy from the day I saw him in *Rose Marie*." Nana dragged heavily on her cigarette. She looked like she wasn't sure how to say what was on her mind, but I guess she figured it out.

"I always liked sex," said my grandmother. Then she turned to look at my mother. "Your father, unfortunately, was never very good at it. Especially the foreplay part."

At this point, whatever thoughts might have been running through my head came to a dead halt, and I giggled. A grown-up talking about sex made me uncomfortable and the idea of anybody having sex with my grandfather—well, that was downright funny. Or something. But if I looked surprised at what Nana had said, it was nothing compared to the look on my mother's face. Mom was in shock. When my mother was a little girl, Nana told her not to wear short shorts because that's how girls got pregnant. Now Nana was talking about foreplay. Next my mother swung back around to look at me, and now she was smiling, too.

"You know, Vanessa, *your* father wasn't very good at that part, either."

With that, both of them started laughing. I didn't know what to say. Certainly I couldn't say what I was thinking, which was that my little brother had better ask somebody to show him a few moves before he grew up and found himself carrying on the family tradition. Anyway, as I said, talking about sex with an old woman and a middle-aged woman, neither of whom were doing it, made me anxious. To be honest, sex made me anxious. My boyfriend was as immature about the whole thing as I was; only he seemed to have twice my sex drive. But I already knew I was going to like sex. I just didn't know which part I was supposed to enjoy—and I wasn't going to ask my mother. Mom said I shouldn't be afraid to talk to her about anything, but it wasn't the talking to her I was afraid of; it was the response. My interest in sex would be treated like my interest in champagne. No, I wasn't going to ask Mom about sex.

It never dawned on me to ask Nana. In fact, until that night it never dawned on me that Nana might know. At thirteen you often misjudge people, automatically attaching their age to your experience.

My mother and grandmother sat there, smoking and grinning at one another. They both smoked all the time, but they almost never grinned at each other.

When I think about my mother, I remember the hard things we've put each other through, but when I think about my grandmother I remember the night the three of us saw dawn together. It only happened once.

(LINDA REMEMBERS)

At thirteen, Vanessa had an answer to any question, and if her excuses were often baffling, they were also, on occasion, stunning.

"Mother, I did not *leave* all my clothes on the floor. I put them there on purpose so my guitar, if it fell onto the floor, wouldn't break."

Right—only her guitar, instead of having the good sense to fall onto the floor, lay on top of the radiator all night and by morning was warped beyond repair.

"It's not my fault, Mother. How was I to know you would choose last night to turn on the heat?"

The snow that began falling about sundown might have given her a clue, or so it seemed to me, but Vanessa claimed she was too busy doing her homework to stop and look out the window. I was to blame because I had not told her about the snow, probably intentionally, just so her guitar would be ruined.

Reality, to Vanessa, was a piece of Silly Putty.

It's not that she was thoughtless. She was the most thoughtful person one might imagine—about herself. *Her* feelings counted. No one else had feelings. If she saw me as her enemy, I saw her as my losing battle, the girl-child who lied to me regularly, shut me out of her life and, oblivious to my love or good intentions, openly preferred the company of her grandmother merely because Vanessa could say and do almost any damnfool thing in the world and that woman would smile at her, and tell me I didn't understand what a fine daughter I had.

All this was painful and very confusing. Oh, how I resented my daughter's perfidy. Had I not done my best to give her the sort of mother I wanted but didn't get? After all, I was interesting. Not like my mother. Not like Hallie. Hallie was a housewife. That's why the idea of asking her what she had wanted to do when she grew up struck me as silly. Hallie obviously had never wanted to do anything when she grew up but be the wife of a man with a career and the mother of a daughter with no mind of her own. If I said what I thought, I was always wrong, unless it happened to be what she thought, too. If I spent my afternoons at the library, which I did, she said I'd better learn you couldn't go through life with your head stuck in a book. If I happened to leave my shoes someplace and not be able to recall exactly where, it meant I was too selfish to realize that shoes cost money and money didn't grow on trees. If I expressed an interest in a boy, she warned me that boys would not respect me if I let them know I liked them, and as for sex, the less said the better, as far as she was concerned. I took her at her word on that one and said as little as possible about sex when she was around. Yes, I lied to my mother, too, but that was different. I lied only because she didn't want to hear any truth but hers and didn't know any life but the dull, secondary one she had chosen to live.

Take the piano. She made me take lessons and when I stopped, she made me feel I was a quitter. Maybe I was, but she was never so much as a starter.

Hallie managed to see most movies soon after they were released, and would not sit still until she had a color television bigger than any other color television on the block. But she despised all books, movies and television programs that were what she called "fantasy," because fantasy gave you ideas about things that weren't real; made you believe in things that weren't going to happen, ever.

It was only when my daughter asked my mother what she'd wanted to be when she grew up, and my mother said she'd wanted to go into politics but it wasn't possible, that it began to dawn on me. The question wasn't nearly as dumb as the fact that I'd never asked it. Never even thought to ask it. What else, I wondered, had I never thought to ask this woman?

During that night I would learn that my mother had planned to go to college, but was forced by her family to go to work so her little brother could go to college instead. Then, when she'd married my father, Mama was forced to quit work because he said it didn't look right. People would think he couldn't support his own wife. She was, at that time, the buyer for the children's department of a small department store. She never got to go to college. She never applied for another job. The one time she'd mentioned how she might run for the local school board, my father had explained to her that ladies had no place in politics, and besides, it would cause comment at the company where he worked. His career came first and her career was to help him in it, he said. After that, Mother gave up any thought of politics. When Election Day came, she just asked my father whom she ought to vote for, then voted the way he told her to.

And I never knew any of this.

Jeanette MacDonald? Yeah, I remember how she used to get all teary about Jeanette, but it wasn't until the night in the basement that I realized the only reason she wanted to be Jeanette MacDonald was so she could have Nelson Eddy. All along Mom had been dreaming, not about Jeanette, but about Nelson, dreaming sexually about ol' Nelson and crying because, although she loved my father, sex (especially the foreplay part) had been added to the list of those things in her life that were to remain, like college and career, fantasy.

No wonder she came to hate fantasy.

How curious, I remember thinking, that Vanessa had it somehow fixed in her mind that it was my mother who told me wearing short shorts was how girls got pregnant. It wasn't my mother, but my grandmother who told me that—my wonderful, under-standing grandmother, the one who, during my summer visits, made me a cup of hot tea each night at the same time she made one for herself, then sat next to me and listened to my wandering dreams, never saying a cautionary word, no matter how far my reach exceeded the grasp of our family's women—or its men.

My mother didn't get along with my grandmother. I had thought I knew why. I'd thought it was because Mama had no adventure in her, unlike my grandmother, a very forward-think-ing person, clearly, and me. The day my grandmother told me about short shorts, I forgave her, dismissing such a stupid remark as a quaint Victorian superstition and unworthy of her. It sounded like something my mother would say.

Sometime before dawn that night in the basement, I got around to asking my mother why, if she liked sex, had she gone to such lengths to hide this from me? Why had she chosen to explain The Facts of Life by walking into my bedroom during the two weeks I was stuck in bed with the measles, handing me a thin, green book, and telling me to be sure to read it—but not until she had left the room. The book was quite literally all about birds and bees. Only the very last sentence had to do with people. It said they were a lot like birds and bees. At the time, however, I assumed the book must have something to do with measles, and I might have continued in my confusion for who knows how long if I had not, one month later, been stung by a bee and decided to share with my Sunday school class the news that I was about to come down with my second case of measles or my first case of childbirth. Maybe both. It made for a lively Sunday afternoon around our house, my announcement did.

Now Mother admitted to me, down in the basement, that she had given me the book because she was afraid she might, if she tried to talk to me about sex, end up telling me the truth—which was that sex sounded like a lot of fun but probably birds and bees knew more about it than she did. She laughed again, but this time it was my eyes that filled with tears.

Sometime during the night Vanessa began to talk, to tell her grandmother what a fine politician she'd have made, but that she ought not to feel sad because she'd done something equally hard and, said Vanessa, she had indeed had a career.

She'd been a wife and mother.

She'd cleaned and cooked and washed and ironed and baked cookies for her daughter's class, attended PTA meetings and school plays, and been there, every day, when her daughter came home. She told her grandmother how important all that was to a child and as she spoke, I realized Vanessa was telling me how important those things were to her, too, and how much she wished I had been home every day when she came in from school.

Why hadn't Vanessa told me this before? Maybe she had, but I hadn't heard her, the way I hadn't heard what my mother had been trying to tell me so many years.

My mother wanted me to understand that just because she'd spent her life in a nest, it didn't mean she hadn't ever dreamed of flying. My daughter wanted me to understand that just because she dreamed of nothing but flying, it didn't mean she hadn't needed a nest or that she wouldn't continue to need one. I wanted them both to see what I saw now. Our trouble wasn't, never had been, our differences.

Our trouble was our similarities.

We didn't hear each other because we didn't listen, except to ourselves. I wanted to tell them this. I couldn't wait to tell them this. Then I stopped long enough to hear what I'd just told myself—and shut up so they could hear themselves, too.

Yes, I remember that night. It happened only once.

(Dawn)

By dawn, the three women had finished their first lesson in bridge building. Two months later Hallie had her next-to-last stroke. She couldn't speak, so Linda talked for them both when she visited her mother at the hospital, sure her mother hated that as much as Linda did. Their closeness was still that new.

On Linda's birthday, in August, she went to the hospital to see Hallie, to say happy birthday to herself *for* her mother, who couldn't. The minute Linda walked into the room, Hallie's face began to redden, the way it did when she was very angry. The way it had so often when her daughter was around, thought her daughter.

Hallie worked her mouth, trying to say—trying to say what? Linda wondered. Hello Linda I love you happy birthday? Or, Linda I still don't forgive you do you forgive me? Or, hold my hand whoever you are I'm scared? Linda couldn't be sure.

"What, Mama? What?" She looked at the woman in the bed, this shrunken but familiar, still fearsome, still beloved enemy of hers. What, Mama, what? A nurse came into the room. She smiled at the two women and picked up Hallie's chart.

"Sheeeaaaaghh," said Hallie.

Linda asked the nurse if she should get the doctor. That sound. Something might be wrong with her mother's throat. The nurse shook her head. "Your mama's talking to you, that's all." The nurse leaned forward over the bed, as if Hallie might be deaf, too. "Try again, Miz Smith. Try again."

Hallie tried again. "Sheeeeaaaaaghh."

"Oh, my," said the nurse, turning to look at Linda. "Maybe you can't make it out what it is she's saying, but don't worry. You be happy your mama's alive and trying so hard. You don't know. I'm here all day. That woman don't try to say nothing, not to me, the doctor, nothing to nobody, not until you get here just now, not until you *finally* get here. She was expecting you earlier today, you know."

"Yes, well, I meant to be here sooner, but . . ."

"Shheeeeeaggghh."

This time the nurse laughed, as though Hallie had said the punch line to a joke only the two of them knew. "It doesn't matter you can't understand what she says. We know what she wants to say, don't we?"

Linda had not taken her eyes off her mother. "No. I've never known what she *wants* to say. Half the time I didn't even know what she *was* saying. I didn't listen."

"Why, sure you know. Your mama wants to say she loves you and she's glad you got here, *finally*, and she gonna get well now. That's what she wants to say, don't you, Miz Smith?"

Hallie shook her head, but not very well; it could have been a yes or a no. Her mouth twisted, searching for the shape of words.

"That's fine, Miz Smith. That's real good. You rest now. We understand, don't we?" She stared hard at Linda, who said nothing, but after a minute, walked to the bed, bent down and kissed her mother on the forehead, which felt like old paper and tasted like baby powder. Straightening back up, she started for the door.

"Shit!"

The word exploded in the room, the sound of brain, mouth, throat, tongue and vocal cords finally reconnecting. The sound of victory. The sound of fury.

Linda let go of the door and walked back to the bed. Putting down her purse, kicking off her shoes, Linda sat down on the edge of the bed and reached out, taking Hallie's hand, holding it very, very gently in her own.

"It's nice to see you, too, Mama."

Hallie died eight months later. A year after that, Vanessa ran away from home, but a year after that, she came back. Linda sold the piano.

This time Linda and Vanessa were able to build a bridge to one another without a third person to help them, which did not mean they agreed with or approved of one another any more than they ever did. Or ever would. No. It meant only that they were learning to forgive one another for those sins they'd come to understand and—most important—for those sins they would never understand and which might not be sins at all.

It's a beginning. And even if they don't say so, both mother and daughter know what might have been lost forever if it weren't for that New Year's Eve in New York City, when Hallie and Linda and Vanessa stayed up until dawn broke, bringing light into a windowless basement, allowing them to see each other at last: mother daughter mother daughter mother daughter mother daughter mother daughter . . .

It only happened once. But it happened. .

RUNNING ON EMPTY

Near where I live in New York City is a woman who, for a small amount of money, will print anything at all on any T-shirt you buy from her, although she prefers you buy the turquoise T-shirts, because she has too many of them. In the summer of 1987, I was tempted to buy one of her T-shirts. On the front I would have her print the words: "I don't get it."

I didn't.

Off the air again, cancelled. Again (if you're wondering whether this gets easier with practice, it doesn't). I'd loved working on *Our World*, an ABC News prime-time series about recent history. Most historical series are driven by an event or series of events but in this one, time took center stage. It was a way to put the past in context: "You mean this was going on when that was going on?" Each program was a kind of video scrapbook of a particular time, *The Summer of 1969*, *The Autumn of 1949*, *Two Weeks in May 1960*, etc., and was composed of the sights and sounds, the witnesses and, crucially, the music of a time, which when put together showed and told, in a relatively digestible way, something fresh about the way we were at a particular time—or the way we thought we were, possibly just as important to know.

For one year, it was like being paid to read, to study: a dream job. That *Our World* was to play opposite *The Cosby Show*, the highest-rated show in the history of television, was its beauty, we thought; no one would expect *Our World* to do well against Bill Cosby, so no one would be disappointed when it didn't. One reason we thought this was because it is what the network had told us when *Our World* was begun. Don't worry about the ratings, they said. This time ratings won't count. Really, they said. What they said when the program was cancelled was that 12 million viewers a week weren't enough.

I decided to quit ABC, to quit network news. While my leaving obviously had something to do with ABC having cancelled *Our World*, it wasn't the only reason. It wasn't ABC. It was everything, years of everything and it was me; about this time my own anger (righteous, I had thought, once) and self-absorption had rendered me a significantly unpleasant human to be around. Talk about getting too big for your britches. There was another thing; I had something I wanted very much to do. For years I'd said I wanted to leave the networks and start an independent television production company. However small the candy store, it would be mine. It's one of those all-American dreams and I was one of the all-American dreamers.

But first I wanted some time off. A lot of it.

Hammockville, I said to myself. Spend the summer in a hammock, think things over, figure out what it all means and what's next. Funny thing, though: the more time I spent in the hammock the less I cared whether I ever moved again. From where I lay, the meadows, the river, the sky—they all looked happy standing still, doing nothing. They seemed to know something that in nearly twenty years of chasing stories I had forgotten. Just after Labor Day, we rented a copy of *Cool Hand Luke*. Watching it, I thought of Hammockville. Sometimes nothing *is* a real cool hand. The only other thing I did that summer was to watch television. The soaps. There were three new ones on television: the Iran–Contra hearings, the Bork confirmation hearings and the PTL scandal, a.k.a. The Jimmy and Tammy Show. This was a new experience. For once I was able to stop writing about events long enough to watch them happen. On *television*. That was the good part. The bad part was that for once I watched events happen without being able to write about them. On television. But I didn't care, I told myself. Another winter came and went. It was June again. I was, I told myself, both older and, for a change, wiser. My television series for the summer of '88 would be the two national political conventions and so, when CNN called five days before the Democratic National Convention opened in Atlanta, I was a woman who knew just what to say, finally: No, thank you, I'd say. I have an appointment with a hammock..

> CNN: We were just sitting around talking, some of us, and Ed mentioned you probably wouldn't be going to the conventions this summer . . .
>
> ME: That's right, and I couldn't be happier about that because . . .
>
> CNN: . . . and we were thinking these are probably the first conventions in years that you won't be . . .
>
> ME: . . . I don't care about conventions anymore, except as a spectator sport. These days I . . .
>
> CNN: . . . and we were wondering if you're going to miss not being there . . .
>
> ME: . . . know how to relax and say no. These days I've learned to . . .
>
> CNN: . . . and so we thought we'd ask you to come to both conventions and . . .
>
> ME: . . . speak my mind about what's important to me and to rearrange my priorities so that I can tell you "N . . .
>
> CNN: . . . speak your mind on CNN about whatever is important to you about the conventions. Yes or no?
>
> ME: I thought you'd never ask.

CNN was even nice enough to pay me, and after the conventions were over they continued to pay me and I continued to speak my mind on their air about politics and, inevitably, change, because that's what the story was for me. In every way.

To begin with, we had two political conventions where, if everything went as planned, nothing would happen, because both parties had decided nothing was better than almost anything else. Even television didn't put up much of a fight; when nothing happens it does make it easier to know where to point the cameras.

Trouble is, chaos makes me feel at home; it also makes me feel I'm among Democrats, but in Atlanta, in 1988, I didn't feel much of anything. If it wasn't Michael Dukakis's fault, it should have been; it was his convention, we kept being told, by the same people who kept telling us the convention was about "inclusion" and "order" and, most of all, "brevity." Silly me, I thought Democratic conventions were about choosing someone to go out and stomp hell out of the Republicans come November, but a Dukakis aide said, "We want a convention that's organized, orderly and short, just like our candidate." As fortune would have it, that's just what they got.

Inanities abounded, as usual. Candidates? Give the "Keep Hope Alive Because the TelePrompTer Is Still Rolling" award to Senator Al Gore who, arriving at the convention, introduced himself with the words, "Hi! I'm Al Gore, the former next President of the United States!" Delegates? The "Our Planet Next to the Planet Krypton" award to the alternate delegate who said pardon me but is that Superman's girlfriend talking about first nuclear use? As for the follies of journalism, there were simply too many contestants in every category (and every one a winner), but all our separate sillinesses might be summed up by the "Does Your Bubble Gum Lose its Flavor on the Bedpost Overnight?" award, which went to Tom Brokaw for informing the television audience that Mike Dukakis, at the beginning of a television interview, had taken a piece of candy out of his mouth and, when done, had put the candy back in his mouth.

It was Thurber who said progress was okay but it went on too long; what he meant to say was that covering conventions was a good idea, overwhelming them was not. In the summer of 1948, the national political conventions were broadcast on television for the first time, and it took almost no time for politicians to stop squirming in front of and start playing to the camera. Television was equally seduced, quickly ignoring substance if it lacked style. Was it innocence or ignorance? You must judge. I can't be trusted. I don't run for office. I work for television (off and on); therefore, I look at the presidential campaign of 1948 not as the first time television covered the thing, but as the last time nobody blamed television for its outcome.

In 1984, I had written that there were too many of us with too many pencils, notebooks, tape recorders, microphones, cameras and satellite dishes. By 1988, there were 15,000 of us in Atlanta to cover 4,212 delegates, one candidate and no story. Reporters, it's said, are like alligators; you don't have to love them, you don't have to like them, but you do have to feed them. When what's on the plate is mostly empty calories, we look to the edges, the details, on the theory that even if God isn't in the details, a story may be. We manufactured drama whenever we could and were stopped only by an occasional head-on collision with reality. What do you mean Jesse Jackson and Mike Dukakis have made up; it's only Monday! We did our best to turn the reconciliation of a fight that never existed into a story, with headlines like, "Peace Has Broken Out Over Atlanta," but it didn't help. When *The New York Times* resorts to asking seven Hollywood writers to evaluate the keynote speech, there is no news.

The only ones who had no problem finding something to say on the air were former candidates who'd found more or less honest work on our side of the fence for the duration of the convention. Gary Hart, a man who couldn't keep his pants zipped long enough to run for President, was doing commentary for Italian television. "The Italians," said Mr. Hart, "understand me." I wished I'd written that. The next day I believe I did.

The fire department livened things up for some of us one night. It was crowded inside the hall, hard to explain when you consider that nothing was going on, but so many people wanted to see nothing that the fire department was forced to close the entrances to the hall. You could go out but not come in. The commentator left the hall to get some fresh air. She didn't know she couldn't come back in. When she tried, the convention-hired security guards turned her away at the door. She argued with them; she explained she'd only stepped outside for a moment and had to return immediately. Networks don't like it when you disappear, she said. They don't pay you if you disappear. All three guards smiled large smiles. (There was a scene in that remake of *The Front Page*, called *Switching Channels*, when Kathleen Turner and Burt Reynolds, playing two television journalists, tell a man holding a gun on them he can't go around shooting members of the press and the man says, "Why not? Half the country would stand up and cheer.") But then two Atlanta policemen standing within hearing distance spoke to the security guards.

"She's telling the truth. We saw her on television just a few minutes ago. She has to go back in there."

"No."

The Atlanta cops shrugged. It wasn't their job. They were there to keep order, not man doors.

"But," said the woman to the security guards, "if you'd told people when they left that they couldn't return, I never would have left."

"Yes," said a guard, "that was our little secret."

The woman turned to the real cops. She liked many cops and sensed these two were not hostiles. And she knew something. The Atlanta Police Department had a kind of mini-precinct set up inside the hall, their own little station house. She looked at the nearest policeman and whispered under her breath: arrest me.

Then the commentator turned and moved for the door, saying to the security guards in her best to-the-barricades! voice, "Out of my way, weasely fascist tools!" The security guards began to yell things at her. A commotion ensued. The two cops moved to grab her.

"Take your hands off me, weasely fascist pigs!" shouted the commentator.

"You're under arrest!" shouted the cop.

They took her by the arms and hurried her through the door into the hall, telling the hired guards: we'll take care of this— not your problem now.

Once inside and around the corner out of sight of guards, they let her go.

"Have a nice convention," said the cop. "Say something nice on television about the Atlanta Police Department."

"Thank you very much," said the commentator, "I will." And I did.

The best you could say about the convention was that, deep down, it was shallow. Gone were the bitter, drawn-out, often arcane, but equally as often important (and rowdy) platform debates—a dirty shame; if there's no fight, there's probably no platform worth speaking of. In 1988 the Democratic National Committee bragged it finally had a platform that could fit on a poster, which it intended to do and to give one to each delegate as a souvenir. Maybe they hoped that by giving people posters of the platform someone would remember what the platform said ten minutes after the convention ended, but for that they'd have had to put it on a gum wrapper. Gone, too, were mighty speeches, the ones that went on for hours and once in a while said something.

There was oratory in Atlanta, but they had to orate fast; red lights were installed on the podium to let the speaker know when he or she had run out of time. So what?—I thought when I heard about it; I've never seen a real Democrat slowed down by a rinky-dink light. The planner people (geeks who take all the fun out of conventions and, no, I don't know if they work for politics or television or both) were ahead of me. Speakers were informed if they went over, someone would shut off their TelePrompTer. That was mean. The sorry part is, it worked. All of it. There was no heat, no lightning, not much smoke, except for a few brief moments one night and not surprisingly—Mike Dukakis was seldom confused with William Jennings Bryan—it wasn't the candidate talking.

Political speech making is tougher than it looks. As Gerald Ford said, when a man is asked to make a speech, the first thing he has to decide is what to say. Ed Muskie, as usual, put it plainer; he said there's no point in speaking unless you can improve on the silence. I know deep noises from the chest are different from messages from the brain, I know you can speak well, and still be a fool or wrong, but I've a soft spot for those who do speak well and if there's a place for rhetoric, a political convention is it. However, during most speeches I was in the CNN newsroom and while the television monitors were always on, nobody watched them much. Newsrooms are noisy places. They are supposed to be, or so we believe. What they're not are good places to listen to a speech; how can we listen to anybody else when we're so busy talking to each other?

Ted Kennedy thunders. He speaks as though he had no microphone, as though he'd taken his training speaking on the town bandstand (or in the United States Senate). Jesse Jackson speaks with the natural rhythm and power of the preacher he is; when Jackson speaks, no matter what you were when you came in, you're Baptist when you leave. These men qualify, I suppose, for what passes as industrial-strength orators today: it was no accident they were asked to speak at the convention, and yet while they did, life in the newsroom went on more or less the same.

"It was more than a quarter of a century ago that my father stood here to accept your nomination for President."

The young man was nervous as an understudy, but a nation's memories were joined at the hip and it didn't matter what he said, in our hearts we saw, first, a small boy salute a large casket and then a different man, his father, older and forever young, and in our memory fire was loose in the room and he caught it with both hands and he held it up and said to us, "Now." In the hall and across the nation those who could remember said to themselves: this is what it felt like to be a Democrat.

And even in the newsroom, there was quiet when John Kennedy, Jr., spoke. But it didn't last; in newsrooms, it never does.

In the end the story of the convention was unity, always a news story, I suppose, when applied to Democrats. For four solid days, the Democrats, the journalists and the citizens of Atlanta told each other we'd come a long way. We pointed to the Reverend Jesse Jackson, a distinct, possibly a major force in American politics, certainly a major story at this convention. We reminded ourselves this convention was being held in the South, a part of our country that had once gone to war to keep its slaves. We remembered that this convention was being held by the party that once opposed Abraham Lincoln because he wanted to free the slaves. We pointed out that this convention was being held in a city which had once refused to let the Reverend Dr. Martin Luther King, Jr., drink water from the white people's fountain.

We honored the Reverend Jesse Jackson. We honored the Reverend Dr. Martin Luther King, Jr. We honored Rosa Parks, who in 1955 sat down in the front of the bus because she was tired, and whose simple, understandable act changed many things. We honored the millions we once humiliated, and in honoring them we tried to honor ourselves. See, we are not what we were. The Old South is not the New South. The last night of the convention, two women came into one of the bathrooms off the floor of the convention. One was black, one was not. They were not together, these two women. Both went into the stalls, and when they came out the white woman turned and said to the black woman, "There's no toilet paper in my stall. Don't you think you ought to fix that?" The white woman left and I am compelled to point out that this woman was not from the South—Old, New or Deep. She was from the Midwest, the convention credentials around her neck said so. Wherever she was from, I wondered if she knew that the woman she had spoken to, the woman she had insulted, was Rosa Parks.

New Orleans with the Republicans was the same as Atlanta with the Democrats, only different: hotter. And sillier. On the theory that good taste and humor are often a contradiction in terms, someone was selling a button in New Orleans that was meant to combat the Atlanta war cry: "Where was George?" This button had printed on it the words "Where was Teddy? USS Chappaquiddick." If you think a button based on an automobile accident in which a young woman died and Ted Kennedy swam to safety is tasteless, you're not unlike most of the people who were standing in line to buy one anyway. The Republicans banned the sale of the button inside the Dome, but their attempt at good taste backfired; the button sellers moved out of the Dome and into the street, where the crowds and the sales were bigger. Then the media was alerted and covered this piece-of-shit story as if it were real. The result of all the attention was that they started printing Chappaquiddick T-shirts and taking orders for bumper stickers; the price of the button went from $3 to $5. I asked the gentleman whose idea the button was if he felt no shame. He felt no shame. "We try to capture the political mood of the moment," he said. I don't know what that says about Republicans, but it may tell you something about the eighties that the man who invented this button was a Democrat.

The planner people at the Republican convention decided the big story was Ronald Reagan's last convention as President, a story with no second line. As governor of California, Reagan said, "The thought of being President frightens me. I do not think I want the job." In 1986, the same man said, "I have come to the conclusion that the twenty-second Amendment limiting the Presidency to two terms was a mistake. Shouldn't the people have the right to vote for somebody as many times as they want to vote for him?" We didn't change the Constitution. Reagan was history. Or about to be.

The real story of the Republican convention was another man. When it comes to figuring out important stuff, my brain generally likes to wait until I've left the room. For instance, from the minute I saw him on television, I knew *exactly* where I stood on the Dan Quayle issue. Where I went wrong at first was in assuming it had something to do with his politics. Instead, it had to do with the fact that I couldn't stand the man. I never could stand him.

And I'd known him all my life.

I remember the first time we'd met. It was 1954. The fifth grade. He had little blue eyes, big white teeth and the only crew cut I ever saw that didn't look as if it were a mistake. He also had great legs, cheated on his arithmetic homework, played the prince in all the school plays and swore his father, who had a boat, a ranch and two Buicks, had promised him "no matter what those fools in Washington said, he would never, ever have to go to school so much as one day with the niggers." His name at the time was Mike Jamieson. That spring our class was locked in mortal combat, softball-wise, with the other fifth-grade class. There came an inning, a final inning, two outs, bases loaded— classic situation. I struck out. Everybody in the fifth grade told me about the awful death I deserved, everybody but Mike Jamieson, who said I shouldn't feel bad because I'd done the best I could ever hope to do, considering my abilities.

I remember high school when Dan Quayle sat next to me in American History, only then his name was Chuck Thompson, and I loved it when he told me I had special qualities most people didn't notice and I blushed when he told me he hadn't decided who he ought to take to the Harvest Ball. I worked hard writing his midterm paper in American History and tried not to notice when he copied off my paper on tests. I hugged him when he got an "A." And tried to understand when he explained he had to take this cheerleader to the Harvest Ball.

When I was a college freshman, the Dan Quayle who asked me out was called Brandon Butler Gaylord, III, the president of the Honor Council, which meant he got to try, judge and punish other students so the faculty wouldn't have to; he was very good at it. We went to his fraternity house for a party. It was a Saturday night. There were several couples and one garbage can, which was filled with something that looked like Welchade but wasn't, still, everybody was drinking and giggling so I drank and giggled, too. Looking back, that was a mistake, because if I'd stayed sober maybe I wouldn't have hit him where I did when he did what he did and then he might not have told all his buddies what he did, which he did, which was not true, but I was not president of the Honor Council. They believed him.

There have been other Dan Quayles in my life. Probably in yours, too. The last one I met was anchoring the most popular television newscast in town and, no, I can't remember which town or whether his name was James Glenn or Glenn James. He was good at his job, though; he was so good he was planning to quit television and run for office. He'll do well. He always has.

Money, sex, power, N'awlins and Dan Quayle. What a party.

And the planner people almost won. They came within one night of having their way. In Atlanta and in New Orleans, we in the media, notably at the networks, had publicly commented on, while being subjected to, the heavy hand of party manipulation; both Democrats and Republicans had worked particularly hard to make sure there was no news but good news, which to a reporter is not good news at all. But then Dan Quayle, looking as if he didn't want to run the country so much as co-anchor it, had come into our lives and suddenly, for a moment there, it was good night, George, and Good morrrnnning, Vietnam!

Remember that moment? Talk about a time warp. It was, astonishingly, 1969 again, the summer of Woodstock and moon landings and Manson. The summer Dan Quayle joined the National Guard. I remembered that summer very well, and that was part of Dan Quayle's problem at the moment; not me, necessarily, but the fact that many of the 13,000 or so members of the media attending the convention were baby boomers. *The reporters were baby boomers.* The planner people forgot that no matter where baby boomers had been in 1969, they sure as hell remembered where they'd been, especially the men, each of whom had known exactly where he stood with the draft and what decisions had to be made. Dan Quayle did what no one else had been able to do; he woke us up. They could plan the hell out of the spontaneous demonstrations, they could keep the real demonstrations, the protesters, fenced into little corrals outside the hall and limited to half-hour soapboxes, they could keep the delegates looking sharp and they could keep to a schedule. They could even keep food, drink and cigarettes off the floor of a political convention, but when all was said and done, and most was, what they could not keep out of their halls was politics. Nice.

Meanwhile, I found that working at CNN was different from working at the other networks, what we once called the "real" networks. I was employed by NBC News in 1980 when CNN first went on the air. I remember what everybody said. It won't last, they said. They sounded just like our parents in 1956 talking about rock 'n' roll. When I say "they," I probably mean management (the usual suspects), because most of us mere workers thought the advent of a fourth network, particularly one devoted to twenty-four hours of news, was a journalistic blessing: it gave us one more place to work. This is not a business known for steady employment, at least it certainly hasn't been for me. Ted Turner was smarter than the networks thought. He did it cheap, and then he did it right and cheap, and kept on doing it, and one day, about two years later, on the wall in the NBC newsroom in New York, where there used to be three monitors so we could always see what we and the other big guys were doing at any moment of the day or night, there appeared, without comment by management, a fourth monitor. The thing is, you can watch four television sets, but you can't listen to four. Would you care to guess which monitor in the television newsrooms of this country today is usually the one with the sound turned up? And why not? CNN is the news junkie's dream, and in newsrooms one finds the odd (is there any other kind) news junkie. And CNN. These days, one always finds CNN in the newsroom.

Working with CNN gave new meaning to the word "chaos" (they could have been Democrats). Of all the networks—well, all the networks I'd worked around, which was only NBC, ABC, CBS, PBS and CNN (so far)—there was no question that CNN had the smallest bureaucracy, even after eight years on the air, and I liked that; everybody who worked there liked that, except possibly the pencil pushers, who never like that. Energy was high, people were nice and the whole place was so scrappy it almost made up for the politics we had to cover, which were so constipated they were like the worst thing about baseball: the no-hitter.

I like baseball, but I don't like no-hitters. They're dangerous, probably un-American. I remember a night game. It was sometime early in the fifties and late in the seventh inning, and all I did was suggest to my father that we leave the game early, I was sleepy. The Houston Buffs, our team, were way ahead. So far the other team didn't have one single hit. Not one. Not a single hit, Daddy. Can't we go now? Hush, said my father. Don't you know you never, ever say there's a no-hitter in progress while there's a no-hitter in progress? It's bad baseball manners. You might jinx everything.

No, I didn't know that, nor did I know why anyone would want to watch such a boring game; sure, it was great pitching, but pitching was about deceit. Pitching was about fooling people, manipulating them, making them believe in something that ultimately wasn't there. Great pitching was great lying. I liked great hitting better, but I kept my mouth shut: going to baseball games with my father was more important to me than anything as inconsequential as plain, honest truth.

Thirtysomething years later, I was watching this no-hitter presidential campaign. Two flat-feated men forever arguing over who had the most to be modest about. These guys weren't running for President, they were *jogging* for President. By 1988, with the enormous help of television, the whole point of presidential politics seemed to be "Don't screw up." It was okay to do nothing. It was better that way. Tell a few jokes. Ride a few tractors. Dance with the folks. Turn a phrase. Sling a little mud. And disappear. Lie? Of course you can lie. You can do whatever you feel you have to do, say whatever you have to say, as long as you don't really do or say anything that means anything, because that's chancy; you might get it wrong. That's not how you win.

And did you notice? Up here in the stands nobody said much, either. Did we think we were watching a baseball game? Were we afraid to speak up for fear we might jinx our chances of seeing that wonderful, much-admired, heroic piece of total deceit we call a no-hitter? I like my politics like I like my baseball: noisy, full of hits, runs, errors and surprises. What this campaign needed was a Charlie Grimm. Once, when Charlie was managing the Chicago Cubs, who were (need I say it?) losing, he got a phone call from one of his scouts. The man was excited and began to shout over the telephone. Charlie, I've landed the greatest young pitcher in the land. He struck out every man who came to bat. Twenty-seven in a row. Nobody even got a foul until two were out in the ninth. The pitcher is right here with me. What shall I do?

Said Charlie, "Sign up the guy who got the foul. We're looking for hitters."

So was I, but there were none. I said I blamed television for what happened to campaigns and I do, but only partly (and only for cause). Really, it's the *combination* of television and politics that made our primaries and our conventions resemble nothing so much as a frog-jumping contest, where it doesn't much matter which way the frog jumps, as long as it jumps. All we had left were the Great Debates, but in the eighteen years since Kennedy faced Nixon, Great Debates had stopped being great, then stopped being debates. When it came to choosing the next leader of the free world, debates no longer worked. How many have we had now? How many more do we need? And what's a citizen to do?

You can stop watching television. Or you can decide whom to vote for entirely on the strength of a candidate's record. But "What have you done?" is the wrong question; it's a résumé question and as anyone who ever wrote one knows, résumés don't necessarily have to tell the truth as long as they look good. Besides, an election, any election, is a gamble. One bets on the future by betting on a particular person who will have enormous power to shape that future—your future, my future—and while I don't know about anyone else, I do know that when it comes to my future, I've come to believe that the thing of most importance is not so much what the candidate's done or what he plans to do, or even what he thinks. No, sir. The first thing I want to know about a candidate these days is what he *knows*.

There's a way to get the information we need. It came to me while talking to an eighteen-year-old man in Minot, North Dakota, who wanted to know why President Reagan continued to defend Ollie North when Mr. North, no matter how finely motivated, had tried to set up what amounted to a tiny government of his own inside our government, a cottage industry, which did not rely on the Constitution to supply the raw materials. In principle, North might have been right, but what happened in the White House basement wasn't how it was supposed to work, said the student. It wasn't what he'd been taught in his American Civics class, the one he'd had to pass to be graduated from high school.

"Right on!" I said. (Does anyone born after 1955 ever say "Right on!" I wonder?) The kid, as kids often are, was on to something.

It's so simple: we get the candidates on television, not a difficult task for your average network, and invite four or five high-school seniors to ask the questions. The same questions those students had to answer to get a diploma. Questions like: What are the three branches of government and what are the powers of each? Why did the men who wrote the Constitution do that? If you don't like it, what are the *legal* ways to change it? Questions like: Explain the doctrine of the separation of church and state. What are the names of the fifty states? What are the ten rights in the Bill of Rights? Not to mention questions like: What is the price of a Big Mac?

Fair questions, those. Why should we vote for a President who doesn't know as much as an eighteen-year-old? And if one day our President decides to alter the Constitution, don't we have a right to know ahead of time whether the man knew what it said before he came along? It would test, really test, in a way neither television nor politics can skew, the mettle of the men who would run the republic. The Great American Civics Test, we'll call it. If only we could make television journalists take it, too.

In this case, it was clear to even the most casual observer, and almost immediately, that the no-shouldered Mr. Dukakis was not going to be riding down Pennsylvania Avenue in January. The play *Waiting for Godot* is a tragicomedy in which nothing much happens. Two tramps wait for Godot who sends a boy to them each day to tell them he will come the next day. The tramps quarrel, contemplate suicide, separation and departure, but they remain dependent on one another and never do anything. If that sounds familiar to you, you're probably a Democrat.

Now CNN invited me to come on the air and contemplate life's little incongruities some more, or as CNN put it, Ellerbee found steady work shooting off her mouth. They said they wanted me to tell people what I thought. On a regular basis. I said, okay, what I think is that whatever hits the fan will not be distributed evenly. On a regular basis. CNN called this commentary. I called it objective reporting. And so it went. On a regular basis. I was really starting to like this place a lot. I was beginning to trust a network. Mainly because they trusted me.

I continued to shoot off my mouth for fun and profit. Meanwhile, it's comforting to know that while I was concentrating on politics, the business of television didn't really get any saner (I hate surprises). It's not that my relationship with CNN didn't work out. It worked out fine. The people there had welcomed me at a time I wanted to be welcomed one more time; *Our World* had taken more hide off my ego than I first thought. So had life in a hammock. Nothing was the hardest work I'd ever tried to do. CNN had made me a happy camper again.

As anybody will tell you, nobody gets rich working for CNN, but there's something about the place: a hunger, an energy. And a lot of time to fill. They had a whole passel of us doing what I was doing, saying what we thought (Ed Turner, my friend and boss at CNN, said the only scary thing about asking Linda Ellerbee to comment on the news was that you couldn't trust anybody to be wrong all the time). This was in addition to people on shows like *Crossfire,* where dueling commentators pontificated *at* one another; that was called "answered" commentary. What I and several others did was called "unanswered" commentary. The network spoke with many voices, and this, I thought, was the way a network should be. Another thing I liked was that CNN seemed the least sexist of the networks, or so I found it in the context of my previous relationships with networks. And I knew I was right about that after Ted Turner did what he did to show his solidarity with women. One of the other commentators on CNN was a weatherman named Flip Spiceland. In one of his commentaries, Mr. Spiceland was, pardon me, flip. About women. He was said to have made derogatory comments about women. And there was no one to answer him. I don't know, I didn't see that particular piece of commentary. I've never met Mr. Spiceland, but I suspect from what I've heard that it was a case of a writer trying to be funny and falling short. It is an experience with which I'm familiar. Whatever he said, it must have offended Ted terribly. On the part of women, I mean. I know this because the next morning, in defense of women, he cancelled all unanswered commentary on his network. That's what you can do when you own it and I agree with that philosophy. It was his candy store.

His choice. Besides, I always appreciated Ted Turner's feminist stance. It meant a lot. And it hardly bears mentioning that in responding the way he did to Flip's flap over being insulting to women, Ted inadvertently also cancelled the only woman commentator on his or anybody else's network. Ah well, it's a new and rather pleasant feeling to look people in the eye and say, yes, I was cancelled, and be sure that for once in my life it wasn't something I said.

Do I miss television news? When I watch television news, half the time I can't figure out what those people are talking about, or whether the problem is them, the world in general or me. Have I changed or has television news? All those years, I'd loved working in television news. Even when I criticized it, I still loved it. News isn't complicated, I said; it's merely the answer to the question: What happened? Once you know the answer the rest is storytelling. But there were too many changes for me to sort out any more. Maybe where television news is concerned, a part of me can never be anything approaching fair, or even rational. Which doesn't mean I'm wrong, either.

Imagine the following. Think of it as a little slice of corporate humor. Once upon a fairly time, a giant corporation held what was meant to be an extremely top-secret meeting of some of its extremely top executives (they met at a deer-hunting lodge in West Virginia, in April. Appalachian spring always makes me want to talk business, how about you?) to consider what might be done about this thing it had bought but could not control—an unwelcome, unpredictable, unprofitable and probably un-American thing called a network news division. What was it, really? It wasn't a business. The giant corporation knew business, knew how to make a profit. But television news? You had to keep people on the job to cover fires when there were no fires to cover, and when there were fires you still had to add extra people. Was this good business? Where was the profit in that? You were supposed to pay people to go on the air and say things you knew damn well would offend those people in Washington you paid other people to make certain were never offended by you, because you wanted them to buy what you sold, like missiles. But how could you sell them anything after your White House reporter said what he had to say about whoever was in the White House? Was this good business? Where was the profit in that?

The giant corporation had tried. But it was all taking too long. And so it may have come about that somewhere in West Virginia, during this meeting, someone from the giant corporation might have felt the light bulb ignite over his head and, filled with that inner glow which comes from suddenly knowing the perfect answer to a problem, stood up and made a joyful noise.

"I've got it! What we do is simple. We eliminate the news division."

Surely there was a murmur in that room. And maybe the man paced as he talked.

"We've been looking at it backwards. We've been thinking we had to make the news division into a business in order to get on with our business, but we don't, we don't have to fix the news division at all. We don't need it. Nobody needs it. They've got three other networks and local news. We could never be the last to go, that wouldn't look good, but we can be the *first!* The affiliates will love it because their own news shows will make more money. The entertainment division will love it because they'll have more time for their programs. The stockholders will be happy because nobody will be coming to them anymore saying things like 'We're sorry but you see covering that hostage story has really eaten into our profits and we sure hope you understand.' And the people who work for the news division will—the people who work for the news division will—well, what the hell, there aren't that many of them left anyway."

You're right. It probably didn't happen exactly like that—but there was a meeting at which someone from GE suggested eliminating NBC News as a solution to their problems, and nobody laughed at the suggestion. Not until the story leaked to the newspapers and the man who was president of NBC News at the time rushed to say the suggestion had been made "facetiously." Why don't I entirely believe him? Why don't any of us? I'll tell you why not. *If they can consider it, they can do it.*

The imaginary network in the movie *Broadcast News* decides it can make even more money if it trims the news budget by $24 million, which is television-talk for "Go forth and fire a bunch of people." Says one newsroom character in the movie, a man who, after thirty years, has just lost his job, "You're lucky if you get out while you can still cry." I was lucky. I did. I was damn lucky not to be run out (it was close, I believe). And I know hundreds of people, former employees of the networks, all of them, who agree that the funniest scene in that movie is when a smarmy but smiling network president tells an experienced but expendable producer that the producer is not being fired, he's merely being retired about fifteen years early, then asks the poor producer if there's anything he can do for him.

"Well," says the graying, soon-to-be-out-of-work veteran, "I certainly hope you die soon."

You have to feel for the ones who are still there, the good ones, who know what counts, which is everything. There are plenty of them, don't forget that, no matter what I've said or written. Do not judge television news by my assessment of what's wrong with it, which by nature is bound to be self-centered. Television news does not eat its young, at least not yet. Because of these dedicated, hard-working, competent men and women, much of television news is good, sometimes stunningly so.

There was a reason television journalists were forbidden by the government of The People's Republic of China to speak to the people of The People's Republic of China or take pictures of The Army of The People's Republic of China during most of 1989, and I'm sure if it weren't for a certain incurable aural impairment quite common to the trade (good journalists cannot actually hear the word "no"), China would never have been forced to kick so many of them out of the country. Not that China's a country afraid to do what needs to be done. In the last ten years, China has thrown out television journalists from Australia, France, Japan, West Germany, Italy and, naturally, Great Britain and America. Plenty other right-thinking nations have caught on to their scam, too. In 1988, NBC News correspondent Rick Davis was evicted from Jordan for grossly misrepresenting the facts (he said it was a repressive society). That was about four days after Israel had thrown out NBC correspondent Martin Fletcher because he violated the Israeli "Censorship Law." In the same ten years, the Soviet Union, Iran, Cuba, Nicaragua, Fiji and South Africa also booted some or all members of the world television media at least once.

And guess what?

It worked.

Kick the media out of South Africa, and South Africa seems to disappear from the newscast, the front page—and our consciousness. No show-and-tell? No repression in Jordan. No censorship in Israel. No Intefada. *The Middle East—no problem.* (Are we invading Jamaica yet?) Pull the satellite plug on China and there is no trouble in China.

And we look at those other places, shake our heads and say, "My word, it's a good thing we live in America, where we have freedom of the press." Except for the tiny fact that our own government tried to keep our journalists out of Grenada for the same reason our journalists were kicked out of China. "Yeah," you say, "but only because journalists aren't *real* Americans, after all, and anyway, didn't we find out absolutely everything our government said we needed to know about the Grenada invasion as soon as our government said it was safe for us to know it? It's not like our government lied to us or anything." No, of course not. Our government just didn't trust the media, but neither did you, and now that I'm no longer a journalist, I don't trust 'em, either. *They are not trustworthy.* Even Thomas Jefferson knew that and although you may not know this, he tried to warn others when he was President. It happened like this: one day Baron Alexander von Humboldt, the German scientist and explorer, came to visit Jefferson and was outraged to find in the President's own office a newspaper containing the most awful abuse of the President.

"But, sir," asked the Baron, "why is this libelous journal not suppressed? Or at the very least, why do you not fine the editor, or imprison him?"

President Jefferson smiled. "Put that paper in your pocket,

Baron, and if you hear the reality of our liberty or the freedom of our press questioned, show them this paper—*and tell them where you found it.*"

You gotta like the man.

Jefferson's is an attitude seldom found in the modern White House, or in our own houses. Too bad. How can we not continue to admire the courage of those who still work in and still do right by television news, in spite of the best efforts of governments, big business and ordinary stupidity? And how can we ignore them? It? Television will be, is and *has been* a major force for change. Television was a major player in every reform that's taken place throughout Eastern Europe. In Czechoslovakia, it is fair to say the revolution that threw out that country's communist government grew by rating points. Every time a mass demonstration was shown on live TV, the next demonstration was bigger. In East Germany, Erich Honecker tried to use television to persuade people to buy his act. They tuned him—and his government— out. In Poland, a Solidarity economic minister now holds "fireside chats." On television. In Romania, the television station that was the voice of Nicolae Ceausescu, the voice of dictatorial power— the voice which no one believed—suddenly became the voice, if not the heart and soul, of the revolution that brought him down. A television station that before the revolution had broadcast only two hours a day, filling those two hours with Ceausescu's propagandist pap, now was on the air twenty-four hours a day, and the screen was filled with the people of Romania. The screen was filled with freedom. The National Salvation Committee dug in and hung on to that TV station with all it had, barricading themselves in the studio as if it meant life or death, which pretty much described the situation.

"We've won! We've won!" shouted Romanian poet Murica Dinescu, over the air, and it was so. But it was close. The station was attacked repeatedly and might have gone off the air if not for the brave few inside and the brave many outside who literally put *their* bodies between the dictator's guns and *their* television station. There was a human shield ringing that station, and it worked, and suddenly nothing that happened in Romania was believed until it was seen on Free Romania Television.

Not too long ago, something happened in the news (the world is changing so fast these days I actually forget exactly what it was, but it had to do with the Soviet Union) and I turned on CNN to find out more. There was a Soviet official commenting on what had happened. When he finished, the CNN correspondent asked him if his government would be making an *official* reply to the United States government on this matter.

"We just did," snapped the Soviet official.

Now, in China, where the government made sure to pull the plug on television before pulling the plug on the students in Tienanmen Square, protest is back. At both Beijing and Qinghua universities, there are posters again, one of which says, simply: "Learn from Romania."

This is what television can do.

This is the power of TV. This is the medium we abuse so regularly—including those of us who work in it, and I still say when it comes to television, there must be a way to raise the ceiling other than lowering the floor. It would be nice to think that in the 1990s, we could learn, when we sit down around our national video campfire, to show a little more respect for the damn thing. *On both sides of the screen.* This was what the movie *Broadcast News* was about. This was all it was about. You don't have to be a television journalist to get the point of this movie; all you have to be is a card-carrying member of the human race, struggling to survive the last decade of the twentieth century with your heart and soul—and dignity—more or less intact. There are people who claim *Broadcast News* is basically just another love story. Well, yes, it's a story celebrating the love of competence, of doing things right. There are other people who claim *Broadcast News* isn't really *like* broadcast news; it's only a movie, they say, like *Network*. It's not. *Network* was satire.

Of course, I am prejudiced in this matter. In 1975, a major American television network hired this hotshot local reporter to be a national correspondent: female, not too well educated, not too experienced, not that good a writer. Nevertheless, she was hired to cover the U.S. Congress. She moved to Washington, showed up at the bureau and was told by her new boss to take herself down the hall to Room 163. Her new office. Her very own office. Only problem was, when she opened the door to her very own office, she found a man already in it, working. The woman went back up the hall to the big, big office of her new boss to tell him that someone had made a mistake. Her new boss paled. Her new boss sputtered. Her new boss told her to come back tomorrow. Someone, he said, had most definitely made a mistake. The woman, worried that the network had decided not to hire her after all, asked what he meant.

He explained. It seems there were these budget cuts, and well, there was this reporter—oh, he had plenty of experience and all, but he wasn't, you know, a communicator. He wasn't cosmetically sound. And so, said her new boss, the network had decided to, uh, relocate the man. The woman asked what that meant and was told that meant the fellow was being relieved of his responsibilities as a television journalist, so he could have plenty of time to devote to his new responsibilities as a radio journalist. Trouble was, they'd sort of forgotten to tell him this before they'd hired someone else to take over his television office. And his television job.

The gentleman in Room 163 might have reacted in several ways. He might have strangled the boss or the woman or both. What he did instead was to clear out his office, introduce the woman around Capitol Hill, answer hundreds of questions from her about how things worked and which one was the Speaker of the House and where was the bathroom. What he did was make it possible for her to do what they wouldn't let him do anymore. A class act, he was. Soon, during another round of budget cuts, he was "given" early retirement. Just like in the movie.

Cut to many years later.

That same woman, now a former network news reporter herself, sits in a theater watching *Broadcast News*, grinning from ear to ear at the smarmy but smiling network president, played with visible ironic glee not by an actor, but by a former network news reporter. And class act. His name is Peter Hackes.

The trouble with living in what they tell me is The Information Age is not *television*, not the technology; the trouble is the information it keeps giving me about the age I'm living in.

You know, Peter, sometimes I wonder who has our old office now.

Do I miss it? Do I miss television news? Hell yes, I miss television news. You never know how deep a puddle is until you step in it. Or out of it.

PUTTING IT TOGETHER

The art of making art is putting it together.

—STEPHEN SONDHEIM

Suddenly it's *that* night again. That other night. Always that other night. Always me lying in Van's bed, him sleeping, me awake, knowing all at once and without any doubt that what you had to do sometimes was choose between your ideals and your children, an easy choice unless you had children. And that was what was true. God, I hated knowing that. That night had changed everything, and that night never left me; it was always right there, looming, and that was always enough to get me up, shut me up and send me off to my job one more day. No matter what. Was it not a noble excuse? But now the excuse is gone—both of them—grown up or mighty near. So now I've quit my salaried job. Quit broadcast news. *Oh, Jesus.* Does it make me a coward to have waited so long? Or a fool to have done it at all?

Depends what happens next, doesn't it?

Starting your own company turns out to be real interesting. As Garrison Keillor says, more happened after that. Lucky Duck Productions (if you want to know why I called it Lucky Duck Productions, please buy my first book. I still need the money) was never meant to rival MGM or Lorimar. What my partner, Rolfe Tessem, and I had in mind from the beginning was a small, full-service production company specializing in nonfiction film. Now that sounds dull enough, doesn't it? We would make some good television, I hoped, the kind that neither talked down to people nor skidded around 40,000 feet above their heads, the kind of television we would be proud to make.

The time, it seemed to us, was right. The three networks were losing some of their audience, enough to make a difference, and other television was expanding. There were basic cable channels. There was first-run syndication. There was at least one new broadcast network. We didn't know how much we didn't know then (and sometimes I wish I didn't know now what I didn't know then). Our introduction to the part of our new business I would come to hate most began in Hollywood, where they make a lot of television. I'm speaking of meetings. Like summit conferences, most of what takes place at a meeting could be accomplished faster and more efficiently on the telephone, but that will not do; you must have meetings, go to meetings, *take* meetings. Sometimes you have to "do a meet." Those are the worst. People who ask you to "do a meet" often are not in constant touch with reality as you and I know it. We were invited to do a lot of meets. Take this as a sign.

However, our first Hollywood meeting after we started Lucky Duck wasn't about a program we wanted to produce at all; it was about a movie Hollywood wanted to make. I was a movie brat, movies were a big part of my childhood, so how could I not be excited the day Hollywood called to say they wanted to make a movie of a book I'd written.

My book a movie? Really and truly? (*"Pinch me, Rosie, Here we are going down the river like Antony and Cleopatra on that barge." The African Queen,* 1951.) What a trip. All I had to do was sign the contract. My mistake, I believe, was in reading the contract first. There were these three tiny, hardly-worth-mentioning problems, the first of which was that certain events in the book (a nonfiction account of some years spent in television news) would have to be changed in order to make it a better story for the movies.

"Okay, but we're talking about real life here. Be careful."

But surely I understood a movie could not possibly include everything in the book; choices must be made: what was good, what was bad? (*"I got brown sandwiches and green sandwiches . . . It's either very new cheese or very old meat." The Odd Couple,* 1968.) The second thing, said Hollywood, was that although the story must be altered, it would be better if we didn't change the real names of the real people about whom I'd written because it would be more real that way.

"Okay, I guess it would have made a sexier story if Ford hadn't pardoned Nixon but . . ."

Hollywood said that was no problem; most thirteen-year-olds' memories weren't very good for such things and it was *thirteen-year-olds who went to movies.* It was thirteen-year-olds for whom movies were made. Dumb thirteen-year-olds, they said. The third thing, explained Hollywood, was that everyone would feel better if I agreed to indemnify everyone against any lawsuits that might arise if some unstable persons didn't like the way we'd rearranged facts but not their names.

"Trust me," said Hollywood. (*"What do you get in place of a conscience? Don't answer. I know: a lawyer." Detective Story,* 1951.)

Not knowing any better, I said no.

Cut to the Hollywood office of the head of the studio—and me, chatting with the mogul, the producer, the director, the screenwriter and the movie star. Yes, movie star. This woman was going to play me. I am a normal American girl; wow again.

"The way I see it," said the screenwriter, "this is the story of a woman who succeeds in spite of always choosing the wrong man."

"One minute, please. While that may be true [*"Tell me Scarlett, do you ever shrink from marrying men you don't love?" Gone With the Wind,* 1939], I never wrote about *that* in my book, so what's it got to do with this movie?" A meeting was being taken around but not with me.

"That's not how I see it at all," said the mogul. "I see it as a female *Rocky*—the story of a woman who succeeds in spite of being not too smart, not too educated and not too talented."

Excuse me? (*"Mrs. Robinson, if you don't mind my saying so, this conversation is getting a little strange." The Graduate,* 1967.) And good-bye.

Hollywood said I didn't understand.

This was true. Over the last few years, we've found ourselves perilously entwined with people who make decisions about what you'll see at the movies and on television (and who have a direct effect on my livelihood) and more often than not, I don't understand. It tells you something that I once sat in the office of a man who swore to me in all seriousness that he had the "hardest job in all Hollywood." He sorted game show proposals for a television syndication company. On the other hand, he did not dress to match his office, like the female cable executive who claimed she found herself unfettered by having to find something blue and gold to wear to work every day. Nor did he take out a fly swatter and swat his way about his office, as the major network executive did while we were describing a documentary on adult illiteracy. Nor did he glare at Rolfe the whole time, like the woman head of programming who said she didn't understand why a feminist like me would have men on her staff in the first place (Rolfe, I explained, was not "on my staff," Rolfe was my partner and one of the best damned television directors she'd ever see, if she ever got that lucky, which she didn't). Nor did the man who sorted game show proposals spend an hour explaining to us why a series based on the World Federation of Wrestling would teach young people a lot about "the real values in life," as a network executive who claimed he had "farsight" did one morning over a power breakfast. Educational television, the man had called it. Like PBS, he said.

Ah, PBS. Public television. The sanctuary. At first we thought we'd never have to get involved with Hollywood because we'd be spending all our time making glorious, impeccable television for PBS. Even before we'd left ABC, Rolfe and I had been approached by WNET in New York, to see if we were interested in producing a series similar to *Our World* for public television.

It will come as no surprise to anyone that we were. Like nostalgia itself, *Our World* aimed for the heart as well as the mind, but when you considered how many of us had become accustomed to learning what we knew from television, the educational value of *Our World* seemed obvious (when it was on ABC, 32,000 teachers had used the show to teach history). Also, this would allow us to keep on doing a program we'd loved but weren't going to be able to do, once ABC had cancelled it. To do it for public television—how nice. How civilized.

I was asked by a media reporter who should have known better, to explain how the show would be different on PBS. "Well, to begin with," I said, "there will be no commercials." (Where did you say you get these guys?) There was a short but loud noise made about the title. Reporters wanted to know if ABC would let us use the title *Our World*. We found ourselves explaining to many people who should have known better that ABC did not own the title—you cannot copyright a title (you can trademark one, which ABC had not done)—and that the *Our World* we'd been associated with at ABC was in fact the third television show called *Our World* in twenty-eight years, then confused them further by saying none of it mattered, because we didn't want to call the show that anyway. We wanted to call it *Our Time*. The show was about when, not where. The only reason ABC had insisted on calling it *Our World* was to match *World News Tonight, World News This Morning,* etc. Okay, but would ABC let us use the concept? We explained one couldn't actually copyright history, either. These are the things that are written about by grown-up humans writing for real newspapers.

A deal was struck, announcements were made, and after leaving ABC, we moved into offices at WNET, sort of; we weren't there a lot after we discovered nothing much was happening about our show. It wasn't WNET's fault entirely; certainly it wasn't the fault of its new president, Bill Baker, who had just gotten there himself and was the man who wanted us to move *Our World* to public television. Baker was an enthusiastic champion, but he, too, was new to non-commercial television. In his first year on the job, he found himself immersed in administrative duties; he had to streamline the station's considerable bureaucracy and raise money to keep the station going, leaving him less time to concentrate on creating new programs.

Like ours.

We waltzed into this thinking non-commercial television would be so much finer than the networks. For one thing, it was lean and therefore, there probably wouldn't be as much waste—and not so many meetings. Yes, we did think that. Soon we discovered that where commercial television has one meeting, non-commercial television has three, plus too much correspondence and paperwork. Everything took too long, it seemed to us. It took WNET six months to put together a written document explaining a show that had already aired on national television, in prime time, every week for one solid year.

We also discovered that most of what you do in non-commercial television has very little to do with television at all; it's about raising money, something of which we knew nothing. When you work for a network news division and have a good idea for a show, or think you do, you try to sell the network on your idea. If the network likes it, they give you the money and you do the show. The money indirectly comes from profit made on shows like *Roseanne* or *Cosby* or *The A-Team*. They support the less profitable shows, such as news and documentaries. One reason we'd signed a deal with WNET was our certainty that this was an area where they were experts; we thought they would raise the money and we would put together the program. Unfortunately, they thought we would put together the program *and* raise the money, and we would have been happy to do so, if we'd known how. We said we were ready to learn. The first thing we learned about money-raising in the fall of 1987 was that just after the stock market has crashed is not a good time to ask corporations for money for non-commercial television.

Not surprisingly, during this time we began to listen to other offers and to explore other ideas that were being proposed to us, until we figured out that most of them could be boiled down to one offer, one idea: have Ellerbee do a talk show.

"You can be the next Geraldo! Only with substance!"

"But I don't want to be the next Geraldo."

"What are you—too uppity for talk shows?"

"No, not at all. It's only that I don't think the world needs another show about women who kill their mothers with ash-trays."

"All right. You can be Joan Rivers."

"Nope."

"Why not?"

"I never much cared what celebrities sleep in. Or with."

"So what have you got against interviewing Bob Hope?"

"The truth is, I'm not real fond of interviewing people. And I'm not very good at it. They always win when I interview them. I'm not Mike Wallace."

"Funny, everybody says you're abrasive as hell."

"I think they mean personally."

"But you'd be great interviewing people! Trust me."

"Yeah? Did you see me with Hubert Humphrey?"

"No, why?"

"Trust me."

"It's the trash thing, isn't it? You think we want you to do Trash TV. You think you're better than that, don't you?"

"I have nothing against Trash TV. Basically, I'm a pretty trashy person, you can ask anybody, but this isn't the television I want to do. It's not what I quit the networks to do, that's all."

"What kind of television do you want to do?"

"Picture stories. Put the power back in the picture, not do more radio with pictures. I'm a writer, not a talker. Don't you like writing?"

"Don't you understand where the money is?"

"I thought I just resigned from where the money was."

"Call us when you're ready to do a talk show."

There were a few people who wanted me to do something that wasn't a talk show. One syndicator wanted me to host a "reality-based" show (another phrase that I would come to understand meant the exact opposite of what it said. If something was "reality-based," it meant it wasn't real) about vengeance. *In Your Face* was the working title. Then there was the cable channel that wanted me to host a celebrity game show about the news. That was special.

Nobody seemed to want to hear much about the kind of pro-grams we wanted to do, nobody in charge, that is. We were on the wrong track, we were told, regularly. For example, I thought there was some fine television to be made having to do with illiteracy. One in five adult Americans is functionally illiterate; they can't read a bus schedule, follow written map directions, fill out a job application or order off a menu. They can't bake a cake from a printed recipe or get a driver's license. They can't read bedtime stories to their children. They can't participate. Another 34 percent are only marginally literate, only marginally able to participate. As much as I hated to admit it, after having worked so many years in television, it was clear that television had contributed to the illiteracy problem in America.

I cared because I'd always known I was one of the lucky ones. I can't remember when I couldn't read. Apart from the purely practical applications of literacy, reading has enriched and stretched me, pulled me outside my own existence and into the lives and worlds of others, enabled me to travel without leaving home, to take an active part in democracy, to hear the voices of others, to question and to understand. I cannot imagine not reading, not being able to read. I cannot imagine illiteracy.

Our idea was that what television helped take away, television could help give back. You see, there's one huge stumbling block to offering regular reading classes for adults, and that is this: to attend such classes is to admit you *can't* read and write—to tell the world that you have not been able to master the basics and are, therefore, a *dummy*. No wonder more don't go than do. But we could use television to teach adult Americans to read and write in privacy, where they live—where they watch. Use the pictures to teach the words. We would produce a kind of *Sesame Street* for grown-ups, using MTV techniques, using popular music, pop heroes, fancy graphic art, humor and fast editing to make a clever, simple show people could enjoy watching and learn something from, too. It was time, we said, for television to stop making programs about illiteracy and start making a program for the illiterate.

It was give-back time.

What it was not, we learned, was a commercial idea, especially to those outfits who claimed not to care that much about what was commercial.

We tried to sell a series about certain Americans we considered to be national treasures, people in entertainment we felt deserved to be profiled definitively and with dignity in a one-hour show about each one of them, shows that concentrated on their work, not their personal lives or celebrity, shows about people like Ella Fitzgerald, Jim Henson, Frank Capra, Count Basie, Fred Astaire, Ray Charles, John Huston, Red Barber, Pete Seeger, Gene Kelly. They were at the time still alive, all of them. The shows would include performance footage, a long interview and original material. It would be, in a sense, their obituary, only they wouldn't have to die first. Some did anyway. The rest may before this series ever gets made.

We tried real, real hard to get syndicators, networks or cable interested in letting us do a daily program about television. We thought it a swell idea. The real question was why there wasn't already a show about television *on* television. The thing that connects us to one another in this country and throughout the world is television. What made *TV Guide* the biggest-selling magazine in America? Why does every newspaper have a TV critic, usually a whole TV section and often a magazine on Sundays? Why are people always talking about television?

Only television ignores television.

What we had in mind was a daily show about television, put together by people who loved television. *The Television Show*, we'd call it (we are downright terrific with catchy titles). We would explain, entertain, show and tell. We would go backstage: How does *60 Minutes* get those stories? How do you get on a game show? Who are the Neilsens, anyway? We would go back in time (memory is a powerful tool and this is the TV generation we're talking to) to visit old television shows, briefly, nostalgically. We would watch a little TV together, then talk about it, review it, argue, laugh, question. We would give the viewer a voice, let people come on the show and ask the questions themselves: Sam Donaldson, why are you so mean to that nice President? Bill Cosby, do you really think all of life's problems are solved in twenty-two minutes? Morton Downey, explain yourself. We would be user-friendly and, yes, friendly to television, too. We saw this as a show that filled a need, a perfect seventh-inning stretch that could play every night after the news and before the evening's prime-time entertainment programs. We saw it as a show that could, once established, become something of an institution itself. TV on TV. We wanted to make waves. Airwaves. Well, my child, you simply would not believe how many different people hated this idea for a show.

"You can't do a show about television on television! You can't give a bad review to a show that's on our network—or a good review to one that's on theirs! You can't make fun of television! Not on television, you can't!"

"No, see, we review everything. And we don't have one reviewer—we have several. Several voices. For fairness, for variety. And our reviewers can't hate television. They have to like it. Yes, we'll be critical sometimes, but the whole show is a kind of celebration of television, so I really don't see this as a problem, do you?"

"Call us when you want to do a talk show."

We kept on truckin'.

When I quit network television, one of my intentions was to write more and talk less, so when asked if I wanted to write a syndicated newspaper column, I said yes. At the time, I wasn't aware I was about to commit an unnatural act. It didn't occur to me there were people who would think it perverse for a television person to leave television, then begin writing for a newspaper. This is not the direction *that* river usually runs. Newspaper writers become television people, not the other way round.

"Why are you doing this?" they asked. Who asked? Mostly, they fell into one of two categories: those who worked in television, and those who worked at newspapers. What half of them really meant was, "After sixteen years in television, do you know *how* to write?" while the other half really meant, "After sixteen years in television, can you afford the pay cut?" (Can you guess which half was from TV and which half was from newspapers? *Wrong.*) The only people in print *or* broadcast who didn't ask me a thing were the working reporters. They didn't have to; they knew what I was up to, and that it had little to do with any differences

between television and newspapers, even less to do with writing and nothing at all to do with money. It's a medical matter. I did it for my health. When you're a reporter, you're paid to get the facts, but facts are hard to get; they don't come when you call, they hide in crowds, won't take orders, can't be trusted and don't stay put. As bad fortune would have it, facts count. Objectivity, though impossible, is desirable. Opinion is not, which is why reporters are paid to keep theirs to themselves. This is good for journalism but bad for journalists; you *do* have opinions, you *do* think, and if you can't *stop* thinking (some can, in which case they are known as editors. It's a technical term) and you can't do anything else, you get constipated. Journalistically, I mean. Stuff builds up inside and keeps on building and that's why God, who hates a mess as much as anybody, created commentary. And it would be a perfect gig, if it weren't for the hard part. If you're getting paid to say what you think, they expect you to know what you think. Sometimes it is too much to ask.

In 1988, Bruce Paisner, the head of King Features, which was owned by Hearst and syndicates my newspaper column, read my first book on an airplane (half the people who read that book tell me they did so on an airplane; the other half read it in the toilet) and called to set up a meeting; he wanted us to produce a pilot for late-night television (late-night television; seems to me I remembered something about that), a program that would run five nights a week. Not exactly a news program but not exactly not a news program, he said, and did I understand? Not exactly, I said. But that was okay; I was used to not understanding. These people wanted to do a show I wanted to do. There was a God, I said. Our troubles were over, I said. I was much younger then.

We came up with a show King Features thought we should call "*. . . and so it goes*" (they're good with catchy titles, too). We would not call it a comedy program, which would make it easier to be funny. We would not call it a news program (what it truly was), which would make it easier to slip some in (companies that do not actually have news divisions—and some that do—are afraid of news; they think it's dull). Perhaps we would call it a situation comedy about a situation called reality (we were moving toward "reality-based" pretty fast for beginners). By re-editing footage of people, places and events from sources all over the world (a video-exchange club, m'dear), by juxtaposing seemingly unrelated local and international events in a way that showed how they were related, we would mold a half-hour program that tried to make sense of what was going on. It was a little bit of *NBC News Overnight,* a little bit of *That Was the Week That Was* and a little bit of something new. One segment, "Videosyncracies," was made up of home movies conceived and shot by famous people. Bill Cosby made one for us. Jane Pauley and Garry Trudeau made one for us. The form was a way to use the latest video technology to "interview" people by letting them turn the camera on their own lives. (Two years later a version of this particular idea proved to be the most popular show on television. Too bad it wasn't ours.) We shot the pilot for our show and waited for King Features to sell it into syndication. And waited. There were problems. Said one of the salesmen, "How can we tell the stations what stories will be on this program every night?"

"Do you mean: what are the news stories of the future?"

We're still waiting for King Features to shop that pilot, but, oh, well, golly, as the broad said, "and so it goes."

Meanwhile, as part of our continuing education in the world of television outside network news, we were becoming accustomed to the new manners of business. We now understood, for instance, that if you telephoned someone and his secretary said he was in a meeting, it may have meant many things but the one thing it seldom meant was that he was in a meeting. Usually, it meant he just didn't want to talk to you. We heard a lot of "He's in a meeting right now, but can he call you back in ten minutes?" Naturally, "he" is in on the west coast and it's six o'clock New York time, so you sit there waiting until ten o'clock before you figure out "he" or "his" secretary is lying to you. Great manners, some of these people have. No wonder they run the world. People who work at Lucky Duck are instructed never to tell anyone I'm in a meeting. They say I can't come to the phone right now. The "and you can go screw yourself" is only implied. That's the polite way.

During this time, I hosted a public television program called *AIDS in the Heartland* (part of the series *America in the Age of AIDS*), a finely crafted documentary following the progress of a disease through one town, Fort Wayne, Indiana, from the first case reported there to the present time. It was a show about how people's emotions and attitudes changed when they came face to face with something that had previously been no more than a news story about something bad that happened to people far away from them. It was produced by the public television station in Seattle and I was pleased to be asked to be a part of it. And we continued to propose new shows to the television marketplace in general. A six-part history of the contemporary American women's movement. A documentary about book-banning in the 1990s. A series about people who successfully fight city hall. A television history of radio. A documentary on the infant-mortality rate in America: *Stillborn in America,* I wanted to call it, rather unfortunately, I think.

"Concept." There was a word. Used to be, you had an idea for a show. Now ideas were bad. You had a "concept" instead, and if your "concept" was not "high," you didn't have a show. My trouble was, I thought low, conceptually speaking, but not, apparently, low enough to be high-concept. We proposed a program for women, a program specifically designed not to shout at its audience, one that would deal with the get-through-the-day issues of life with a little perspective, a little humor, even a little music, a cross between the old *Arthur Godfrey Show* and *A Prairie Home Companion,* a show meant to raise no one's anxiety level. Said one syndication mogul: "Can't you be a little more exploitive? No, not like Geraldo. Linda Ellerbee-exploitive, I mean." I really didn't know they used words like "exploitive" except to one another and in secret. They used to at least deny in public that "exploitive" was what they wanted, was their overt aim. But, hey, "Ellerbee-exploitive?" I can handle that. Just let me get my coffee can and I'll be right on down.

That's right. Enter Maxwell House.

Once upon a time, I was a journalist. I didn't understand at the time that journalism was a calling; I thought it was a job.

While I worked at this job, I played by its rules. Then I left the networks, but one year after starting Lucky Duck Productions, because of some chicanery of another person (not Rolfe, my partner, but somebody who worked for us—we thought), my misunderstandings about how television got made and my own lack of business knowledge, we lost a large chunk of money. Lucky Duck was about to go under.

But wait! Not so fast! *Please!* This company was my dream; I didn't want to fire everybody and go back to being just another salaried employee (if someone would hire me). I didn't want to give up my company—or my dream. Nor did I want to take in the venture capitalist who offered us lots of money as long as we wouldn't do any more documentaries about AIDS. As Mr. Sondheim said in his song, advancing art is easy; financing it is not. Welcome to the cold, hard and very real world, Linda Jane. (Is it *that* night again? Do you hear the dragons roaring? Are you scared? How scared? Real scared? Are you going to lose it all? Everything? How scared are you? What are you going to do now?)

I agreed to do a commercial for Maxwell House coffee.

Some people said I was wrong to do that because I was a journalist. However, I hadn't worked as a daily reporter since 1985. I wrote true stories about real events and people, but I did it as a columnist for newspapers, a commentator for television and an author of books. I was not a journalist, I was a writer. However, what counted most in this particular instance was that I was also the owner of a small business, with a payroll to meet.

The choice was all mine. Nobody twisted my arm. Some people might object to me doing a commercial, I reckoned, but my company would survive, no documentaries would be cancelled and no one who worked for me would be fired.

The commercial began airing May 1, 1989. Within two weeks I'd been derided and defrocked by any number of serious folks. *The New York Times* ran an editorial saying it would be just fine if Walter Cronkite wanted to do a commercial for Hathaway shirts but it wasn't okay for Linda Ellerbee to drink coffee and *say so,* not that I did say so. The same editorial suggested I had attempted to fool people by passing a commercial off as a news program. Sure. The commercial was thirty seconds long, just like every news program I've ever done. I sat in a big easy chair next to a five-pound can of coffee, just the way I always did on NBC News.

The implication of the editorial was that the people who watch television are so dumb (unlike the fellow who wrote the editorial) they wouldn't know it was a commercial. Gimme a break. As I've said before, the people who watch television are just as smart as most of us who do it—or write about it.

Not everyone reacted negatively to the commercial. My favorite memory is of a telephone conversation with columnist Jimmy Breslin.

"Elluhbee? Breslin here."

"Yeah, Jimmy. How are you?"

"Elluhbee—I did a commercial for beer and know what?"

"No, Jimmy. What?"

"They let me keep the Pulitzer."

My writing may never be good enough to win a Pulitzer Prize, but Jimmy Breslin made me feel better and when the dust had finally settled I could laugh, too—at me, at them, at the whole damn thing, because, you know what? It was funny. For too many years, too many of the people who write about television had written that I was a maverick, which, they'd said, was *good*. But they thought being a maverick meant going your own way, only as long as I went *their* way, bucked the rules they hated, spitballed their targets, took on their enemies.

There was something else.

For too many years, too many of those people had written about me in a way that made it hard for me to recognize myself. Some of them seemed to think I was, somehow, better *than I knew I was*. Eleanor Roosevelt once made a commercial for margarine. Afterward, she said her mail was pretty well divided. One half was sad because she had damaged her reputation. The other half was happy because she had damaged her reputation. That was sort of how people felt about me after Maxwell House—and how I felt about myself. It was not one of my proudest moments. It is not one of my proudest memories. But given the same set of circumstances, I would do it again. And now I don't even have my kids to blame these decisions on.

It ain't easy being grown.

One last, not so little thing concerning this subject. These days I find I'm much more careful what *I* write or say about other people. Cheap shots are called cheap for a reason. It's a lesson every writer ought to have to learn. It changes you. It should.

The company survived and began to get more business. We produced a program about food for *Smithsonian World* on PBS. *A Moveable Feast* explored diverse, important developments in the history of eating in America, following food as it went from sustenance to a tool of power—sieges in war and lunches in business. The subject, food, seemed to us a little bit broad but that was what *Smithsonian* wanted. *Food—The Movie.* By necessity, more was left out than was included; a researcher quit, saying we were intellectual philistines for not including communion in the program. Tom Shales, writing for *The Washington Post,* gave it what I think was a good review; he said it made him hungry. He also said it was "livelier than the usual stodgy *Smithsonian World* show, perhaps because it was made by feisty Linda Ellerbee's company, Lucky Duck Productions." But Ellerbee did not appear on or write the program. We persuaded Lloyd Dobyns, my old pal and partner from *Overnight* and *Weekend* days, to do that. One of the goals of Lucky Duck was that it would be a real production company, not a loan-out company for me. We wanted people whose work we respected to find a happy home at Lucky Duck. But we hired Lloyd anyway.

This is where I have to explain again, I guess, that I really do like Lloyd Dobyns, he is one of my dearest and *oldest* friends. I simply don't like saying nice things about the man. That's just the way we work this friendship. Having Lloyd around again was even better than I expected. From the beginning, when first we'd called him and offered him the job, he'd been his usual courteous, soft-spoken self.

"Work for you?" he shouted. "Work for you, Ellerbee? Not on your fucking life." He paused. I could hear the smile. "I'll work for Rolfe."

And so he did.

But I got to go over his scripts, too, and, my, but that was lovely to do. "Excuse me, Lloyd, but wouldn't it be better to say . . ." Most lovely of all was that during this time, Lloyd lived with us. Targets of opportunity ranneth over. Lloyd and I have always enjoyed playing something we call "Shoot the Wounded." It's a game in which each person tries to insult the other worse than the other has insulted them. There are no rules, no boundaries and no prisoners are taken; you have to know a person really well to be truly good at this game. Or so I used to think. However, a charming, pretty and, by comparison, terribly innocent young woman named Kristin showed me some new ways to put the man down, way down, and leave him there, bleeding bad.

It began with Lloyd's coming on to Kristin daily. It was nothing personal; it was only that Dobyns was a dirty old man before he could vote and he's too old to grow up. He doesn't mean anything by it and everybody knows that but him. Kristin put up with his ways with considerable natural grace. That she didn't understand half of what he was talking about helped. Lloyd continued to chase Kristin (he does this mainly for practice, I believe, being happily married to Patti for more than thirty years), until one night Kristin said something about marriage being a fine thing and one day she wanted to have the kind of marriage Lloyd had, the kind her parents had had, you know, a good marriage, a *lasting* marriage. Dobyns made his eyes very large and leaned into her face to announce, as if from a great distance, "Kristin. People who are married for a long time despise one another. *Don't you know that?*"

He proceeded to do a number on marriage for ten minutes or so, until finally he wound down and was reduced to glaring at the young lady, at which point Kristin smiled sweetly into his red face and said, in all innocence, "Lloyd, I'm sure your wife loves you for what you are."

Sound of rim-shot. Sound of silence.

And I assure you nothing was helped when, five minutes later, Kristin's father showed up to give her a ride home. Kristin's *father* was younger than Lloyd. For a man with no juice left in him,

Lloyd Dobyns did a fair job writing the food show, I thought.

Another truly lucky break was when another friend from the past, one much smarter than Lloyd or me, joined Lucky Duck. Reuven Frank had been executive producer of *Weekend*, the magazine show I'd done with Lloyd at NBC News and the creator of *NBC News Overnight*. He'd also been president of NBC News, twice, and if you asked me, had practically invented television news, for which I never held him accountable; things get out of hand everywhere. Having Reuven as consulting producer at Lucky Duck cheered me up almost as much as being asked to do *Overnight* one more time would have done. Reuven was helpful in a variety of ways, besides thinking, which he does better than almost anybody. For one thing, he was great at throwing his weight around when a little weight-throwing was what was called for. We were meeting with the mucky-mucks of a cable company about a series of documentaries on American education, and one mucky-muck (one mucky?) said to Reuven, "Now, are you sure you understand how important the writing is to this series?"

"Well," said Reuven, "as one of the founders of the Writers Guild . . ."

At Lucky Duck, our plan was to gather people who were older, who had a lot of experience and at least a little wisdom, and people who were much, much younger, who were just starting out. We thought the two groups could learn much from one another. It has proved to be so.

At last people were beginning to come to us with projects (other than talk shows). Occasionally we even had meetings with people who behaved normally, and when that happened it generally confused us a great deal. We had lunch with Tim Forbes, during which we outlined our idea for a series of four television specials a year based on one of Forbes's magazines, *American Heritage*. We explained it once. Tim asked two questions then said, "I like it. We'll do it." None of us knew quite how to take that. Later, when the shock wore off, we decided we liked Tim Forbes a lot and wished everyone could be like him. A simple "yes" or "no" and forget about "I have to take it up with three or four committees first," or "Let me run it up my boss and see who salutes," or my favorite) "Let's see what a few focus groups have to say about it."

But there were always some who made us offers we could refuse, even when we tried not to. One syndicator wanted us to produce a daily, hourly version of *20/20* for women. It was a dandy idea, we said. Yes, we said, we can do that. Unfortunately, they wanted to do it for about fifty cents, and when we explained that while we would love to have their business, what they wanted could not be done on the unrealistic budget they had in mind ("But we won't use union camera crews!" they argued, as if that would make the difference), they told our agent we were uncooperative and lacked the right attitude. We agreed and promised to practice lying, which made our agent happy at least.

As I write this, we're working on a daily information show to follow the *Today* show (I suggested we call it *What They Meant to Say Was . . .*); a biographical series for cable; a documentary that follows a woman elected to Congress through her first year in office (*Ms. Smith Goes to Washington*); a network special on the environment, this one a spectacular combination of photographic essays on the places we call home, places whose character if not their very existence are threatened, to be shot by three internationally known and respected cinematographers; a hip roundup of the week's news called *The Weekly Rap;* and a weekly *Sunday Morning*-type news program, airing internationally, to be reported and anchored jointly from the United States and the Soviet Union (the old Global Village come to life). To understand independent production, all you need know is that if all those shows come through, we will be rich and dead from too much work. We are not going to be dead. I am not *that* young anymore.

We still have funny experiences with meetings; I still have trouble between the people who never heard of me, don't know me at all, and the people who know me all too well. At a meeting with the Fox Network, an executive, when I suggested an historical series, said to me, "Nah, ABC tried that a few years ago, can't remember what they called it, but it was a terrible failure."

Our World. They called it *Our World.*

Among those who knew me too well were the producers of the

successful and regularly funny sitcom *Murphy Brown*. This was a show any woman who'd worked in television news had to love. Murphy Brown was a wise-assed, irreverent newswoman whose smart mouth wrote more checks than her smart ass could cash. Murphy was a graduate of The Betty Ford Center, a bemused survivor of the sixties, a lover of rock 'n' roll, hater of all things disco and a helluva reporter. What was not to like? I wondered. When they were shooting the pilot for the series, Candice Bergen, one of the best unrecognized (at the time) comic talents in the business, had called to ask if she could follow me around for a while. Her job on the show, she said, would be based on Diane Sawyer's at *60 Minutes,* but the character would be based on, uh, well, you know, someone like, uh, me. Sort of. I wished her better luck than I was having being someone like, uh, me. Months later, the producers called and asked would I appear in an episode of *Murphy Brown.* I wouldn't have to act, they said; I'd only be playing myself.

Like a fool, I said yes.

During my week in sitcom land two things were made clear to me. One, no matter how much actors get paid, it's not enough. Two, playing yourself is very different from being yourself. Diane English, the savvy producer who'd invented the show and who'd written the program I would be on, told me that every time she'd written a line for me to say, she'd stopped and asked herself, "Is this an Ellerbee-like line?" Later, during rehearsals, Diane stopped me on one line several times. I wasn't saying it to her satisfaction. I kept trying, but it wasn't working. "I didn't," she said, "sound Ellerbee-like." (But, hey. If I say this line and I'm Linda Ellerbee, isn't that "Ellerbee-like"?)

No, it wasn't.

I threw myself at her mercy. Would she please say the line "Ellerbee-like" and I would simply say it the way she did. She did and I did, and we let it go at that. It was, after all, only television.

Yes, yes, yes! It's only television. All of it! Inside and outside the networks! No matter how many times I've said that over the years, the obvious fact is, I still need to hear it. I'm still a baby at it, too, in so many ways. But I'm learning fast now. I suppose that's why the National Association of Programmers and Television Executives invited me to address their convention on the subject of broadcasting twenty-five years from now. That, and my terrific history as a prophet.

The future of television?

"Welcome," I told them, "to the wonderful world of the future." What is broadcasting like these days? Well, there is no broadcasting these days. Not over the airwaves. Not in television. The whole country is hooked into the whole country by satellite or by cable. The networks no longer exist. One of them has become a programming service. One of them is a major multisystem cable operator. The other one budget-cut itself out of existence. PBS? After our government withdrew all its support, things looked bleak, but public television has been just fine since the BBC bought PBS, changed it to BBS and proved that reruns of *Dallas* are just as popular here as they are in Great Britain. Local stations have changed dramatically. Now most of them are primarily conduits for local, national and international news, advertising and first-run programming. Some of them have become so good at it and so well-known that they are available (and successful) nationally, the way certain newspapers like *The New York Times* were in the last quarter of the twentieth century.

All television, I said, from my perch twenty-five years in the future, is now high-definition and in stereo. All new homes have a room where one entire wall is a screen. Sometimes the entire room is a screen. A computer allows the viewer to select programming from a vast line of available shows and to order up a show for viewing in this special room at any time she (or he) wishes. This room has a name. We call it a library.

Television is now used to create works of art, I said. For example, through satellite links it is possible to create a concert in which the band is in one country and the singer is in another. Why this should be desirable remains unclear. Finally, I said, television is capable of being interactive. Yes, through cable, one may sit at home and participate in a game show or vote in a national election; however, according to A. C. Nielsen and the Federal Election Commission, more people play games than vote.

Some programming notes from the future:

You all remember *Leave It to Beaver* and its revival, *Still the Beaver,* and its revival *Be Still, the Beaver.* Well, the Beav is back. His new show, *Forever the Beaver,* will revolve around the cybernetics technicians who keep the Cleaver family alive. Forever. Dick Clark is also back and looking younger than ever. In fact, because of cybernetics, he *is* younger than ever, and because of certain other medical advances, his new program, *World Bandstand,* will feature live appearances by Elvis Presley, Ritchie Valens and Otis Redding. Vanna is as popular as ever, too. In fact, she's more popular than ever, now that she's memorized *all* the vowels. Oprah, Geraldo, Sally Jesse, Will, Phil and Joan are still talking to everyone but each other.

And it will still be only television.

And I will still love it.

Yes, I still wake up at night, sweaty, thinking of that other night, and half the time I think we're not going to make it, I'm going to lose the company, my house, my computer, even—everything. I lie there in my dark night and tell myself it's over. You're a has-been. Nobody wants you on television. Nobody wants to hear what you have to say. Give it up, Ellerbee. You're done. You've lost it. They are the bad nights. But there are mornings, too, and on the morning of my forty-sixth birthday, my twenty-year-old son gave me this note:

Dear Mom:
Maybe it's my eyes; they are young and still focusing. My vision is more narrow. I see the horizon and the other side seems a little too far away to worry about right now; I have no words for house, mortgage, salaries—other jobs, other people depending on me. I have not been "there" yet and so do not understand completely what the loss of it means. I have not achieved to the point where I could feel as if I were descending. I have my dreams, my choices and time (in rude and copious quantities). I have no answers, no consolation to offer in amends for the loss of trappings. Instead I offer the stupid simplicity of youth and its ability to survive in the raw, and the ability to have hope and belief if for no other reason than it makes the mornings easier. And, in my callowness, I tell you that you still have everything you need for the work you love. You can succeed because it requires nothing but you, the gift and the machine. You own the gift. I give you the machine. Love, Joshua.

On that morning, he also gave me an old-fashioned, used, battered-about and beaten-up—and still working—typewriter.

Thank you, son. I am a lot younger now.

Television, Hollywood, Journalism, all of you—you can't scare us with your arrogance, your righteousness, your silly, useless meetings, your half-assed committees, your half-baked brains and your "we program everything for thirteen-year-olds" notions. I've thought it over and the truth is, television and the movies don't belong to you anyway. They belong to us. To all of us. You don't watch. We do. So next time, look out, because I'm bringing my pals with me. All of them. And we're going to make the kind of television we want to watch. New television. And we're going to keep on making it. And you're going to let us. Got that? (*"Captain, it is I—Ensign Pulver—and I just threw your stinking palm tree overboard. Now, what's all this crap about no movie tonight?" Mister Roberts,* 1955.)

And I was eleven years old when I saw it, dammit.

TIME IN A BOTTLE

The Daily Feelings Journal describes what you have experienced during the past 24 hours. By taking time to review your day and reflect on your behavior, you can become more aware of your feelings, actions and attitudes toward yourself and others. Generally one or two paragraphs will be enough. You may choose your own time to write in your journal so long as it does not interfere with other scheduled sessions. Each evening the journal is placed on the desk in the living room, where it is accessible to your counselor. The feelings journal is reviewed daily by your counselor. It is recommended you use at least four "feeling" words per day.

You want to know how I "feel"? I feel like Private fucking Benjamin, only not cute. I'm also not awake, I can't think of anything nice to say and I wish, *oh how I wish* I were home.

"Have you 'journaled' today?" they ask.

"There's a word for people who do that," I snap. "We call them journalists."

I am not doing well at The Betty Ford Center.

The question is, do I belong here? I never meant to be an alcoholic. All I did was decide to drink. They have asked me, for my assignment for tomorrow, to write down the consequences of my drinking. Let's see, there's been perhaps a bit of erosion in my health and some deterioration in my looks, maybe a little increasing sloppiness about my appearance, some puffiness around the eyes and okay, I'm overweight, but nothing I can't fix. It's true my social life's almost nonexistent; I work, I drink, I sleep. My dwindling interest in sex seems hardly worth mentioning. Sure, there's been some isolation from friends and alienation from my children because of certain inconsistent behavior on my part, and so what if I've been overbearing or stopped listening to any voice but my own—it's *my* life. Oh, I admit I've gotten pretty rotten at handling some of the details of my life, say, most of them—this constant forgetting and losing things—and yes, I am depressed most of the time now and cry for no reason or all of them and, yes, I did endanger my son's life that night I drove us to the country drunk in that mean storm. And, yes, I guess you could say that because of my behavior fluctuating so wildly behind my code of values, or what's left of it, that I've pretty much lost all self-esteem. Put another way, I guess you could say I hate myself. But I'm *not* angry. Last Thanksgiving a friend, watching while I sliced the goose in the kitchen, told me in the kindest way that Josh had said something to him about being worried about me, about my drinking, and I was calm, wasn't I, when I sliced my finger to the bone?

And, yes, my father was an alcoholic, goddammit.

I used to love to get up in time to watch the sun rise. I was moved by the wholeness of beauty, the fine way the parts were joined. Little by little, that beauty has broken into pieces for me. Pretty is all that's left. It's not enough.

Do I belong here?

I belong here.

It tells you something when you say to your family and very closest friends that you're going to The Betty Ford Center and no one asks why.

Oh, hell, if Murphy Brown can . . .

> You will be assigned to one of four [4] living units. You are
> not to be involved in any way, or to enter, any other unit
> than your assigned unit. You are expected to be in your unit
> at 10 pm, and you must sign out and back in at the reception
> window in your unit.

My "unit" is North Hall. There are twenty of us, a mixture of
men and women, but not in the bedrooms, which are all doubles
except for one. A retired elementary school teacher from Des
Moines who's been here a week but whose eyes are still blackened
from being beaten up by her husband, also a drunk, told me this
afternoon that "when Betty was admitted to the Long Beach
Naval Hospital she insisted on a private room but they told her
it didn't work that way and in time Betty decided they were right
so when she started her own place, she said each unit should have
rooms with two beds in them and one room with four beds in it
for anybody who demands a private room."

Betty isn't here right now, she tells me. Except in spirit, she
adds. Betty's in Colorado. I don't blame Betty one damn bit. The
temperature today in Palm Springs is 122° and there are no celebrities here, none, but the retired elementary school teacher
says she can show me just which unit and bed Elizabeth Taylor
was in. Both times.

> You will not leave the campus at any time. You will become
> an important member of a new "family" of 20 peers as each
> day you form new and meaningful relationships.

One of the minor versions of hell: my roommate is thin, tanned,
gorgeous and twenty-three. She listens to rap music on the port-
able tape player her boyfriend, the Hell's Angel, bought for her
as a going-away-to-The-Betty-Ford-Center gift. Walkmans, she
says (Walkmen?), are against the rules. Getting sober is going to
be loud. Funny, the people here, the patients, don't look like
drunks; they look like normal people, most of them, not counting
the short fellow from Omaha with the twitch who says he designs
security systems for missile bases.

Last night I went to my first AA meeting. They read from

the Big Book. Every reference was to men. "If the alcoholic says to his boss . . . Some good news for the wife of an alcoholic is . . ."

My "peers" keep their distance. I've been to crime scenes that were friendlier. I am the new kid on their block. Also, some of them think I'm here to write an "exposé" of The Betty Ford Center. I tried to tell them I was here for the same reason they were, but there was trouble about my coffee cup. You're given a coffee cup for the duration. A punch-label with your name on it is glued to the cup. Mine says "Linda Smith." When I was registering, the lady at the desk said sometimes the press got a hold of the patient list and it wouldn't be good for me to be worrying about that while I was worrying about so many other things (she sounded as if there were a great many things about which I ought to be worrying and if I were not, certainly would be soon), so why didn't I pick another name. I said I didn't see how much could be accomplished if I had to lie to other people starting with basics like my name. She said it was only for the books, not the people, and why didn't I just pick one, now. I said write down "Linda Smith."

"Surely you can be more creative than that."

"Maybe, but my parents couldn't."

> You are required to attend and participate in all aspects of the treatment program. You are asked to keep current by checking the bulletin board in your unit. You are responsible for your personal care, for keeping your room clean and for completing your daily therapeutic duty assignment. You are expected to launder your own clothes. No dry cleaning is available. Becoming responsible to self and others is an essential component of recovery.

They gave me a schedule and told me to thumbtack it on the bulletin board over the desk in my room. They gave me a thumbtack, too. Up at 5:30. "Meditation" walk, followed by breakfast, followed by my "therapeutic duty assignment." I am a busboy. After I clean tables, there is exercise, then a lecture, then an hour-and-a-half group therapy session and a community meeting. By now we have reached lunch, it says here. After lunch there's another lecture, another therapy session, more exercise, then study time, dinner, still another lecture or AA meeting, then return to my room to work on written assignments or my "journaling."

I've been examined physically and mentally for three days, the same questions over and over.

"How did you feel when you realized you had a blackout?"

"I didn't have blackouts." *Oh, maybe a few times I couldn't remember some things, but no blackouts.*

"When was the first time you got high?"

"When I was three years old and discovered how dizzy I could get rolling down a hill." *I liked that.*

"Did you use other drugs besides alcohol?"

"I don't recall, I was drunk at the time." *The drugs of my generation. I did the drugs of my generation.*

"What is your drug of choice?"

"Tequila." *Or vodka or rum or brandy or whatever you've got.*

"When did you take your first drink?"

"Sixteen. Cutty Sark on the rocks." *My father drank Cutty Sark.*

"Did you like drinking?"

"Loved it." *In the beginning, the high I got from drinking in some ways did resemble the rush you get falling in love, a sense of well-being, an optimistic view of tomorrow and a desire to see my "lover" again soon.*

"What did you love about it?"

"The taste."

"You loved the taste?"

"Yes." *I hated the taste.*

"Is that why you kept drinking?"

"I guess." *I also liked being one of the "guys." You know, after you get that story you all sit around the bar telling lies about how you got that story. And drinking.*

"Anything else?"

"No." *Yes. Drinking made it easier to talk to strangers. And friends. Drinking made me forget to think about what I never wanted to think about anyway. Drinking made me happy. Drinking made me stupid.*

"Are you an alcoholic?"

"Yes." *Am I really? I hate this.*

"When did you realize you were an alcoholic?"

"Gee, I can't remember." *What time is it?*

They have given me a printed sheet of "feeling words" for my journal in case I've forgotten what "apprehensive," "lonely" and "humiliated" mean.

> You may not use the phone for the first five days. After that you may use the phone during one, scheduled, 10-minute period each 24 hours. Mail is sorted at the reception desk. We have a need to inspect all deliveries, including packages sent or dropped off by family and friends.

Mail for me, a card from Lloyd Dobyns. On the outside of the card, one jellyfish says to another jellyfish (who's floating upside down with all its tendrils rising upright and stiff): "The first thing you've got to learn is to relax." Inside, he has hand-printed: "And the second thing you've got to learn is to answer the question, 'When the cocktail hour comes, what do I do with my hands?' One possible answer, Ellerbee, is to chew on them for a while. That way your mouth won't be busy either. Love, Lloyd." Telling him may have been something of a mistake.

> Once you are diagnosed as chemically dependent, it is your responsibility to do those things necessary to get well. You will learn about yourself and your disease. It is important to become involved during your first week and to increase that involvement daily.

"*Webster's*," says the lecturer, "defines disease as anything which interferes with the human organism's ability to function normally." Does this, I wonder, make a knife wound a disease?

My disease is defined as alcoholism, he says. My disease is chronic, progressive (*progressive as long as I drink*) and incurable (*it's impossible to take an alcoholic and make a controlled drinker out of him—her*). My disease is characterized by a loss of control (*an alcoholic cannot predict how much she will drink or her behavior when she drinks*) over alcohol and other sedatives (*alcohol is merely one more sedative).* My disease follows a natural course *(if untreated),* has specific signs and clinical symptoms, a known outcome *(I will drink until I die, drink until I'm insane or brain-damaged, or stop drinking)* and a very definite treatment.

Which starts with not drinking.

"The cause, like that of many cancers, diabetes and AIDS, is unknown," he tells us, "but it is not, as the post-Freudians thought, the symptom of some larger, underlying problem. There is no set personality structure."

I am not unique.

This right away is a problem. I have counted on my uniqueness for years, relied on it. Being told I'm one of 12 million makes me feel about as good as being told I'm doing the "in" thing by checking into a rehab center or that all the really interesting people these days are at AA meetings. I used to tell Betty Ford Center jokes. Now I am one.

At the lectures I take many and detailed notes, like a good student, or a good girl. I am eager to please, to do well. To *get* well?

"What is known," says the not-quite-retired surgeon with the strong face and no-bull bedside manner, also a recovering alcoholic (he looks like a well-aged Richard Widmark, but then so does Richard Widmark), "is that something happens when ethyl alcohol is taken into the body of an alcoholic drinker that does not happen when it's taken into the body of a non-alcoholic drinker; something happens in the brain that causes a small portion of the alcohol to be converted into a highly addictive substance referred to as THIQ (tetrahydronisoquinalone). This substance is not found in the brain of non-alcoholic drinkers and at this time, it cannot be detected nor removed. Except by autopsy. But testing has shown there exists in some people some sort of biochemical defect which causes the alcohol to be converted to THIQ, and that the defect is hereditary."

I know about my father. And me. But what will this mean to my children?

In bed tonight, I read more on the subject in one of the pamphlets I've been given. They're all I have to read, them and the

AA Big Book. They took away the books I brought with me: a couple of serious novels I'd been meaning to get around to, another book about Washington politics and a handful of mysteries. "Here," they said, "read this, instead." And so I do. "The alcoholic," I read, "while not responsible for having the disease of alcoholism, is entirely responsible for his recovery."

A disease? I'm not so sure about this disease business. I was raised to believe we bring our troubles on ourselves and have done my part in this matter. The American Medical Association defined alcoholism as a disease in 1956; I still think of it as a moral failing. My drinking is not my disease. My drinking is my fault. And my addiction. Alcoholism is an addiction to alcohol. If I am an alcoholic, then I am an addict. Like a junkie. My "feeling word" for the day is "shitty."

> You will become familiar with the twelve steps of the Alcoholics Anonymous program, which is the blueprint to your recovery.

Today a lecture about change happens. And I had thought I was the expert.

"It's really quite simple," says the psychologist. "First you identify the problem. The second step is to develop trust." I ask the psychologist what she means.

"Hope," she says. "You gotta hope."

The next step, she says, is the catharsis ("Ventilate. Ventilate.") followed by insight and then, finally, change. These, she points out, are also the first five steps of the AA twelve-step program, except for change. Change is all the steps after the first five.

Sure sounds simple. But then so does a sex-change operation and I wouldn't want to contemplate trying one of those in thirty days. Or a lifetime.

Tonight's AA meeting is better. Drunks are very funny when they're sober, I find out. The man who spoke to us tonight is not a patient—or "inmate," as I continue to call them. Us.

Us.

He's a retired carpenter and a drunk who's been sober fifty

years now. I ask him how. He says there's nothing to it. All you do is don't drink and don't die.

> You will be assigned a counselor as your primary case manager. There are formal planning sessions for each patient; individual therapy sessions between counselor and patient and daily group therapy sessions. The daily group becomes the nucleus of your recovery program. Your participation is important.

I get it. The basic assumption of AA is that only another alcoholic can help an alcoholic. But I don't like this group therapy business. It's too personal. I don't know these ten people well enough to talk about, well, to talk about what I don't know these ten people well enough to talk about. Today I watched them doing it with one another and could not imagine my being able to be so candid with near strangers. I have used words to keep from saying much for such a long time now, and so deftly, I like to think.

And what of all this chumminess? What am I to make of grownups who hug people they aren't related to and chant: *North Hall had a ball, using drugs and alcohol! Now we're sober one and all! Rah!* This cheer or one like it is performed with the twenty of us standing in a circle, arms linked, five or six times a day. A required exercise. I'm sure it's a polite way to perform regular "bed checks," but I don't know; I feel so damned silly.

They keep telling us, "If you want what we have, do what we do." Do they mean I have to become a sheep? Shit. I tell my counselor when it comes to how things are run around here, I have feelings. I have feelings that are buried alive. She says feelings are always buried alive.

> Our feelings substantially color the way we see life and react to it. No longer are we persons who simply feel resentful; we are resentful persons. We may discover we have become self-pitying persons. What was once a feeling has hardened into an attitudinal posture—a character defect. If we are to change this, we must first discover ourselves at the feeling level.

There's another good-bye party tonight. It's always someone's first day, someone else's last. We have fruit punch; you never saw so many people who know how to hold a glass.

Tomorrow's my turn to "share" my life story.

Is "wordy" a feeling?

Tonight I think about my life. My counselor tells me there is a Linda and a Linda Jane. Little Linda Jane. My counselor tells me I need to go back and find little Linda Jane, but I can't even remember where I left my shoes after lunch, or what I ate. They say it will take at least a year to get my short-term memory back, if it comes back. They do not coddle us about the facts; one of the first things they tell us is that more than half never make it.

Josh's high-school graduation. He was so fine. I was so drunk. And I told him what I thought of his class play, the one we'd all gone to see the night before graduation; I took it apart, front to back, gave it my *professional* best. Over and over, the way drunks do. My son directed that play. Neither of us will forget graduation day, I expect.

This road seems so long and hard and I am so tired and scared. Trying to see myself clearly these days is like trying to look backwards without turning around.

> Most of us think we know ourselves and are afraid of looking bad to others, so it's hard to take the risk of being revealing and genuine. But what have we got to lose? You're only as sick as your secrets.

"My, but you're touchy tonight."

Mike and I are walking back from dinner when he says this. It's not dark yet. We eat at 5 P.M., like convicts or nuns, or children. Mike and I have taken to one another, possibly because, except for a mild case of terminal smart mouth, we are unalike. Mike is from Chicago but lives in Florida now. He has no job; he used to sell shoes, and other things, he hints, but I don't know at what. Michael has pancreatitis. Unlike liver damage, it is irreversible. Sometimes he's in pain. When the pain gets really bad, they let him have an aspirin. Mike laughs about that. And at me. He says women are only good for one thing. He calls me one of "those feminists" and say it's my fault or the fault of women like me that the world's so screwed up because women are far superior to men and we blew it when we demanded equality. It was a step down, he says. Mike does not read enough and he thinks too much and it's nice to have a pal. But not tonight.

"I am not touchy. Please just shut up."

Today I gave my life story to the group. Gave. Now there's an interesting choice of words. I cried once in the telling when something reminded me of something else. When it was over, I felt drained and also part of this group of people for the first time. It was not a bad feeling. So why am I so touchy tonight?

"Alcoholics," says my counselor, "do everything the hard way."

Another card from Lloyd today. On the front, the famous Escher lithograph "Relativity," the one with the people climbing stairs that go every which way, no matter which way you look at it or turn the card. Inside, he's printed, "This is a test. If you're sober and half-psychotic, the drawing on the front is all fucked up. To me it's just a bunch of people wanting to go up or down stairs. Of course, I'm half-sober and completely psychotic. Love, Lloyd."

> Besides a physician, registered nurse, psychologist and chemical dependency counselors, our multi-disciplinary team includes clergy, family counselors, a registered dietitian and an exercise coordinator.

God, this is depressing. Not only am I a sick person, I'm a fat sick person. They gave me a questionnaire at lunch. At *lunch*. "Are you a Fitness Drop-out?" I got as far as the first five questions. "Do you remember the day you last exercised for at least 30 minutes without stopping? Do you hang your laundry on your exercise bicycle? Do your children roll their eyes when you say you're going to start exercising again? Do you know exactly where your walking shoes are?" And the worst: "Do you weigh at least 20% more than you did when you graduated high school?" Does it count that I know at least 20 percent more, too? No? I see.

I've lost six pounds. But who could tell?

The dietitian tells us there are 630 calories in a Whopper. This is information I've been living to hear.

There's a lot of joking goes on among the inmates about this place. It's a victim of its own success; we've all seen the before-and-after pictures of the famous who've been here and said so. We kid each other about when do we get our face-lifts? But there are no face-lifts here, no tucks, no facials, no body rubs, no masseuse at all. There is no fashion boutique, no tanning salon, no golden saving lotions: only the Exercycles, weights and the track. There is a swimming pool, but North Hall's time to use it (thrice weekly) is from four to five in the afternoon and by that time the sun has turned it into people soup. I seem to be waking earlier and earlier, 4:30 this morning, but the coffeepot in the kitchen is always on and I've come to enjoy walking alone at this time of day. Round and round the track, I watch the purple leave the mountains.

This religion thing: the trick, I've decided, is not to allow my lack of it to get in the way of my getting sober. I am not going to be one of those people who runs around saying, "I found God at The Betty Ford Center." Father Joseph says I haven't lost my faith; he says it's just buried under a pile of shit. Do all Catholic priests talk like Father Joseph? Or is it only the Irish? Lapsed Methodists would like to know these secular secrets.

I woke up and heard someone crying in the night. Was it me?

> Those who do not recover are people who cannot or will not completely give themselves to this simple program, usually men and women who are constitutionally incapable of being honest with themselves. There are such unfortunates. They are not at fault; they seem to have been born that way. They are naturally incapable of grasping and developing a manner of living which demands rigorous honesty. Their chances are less than average.

Every day, more confusion in my head. I've become obsessed with the idea I'm one of the ones they're talking about, one of the "unfortunates" incapable of recovery. But how can you know for sure? I've lied to myself so often about drinking; am I lying to myself about wanting to stop drinking? About being able to? How well *does* a person know herself after the better part of a half a century? I look in my roommate's journal to see what she's written about me.

> Most events that occur during your stay fall under the heading of therapeutic. All aspects of this chronic disease must be treated. As you participate in the program you will experience many hills and valleys.

What a remarkable morning! I feel great for a change, woke feeling rested and yes, peaceful. The feeling lasted a whole day. (That's three "feeling words" in one paragraph, except all the "feeling words" are "feeling" words, which probably doesn't count.) Spent part of the morning in the Serenity Room. Can you believe they call it that? "If you're looking for Twyla Jean, she's meditating right over there in the Serenity Room, just past the nurses' station. Look out for the pillows on the floor. Have a nice day."

It *is* nice, though, this day, and this room: soft carpet, the pillows on the floor and a glass wall facing a small courtyard garden with a few desert blossoms and much sky. The first thing everybody says when they see the Serenity Room is, "Jesus, what a great place to get high." I try to meditate. I used to do that in the sixties or was it the seventies; naturally I can remember my mantra. Or can I? Surely a plain old ohhmmm will work.

Ohhmmmmmmmmm . . .

After a while, when nobody was around, I knelt and put my hands together, the way I did when I was a little girl and believed in Jesus, the tooth fairy and tomorrow. Part of me felt like a fool. Another part of me asked the first part just which one was the fool here. When it started to go that way, I got up and left the Serenity Room before I lost the stupid feelings that took me there in the first place, but going out the door I turned back and without thinking said, "Thank you." To an empty room.

Yesterday's card from Lloyd was blue with a star of David and the words "On Your Bar Mitzvah" embossed on the front. His words inside: "What the hell, they don't make cards that say, 'On Your Sobriety.' Love, Lloyd."

They do make such cards, Lloyd. They sell them here at the book and sundry shop (we call it the mall), not too far from the Serenity Room, but I'd never tell you that. You would laugh and then I would laugh and we'd be making up badass cards and I'd forget the point of the whole exercise was to clean the swamp. Lloyd, you really are a shithead. Don't ask me to tell you about the Serenity Room.

This week I got my "Master Plan." There it is in writing: Patient does not understand disease concept as evidenced by her continuing guilt feelings over drinking. Patient exhibits low self-esteem by covering more sensitive parts of her personality with a tough facade. Patient exhibits extreme confusions and shame concerning what her drinking has done to her children.

What they don't know about English they apparently do know about me. The same day I got a letter from Allison. About children. They tell me there are no coincidences.

"Dear Linda: This is great. I can talk at you and you can't talk back! I've been on vacation this week but most of my time is spent worrying about the beastie boy [Tyler is three and wonderful] who has just started day camp. These folks take this whole school/day camp thing far too seriously. There are words like 'structured play' and 'unstructured play.' Before the group started, I went to a meeting and the group leader asked us what we looked for in a play group. Comments like 'meaningful interaction' and 'racial diversity' spewed forth from these suburban mouths. I said I first looked in the closets and if there were no kids bound and gagged, it was probably a swell program. Tyler's taken to going to the bathroom outside. He likes it best when a car is passing. I'm letting his father handle that situation. Linda, I'm bewildered by the one of him. When I think about having two so close in age, the way you did, and then trying to raise them alone, I think about slitting my throat. Don't know how you did it. Again, hope all is well, and Linda, *listen* to them."

I'm listening.

We talked about different levels of communication yesterday morning. This is all so terribly obvious. Or so obviously necessary.

The cliche: "My name is Bob and I'm an alcoholic."

The facts: "I'm from Ohio."

The opinion: "I believe alcoholism is a disease."

The feeling: "When I found out I was an alcoholic, I was devastated."

After lunch, pretending it wasn't a zillion degrees hot, a bunch of us sat outside on the sidewalk and I got to thinking how much I liked these people and what an easy time I had talking to them. There wasn't a thing you could say you'd done that somebody else hadn't done worse. Black humor is made for them, for here; there's much laughter, almost as much laughter as there is sadness.

Yesterday afternoon we talked about co-dependence (basically, taking someone else's temperature to see how you feel) and when Sue said, "the co-dependent parent, the one who didn't drink, is the one children have the most issues with later in life," I was genuinely stunned, having assumed, without giving it much thought, that my anger at Mama, our constant fighting, had to do with my taste, politics, friends, men, choices, life or the fact we were a lot alike. It never occurred to me it had to do with her not being able to stop Daddy from drinking.

> Visiting hours are Sundays and holidays from 1:00 pm–5:00 pm. Visitors are to register at the reception desk and receive a visitor's badge that is to be worn during their visit. The badge is to be returned to the desk upon departure of the visitor.

Watching other people's families come to visit, I miss my own so much I'm determined to do what it takes to get back to them. Today my roommate talked about dropping out, leaving now. She's thinking of it. I was anxious for her but very nervous, because I have not thought about quitting, although I said, "Oh, sure I have," when she asked. "We all do," I said.

I'm too scared to quit. I don't want to go back to where I was.

But I do want to get back to my family; and still it's pleasant tonight sitting in this room at this desk, alone. There's no light but that from my desk lamp, soft and yellow, no sound but the crickets and the sprinklers that keep the desert at bay (for considerable handfuls of money, I suspect). I do like moments like this; you feel most monk-like. It must be the cell-effect. There's a curious peace in distance. Once in a while I think I would like to spend long periods of time apart from the world. Can one meditate and write at the same time? Solitude will always be necessary, I think, but then solitude is not isolation, is it? How is it that so often here I get the feeling I've worked hard to learn something I already know, or knew, once. Is it their purpose to teach us what we know? Or to remind us where to look for it, touching the posts as we go, trying to find our way home in the dark?

The soft yellow light on my desk shines me to sleep.

> Confrontation is defined as "presenting a person with himself by describing how I see him." It takes courage to risk confronting. We are all dependent upon others for a completed picture of ourselves. Confrontation provides that.

Treatment, they tell you, works from the outside in. At some time everyone in the group is asked to evaluate your progress. Each person is given a form and asked to check those statements most appropriate to you. There are two columns. In one column are the phrases that damn: Minimizes use. Doesn't ask for help. Too much outside focus. Seems arrogant and self-centered. In the other column: Realistic about self and problem. Is well focused on treatment. Takes responsibility for own behavior. Socializes well with peers. Both lists are long in case you want to really get down to it. When it was Tom's turn, he was excited because he thought he was doing so well; he could hardly wait to see what nice things were going to be said about him. Probably, he said, he'd be the first person to get no bad phrases at all. He was crushed after the papers were turned in and the counselor read the results. It seems everybody said terrible things about Tom. Acts immaturely. Glamorizes use. Over-intellectualizes.

"But didn't anybody have any nice things to say about you?" I ask him, feeling pretty awful for him myself.

"Only Miguelito."

Miguelito is a gardener from East Los Angeles. He's also a drug dealer who liked his wares and as a consequence has a little trouble now putting two sentences together without large gaps of time between the words. Verbs give him particular trouble.

"What did Miguelito say?"

"He said I 'seemed willing.' Tom seems willing, said Miguelito the drug dealer."

"It's not much, is it?"

On Saturdays, we have two-hour sessions, the four "units" together in the main hall where they can mess with all our minds at once. They are quite good at it. This Saturday was "Lifeboat Drill." They divided us into four groups of twenty each, told each group it was a lifeboat halfway between Europe and America, with food and water on board for only eighteen; therefore each group had to pick two people to throw overboard. And each group had to decide *how* it would pick the two people to throw overboard, with only two rules: no volunteers, none of this "Oh, I'm not worth a damn or I don't care, etc., so throw me over," and no lotteries.

Amazing the way we can become children, cruel children, with the least encouragement. In our group, we decided to go round the circle and have everybody say why it was they thought they deserved to be allowed to stay on board (to live), then we'd vote. People said the oddest things. "I'm a good fisherman or I could learn to be one fast." "I studied astronomy in high school. I could guide us." "I'm small; I don't eat much." "I'm a good person. I sing."

When everybody was done, the eight people who'd been tossed to the sharks had to get up on stage in front of the rest of us and say how they "felt" about it. One theoretically dead woman ran crying from the room. A yellow-haired man I'd seen throwing rocks at a duck one day, also theoretically dead, said he hated us all and we'd be sorry. Others were merely pissed. The woman my group voted to sink said she expected it; she was old and her arm was in a cast (which she'd said would be good for hitting fish on the head when she was trying to think of a reason we shouldn't drown her). I was sad for her. Nobody felt sad for the other one we threw off our boat. He should have known better than to ask the tired, used people in that room (collectively among our group of twenty, we had 500 years of drinking) to spare him because he was only twenty-four and had his whole life in front of him; and still we might have, but he said he was going to be a lawyer.

Taking a closer look at the eight people on the stage, seven now, I notice we've thrown away the old, the injured, the weak, a homosexual, a black man and in the would-have-been-a-lawyer's case, the witless. I'm less sure what this says about us as a bunch of drunks than as a society, but we learned, each of us to some extent or another during "Lifeboat Drill," about how we regarded ourselves and how that affected the way the others saw us. I knew, going in, that if it were a game, I would be voted overboard. I also knew if it were for real, I would survive. I was not voted overboard. Not that day.

The retired schoolteacher from Des Moines said that "when Betty was in treatment they played this same game and Betty said, 'If you don't throw me overboard, you'll all have a better chance of living because they won't give up searching for an ex-president's wife so soon.'" Mrs. Ford was always practical.

Lloyd's card today is a detail from "Garden of Id," an original oil painting by Ilene Meyer of Seattle, Washington, it says on the back. A beautiful blonde woman in a white tunic stands in the middle of a forest, gazing into a crystal ball which she holds above her head. She is surrounded by three male elves and one female elf wearing a red dress. The elves are very ugly and they, too, are looking in the crystal ball. Inside the card, in Lloyd's script, it says, "I figure you've been there long enough I don't have to print anymore. The blonde in white sees a future without all these pointy-eared, little-dick men who can do nothing for her. She is, therefore, pleased. The blonde in red sees a future without the demanding giant bitch and with a different man for every night of the week. She is, therefore, pleased. It's all relative. Love, Lloyd." There's a man to have in a lifeboat.

> For the most part, defenses are unconscious and automatic shields against a real or imagined threat. By pointing out the defenses you are using, you have a better chance of letting down this wall that is locking others out and keeping you prisoner. Since defenses hide us from ourselves as well as others, it is important to identify them.

I hate this place. Today they made me be quiet for two hours. I wasn't allowed to say anything to anyone or explain why I could not, nor was I allowed to be by myself. I had to sit with people, go to lunch with people and the longer it went on the more awful it was. Being silent, I realized how much I talked in self-defense. Being silent, I felt naked. How dare they take away my clothes. I mean my voice. I was in a rage so black the room went dark. No voice. No power. I would get even. I would show them who had the power. I would, I said to myself, drink. Drinking would give me a voice.

When you shut one eye you don't hear so good.

I hate this place. They're so . . . right.

Got to change my behavior, not my thinking. Check. Can't think myself into better living; it was my best thinking got me here. Check. Maybe I can live myself into better thinking. Check. Why have I been sober for twenty-one days? Because I haven't had a drink in twenty-one days. Right. Fear comes out as anger. Anger suppressed comes out as guilt. Check. Remember, you were a co-dependent before you were an addict. And so what? You think you come from a dysfunctional family, Linda? Nobody named Beaver Cleaver can be healthy.

Right.

I wander around The Betty Ford Center early in the morning, noting the many places I have stopped to cry in three weeks' time.

Last night a splendid white-haired, tall woman spoke to us at the AA meeting. She lives in Palm Springs and also is the mother of a man I once saw a lot in, and of. Strange place to meet her. This lady opened with the traditional greeting only more so;

instead of saying, "My name is Maureen and I'm an alcoholic," she said, "No matter what you've been told, this is a confidential society, not a secret one, so my name is Maureen *Jones* and I'm an alcoholic." She waits while we laugh. "And I was one before your mother was born. So don't try to con me."

Maureen Jones is not her real name, of course. None of the names I've mentioned are real, except for mine, but "Maureen Jones" *is* a real person and she's gotten me thinking about what it's going to be like when I leave here, which won't be long now. My struggle is no longer how to live drunk, but how to live sober.

"It's simple," says Maureen. "Go to meetings and don't drink."

It *is* simple. But who's good with simple? No, shut up. Do what you're told. For once.

H: never get too hungry.
A: never get too angry.
L: never get too lonely.
T: never get too tired.

HALT, they say to remember. If you don't want to relapse, *HALT.* More codes for kids. And go to meetings and don't drink; I know. I know. Or hope I know. Recovery is a process, not an event. I must think about that, think about who will expect me to come home "fixed," and what will I say to them.

Even this place is changed. Mike is gone. June is leaving tomorrow. She and I have become close, too, in the way women can in confined circumstances, despite (or because of) these also being circumstances where you spend a good part of the day telling each other your faults. I look forward to visiting her in Los Angeles. We will, I hope, stay friends. She is one of those women who moves things along. Herself. Me. The group. I envy that. June knows many things. She told me when she used to drink tequila and didn't want anyone to know, she'd eat an apple and it would take the smell away.

Now you tell me?

I will miss her.

Them.

They told us the real healing would go on in the halls, by the water fountain and across the breakfast table, but there are so many new people who've come in, so many old people gone. I'm by way of being senior around here now. There's a scary thought.

Here's another. I was walking across what I still cannot bring myself to call the "campus" tonight, walking back to my "unit," and it was so nice out, the air so heavy and hot, so filled with summer, that I stopped, took off my shoes and ran into the sprinkler, dancing a little, a step or two, singing some, until I was wet and cool. My feet squishing in the grass the rest of the way back, I could see the mountains, black holes against the starred night sky of the desert, and nothing happened, but I knew I wasn't alone and hadn't been for a long time, maybe ever.

And to think I could have missed it all . . .

> Women have traditionally been the hidden chemically dependent. It appears that in specialized treatment services for women there is less game-playing, less falling into traditional roles, and less tendency to sit back and let the focus be on others. Special emphasis is placed on helping each woman work on her anger, her guilt, her grief and on helping her begin to build a positive self-image.

My last assignment is to write a letter to Linda Jane, the girl I left behind me. A "hello" letter, says my counselor. My hand must be permanently bent, I think, from so much longhand writing. Not since high school have I been without a machine to make the words. But I have gotten used to what seem nonsensical assignments. I have even come to see their sense.

When quite young, I thought other little girls were not like me because I was aware, and aware that I was. I was a tree, a sun and a feather. I had leaves and was yellow warm and could float; and my leaves could turn brown and die, falling away; clouds could hide the world so I could not shine and somebody could pick at me until all the things that made me a feather were gone and I was a bone. Or maybe a balloon. I could tell you what it felt like to be red or big or salty. What it felt like to be born. To be hurt. I would touch the skin on my knee, feeling it smooth, then bleeding, scabrous, then smooth once more. I felt *everything*. I could do anything. The only thing I could not feel was nothing at all and the only thing I could not do was make time stand still or love last. Or make my daddy stop drinking. And I felt that most of all.

That little girl knew something I don't. I learned how to feel nothing at all—or how to drink until it seemed that way. But drinking never made time stop or love last, either. And my daddy died.

Am I ready to leave here? Yes. No.

What will I tell the people I don't know? Where will I say I've been? I can't tell them the truth, not the people with whom I'll be working. Networks don't like drunks, even sober. They don't like women drunks more, I'll bet. Redemption is not what they're into. I decide to practice my story. I call a network vice president, a man who signs an occasional paycheck of mine. "Hello," I say, all cheery. "How are you?"

"Fine," he says. "Where are you?"

"Oh," I say, ready to tell him I'm visiting friends in the desert, "I'm at The Betty Ford Center." *Jesus Christ,* Ellerbee, you just said you were *where?* To a *network executive?* Have you lost it or what? I start to sweat. There is a short pause while he takes in what I've said.

"My name is Dave and I'm an alcoholic."

Today I got my last card from Lloyd. He called to tell me so. He's leaving for Detroit, which, he says, still sucks. I ask him don't they have cards in Detroit? "No," he says, "they have cards. They have no stamps."

The last card features another detail from another original oil by Ms. Meyer of Seattle (I suspect a sale). This one is called "Sentinel." It shows three women more or less lying, sphinx-like, on a beach, a few steps shy of what appears to be primordial slime. The women have wings growing from their backs, the lower halves of their bodies are leopards and they have long dragon tails. Two men stand in the slime, looking bewildered and somewhat insignificant in the face of such improbable strength. It is the dawn of the world. "Dear Linda Jane," writes Lloyd, inside.

"Since you share my fascination with the language, I believe that you will be as delighted as I was to see for yourself the etymology of that familiar phrase, 'a little piece of tail.' Love, Lloyd." I always will love him, you know.

Hope is the thing with feathers
That purchase in the soul
That sings the song without the tune
And never stops at all.

My name is Linda and I'm an alcoholic.

In the summer of 1989, I turned to my son and said please hold my hand, I think I'm in terrible trouble. I'm going to telephone The Betty Ford Center. I don't know where else to call and if I take the time to find out, I'll chicken out.

In the summer of 1990, I celebrated my first year of sobriety.

"It's the thirteenth month that's the hardest," says a friend with ten years. "We get over the first year: we're successful and we alcoholics can't take that."

"But it's my fourteenth month and I'm still sober," I tell her. "And still here."

"And do you know why?"

"Yes. I didn't drink and I didn't die."

GRACELAND

And I may be obliged to defend
Every love, every ending
Or maybe there's no obligations, now.
Maybe I've a reason to believe
We all will be received
In Graceland.

—*PAUL SIMON*

Perhaps when you've got close to half a century, sentimental journeys are the ones you have to take. Look down there. You say gray's dull and lifeless, the color of old cardboard boxes and dirt—but look. This is the land where gray comes alive. Aren't there more shades of gray down there than you ever saw or thought possible? The water glows back at you, a big luminous gray pearl, and the clouds lie like silver smoke on the mountains. There's steel and stone gray in the scars man makes in these greenblack forests with his buildings, his machines and roads and even his empty places; and polished gray in the mandolin wind that blows, high-wailing and lonesome, down from the mountains and straight into your soul, filling it with bittersweet memories of anticipation. Just look down there. This is the magic place, achromatic: able to emit, receive and even transmit light without separating it into colors, a trick conjured in the air that rides the great ocean, following the warm waves from the west until it hits the mountains and then up it goes, cooling its heels, making the clouds cry every time—cry gray like the rain, like the silk sky, like the days, gray and alive almost every one of them, when you lived in Juneau, Alaska.

There's an afternoon, almost twenty years ago. A small carnival has come to town. It isn't open, but nobody seems to care if you wander around; either I look harmless to the carnival people (I think to myself, they just don't know) or I look *like* the carnival people. It's possible. I'm wearing a flowered skirt that reaches the ground, an embroidered Mexican blouse, a rawhide headband, many beads and dangly earrings, and an old army fatigue jacket with the words "Up The Amerikan Revolution" hand-painted on the back. The hair's long, only not so free as Kirsten's, not plaited into one long braid like Louise's. The feet are muddy (I am barefoot). Slung papoose style over the shoulder is my one-year-old boy-child. My two-year-old daughter holds my right hand, pulling me ahead faster faster Mommy faster, slowing only for us to jump with both feet into the mud puddles (we are both barefoot). The colored lights of the carnival are rain-soft, vaporous, but still they dance, inviting you to believe in their magic, in somebody's magic. And you do. In theirs. In yours. Ours. We are all gypsies, you say to yourself that afternoon. The rain is shiny wet on your face and you're smiling, younger than you've ever been and telling yourself happiness is a manner of traveling, your toes all wiggly and gray from the alive Alaska mud, gray like the wing you see outside this window on the airplane that's bringing you back here. Years back here.

And for what? A man who figured out how to calculate the orbits of planets said there are only three great questions in life and we have to answer them over and over again: Is it true or false? Is it right or wrong? Is it beautiful or ugly? The two years Van and I lived in this place changed everything. I came to Juneau a discontented housewife listing to the left. I left Juneau a reporter, a fan of Ayn Rand and divorced. I know a lot about both of those events, the ones at either end, and those two women; it's the middle that confuses me. Here I lived in a commune and favored the overthrow of the United States government. Here my husband left me for another. That is one version. But what really happened here—*what in hell happened here*—and was it true, right and beautiful or false, wrong and ugly? I am a woman with questions. Gray is not my favorite color. I like red. You know where you stand with red.

At the airport I rent a car. Overcast and drizzling, it's not a gloomy day, only a normal one. I get a little lost driving into town; there are two roads now for part of the way, but the Gastineau Channel and Douglas Island are on my right and the mountain's on my left, where it ought to be. Mount Juneau in June, and snow on it still. No gentle slope, this mountain; it rises straight up, the town a Band-Aid on its big toe. The mountain confuses people who don't live here. "How high are we above sea level?" tourists ask, standing on a dock two feet above what is essentially the Pacific Ocean.

There, you see, the capital's still here. They were talking about moving it to Anchorage or some Alaskan version of Brasilia when I first came to this place. They still are, I bet; half a million people in Alaska and half of those live in one place: Anchorage. Not quite 30,000 live in Juneau, about 15,000 more than when I lived here. That's what oil does for you—and to you.

Downtown looks the same but for more tour ships and tourist shops (T-shirts that say "I ♥ fishing," smoked salmon from Seattle and moccasins from Taiwan) and you'll notice the Red Dog Saloon has moved again. Wooden houses are still stacked on top of one another up the steep streets that cling to the ankles of the mountain like nasty children (when they get too steep, some streets chicken out and turn into stairs with street signs, as in: Annie? She lives two flights up Fourth Street). Frederick always said that when everyone else in the world was trying to figure out how to stop urban sprawl, Juneau went out of its way to create some, and it didn't matter if they were built in the twenties or the sixties, the one thing they had in common was that each building was totally disassociated, architecturally, from the one next to it. Wait a minute. The mural on the wall over there—the Indian with the killer whale—is that Gary's face the artist has painted? If so, he hasn't changed at all. Hasn't gotten older-looking is what I mean, don't I? Do I notice fewer natives or are there just too many tourists in the way to tell? Or is it both things? You don't see many fishing boats, do you? What happened to the fleet? The whole town looks as if it had been left out in the rain too long and by mistake.

And so beautiful anyway. So beautiful.

In the hotel room I wonder whom to call first. Don't hurry the past, I say to myself, as if I know what I'm talking about. Lie down, read your "Welcome to Juneau" booklet and think about what to do next. Ordinarily I read detective stories on the road. All questions get answered in mystery books.

It says here that Juneau was founded 101 years ago by Joe Juneau and Richard Harris, two miners who were led to rich deposits along the aptly named Gold Creek by a Tlingit Indian named Kowee. It does not tell you that the Americans were only the latest to take whatever they wanted, the Russians having already come and gone, carrying full mountains of fur to warm themselves and their countrymen against the cold, the way the animals whose skins they wore once did. It does not tell you that.

It says there's much for the tourist to do here. Try your luck at gold-panning, $10, it says. See the glacier (there are 5,000 glaciers in Alaska and my main memory of this one is that it's large, blue and, when chipped, gives ice that stays hard in your drink all night long). Swim (better have brought your wet suit; 5,000 glaciers do not a Gulfstream make). Fish. Hike. Running's very big here now, I see; next week is the "Only Fools Run at Midnight" run. You can just imagine. But where do they run? There are no roads to Juneau, Alaska; you get here by plane or boat, effectively making this an island and like all islands, something of a fairy tale.

In the tourist booklet you read that Juneau has five radio stations and two television stations, that Juneau has survived both the oil boom of the seventies and the oil bust of the eighties, that unemployment is the lowest it's ever been, that plenty of good housing is available and that Juneau is a place that celebrates the diversity of its people and respects the traditions and culture of Alaska's native heritage. You will not see anything in this booklet about The Chinese Firehouse, the Citizens' Participation Committee or how we bombed in New Haven one gray night in Juneau (in summer at this latitude, even night is an indefinite object). But it's there, if you know where to look.

Call Frederick first.

He seems pleased but not surprised to hear I am in town, as if it were only yesterday I sat in the radio station next to him, watching his hands on the controls, raising this, lowering that; so careful they were, Frederick's hands, cautious, like him. Tell him why you're here. Later.

We arrange dinner. I meet Frederick and Terry, his wife, an expert video repairwoman with a wicked grin and a big, roomy heart, at a restaurant that used to be something else. You ask if you can have fresh Alaska king crab and are told not anymore, it's all shipped south, what there is. Do you remember how you'd send Gary and Jimmy out in the boat with a six-pack? They'd find a crab pot with a few crabs in it and exchange the beer for crabs. As they walked the crab in the back door, Neil would have his "gen-u-wine cauldron" of water boiling on the stove and Marvin would have melted two bowls of real butter, garlic in one, too much Tabasco in the other. Judy and I would take the crab, pull off the legs, toss them into the water then onto a table covered with newspapers to use as plates, next to a couple of gallon jugs of heavy-duty California white. Tonight I eat salmon, blackened, and drink decaffeinated coffee, the house wine of the recently sober, under a hanging plant and save-the-spotted-owl poster.

Frederick says let's have a party, a reunion, tomorrow—we'll get everyone. Terry promises to bake chocolate-chip cookies (it's brownies you still remember, Ms. Toklas's brownies, but that was back when such things seemed socially appropriate and entirely harmless) and maybe Marvin can make some chili. The three of us compose the "guest" list from who's still around. They don't see much of Neil anymore; he has no phone or job (I hear gentle concern about Neil's drinking), but they know where he lives. Gary and Kirsten are over on Gold Street in Gary's parents' old house. Marvin, who still works for the state, is in one of those condos they built down by what used to be a wharf. Pete is into desktop publishing now; his office is up the hill from where Louise works as a computer programmer. Dennis does something with computers, too, but Frederick says Dennis still stirs his stew; last year Dennis organized the protest against that new black box of a hotel someone wanted to build. "Not on my waterfront you don't," said the posters. Judy's married and living in Anchorage, they think, and Jimmy, well, you won't see Jimmy; he left ten years ago and the last anybody heard he's somewhere in northern California. Dealing drugs, is everyone's guess.

And Van . . .

Conversation moves quickly to the present. Frederick and Terry are doing well with their store, Snow-Free Video. Also, he still hosts *Action Line* on the radio on Saturdays and for old times' sake, will I be his guest tomorrow morning on KJNO? And won't that be a hoot, he says.

I go to bed early, but do not sleep. This was a dumb idea. Did you think you could be a reporter about this? You do think that, don't you? But is it possible? When it comes to truth, memory and imagination grow their own. And everybody shows his own movie. I sleep and wake with just enough time to put something on and drive to the radio station.

"Linda, you came to Alaska in 1971, is that right?" Frederick fiddles with dials, ready to adjust me.

"That's right, Frederick [he knows this; we're talking for the audience]. I came to Alaska in 1971."

By boat. In the January night. It was two or three in the morning when the ferry docked, I recall. Van and I, so young, so determined not to seem so. The missionary, Van's boss, was there to meet us, as though it were far Africa which, except for the blizzard, it might as well have been, that's how different it was from the pale, broad land and persistent sun of our South Texas brush country. Poor Van had been seasick for most of the three days it took to sail from Seattle to Juneau. Magoo, the yellow dog, and I enjoyed our ride, thrilled by the icy air, the vulgar, noisy waves, even the storms that rocked 'n' rolled us through Queen Charlotte Straits and partway up the Inside Passage. We met Judy on board the ferry; she was returning home, a native Alaskan but not a Native Alaskan she explained. When you asked her about the rain, Judy laughed as if that were funny and said one day you'd go on a picnic in the rain and never notice.

"Your husband, Van, came to Juneau to work for the Model Cities Program back then, right?"

"Yes, he did, Frederick."

"Perhaps I'd better explain to our audience what that was . . ."

Please do. Explain to them how the Model Cities Program was a chance for people whose voices weren't really being heard not only to get them into the system but to get them so fired up they wouldn't settle for not being heard ever again, and how Van, the cowboy-poet, was not what they had in mind, the good Methodist minister and the City Fathers who ran the program. Explain how they wanted someone who understood the poor, not someone who liked them, certainly not someone who'd join them, egg them on in their rabble-rousing disruptive, unproductive, un-American ways; sure, the borough assembly had allowed that Citizens' Participation Committee to be formed but never expected it to be so loud, so political—so *uppity:* saying how *they* thought the money should be spent, talking about housing and employment and public transportation as though *they* could afford it. It was all a part of the horrible, angry noises you heard everywhere, part of the dreadful thing that was happening to America, a nation with too much to offer and too damn many young people who didn't think so anymore. The most ungrateful people you'd ever seen, even here, smack under the Big Dipper, safe in (what the City Fathers fervently hoped was) the last frontier.

Juneau wasn't like what people in Alaska referred to as "the lower forty-eight" (Hawaii could cut its own deals) in that you couldn't always tell a hippie from the mayor; they both wore jeans and beards, but only the hippies wore beads, unless they were old Russian trade beads, which cost so much that if you had them you could still wear them no matter who you were. And only "straights" called us "hippies." If you *were* hippies, you called yourselves "freaks." We were freaks, we thought, and said. The house we rented on Sixth Street was small, white and wooden, with linoleum floors, and would have been quite ordinary but for the forty-foot totem pole in front of it. I was glad we'd brought that 100-pound sack of dried pinto beans with us from Texas; we were taking enough chances with Alaska as it was.

"Things were pretty interesting here then, weren't they, Linda?"

"Frederick, it was the sixties."

"I thought it was 1971."

"You know what I mean."

We met Marvin and Gary at the Citizens' Participation Committee meetings, fascinating, if rococo, events; I'd never heard Indians speak publicly before. They would open by saying something like, "In the beginning, the moon . . ." then they'd acknowledge everyone in their mother's clan, then everyone in their clan, then everyone in the opposite clan and all their ancestors, individually, it seemed at the time, and after they'd get around to saying what they'd come to say in the first place, they'd finish by thanking everyone in their mother's clan, everyone in their clan, everyone in the opposite clan and all their ancestors. They weren't all Indians at the meetings, but they all talked and everybody argued, usually formally and with great shows of manners, but not always. If it took a while to get anything done, these events were still democratic in the most basic, cumbersome way, and a mighty interesting thing that was. Van and I went for that reason, and because it was his job—and because we were "into" community action in a big way.

The first one we met was Gary, born and raised in Juneau, twenty-three years old and just back from Vietnam. His mother was Tlingit, his father was not. Gary was a "breed." It was not a polite word, yet Gary was so handsome, on him anything looked good. He was the perfect poster-brave. But Gary was getting himself politicized.

Skinny, skeptical Marvin, who was not an Indian, could always make you laugh, and although he had gray in his hair even then, neutral was not his color. Neither was monotonous. Marvin was an actor and, when he arrived in Juneau in 1968, a hairdresser as well. His first day at work they told him about the last male hairdresser who'd been run out of town for being "queer." Marvin went to work for the state the first chance he got; it made sense, and anyway the pay was better. But he was still an actor. Marvin got Gary, who was also doing something or other for the state, to go see a play he'd directed at the local community theater. Gary got Marvin to go to a Citizens' Participation Committee meeting. That's how their friendship started. They had many things in common; there were laws against discrimination but no rules; discrimination was another "gray" area.

One night, coming home from beer and political talk at Dreamland following a CPC meeting, they were stopped. Both Gary and Marvin were drunk. The cop arrested Gary, the Indian. He drove Marvin, the white man, home. If only he'd known, said Marvin. If only the cop had known.

Gary was turning into a radical Indian. Marvin was becoming an angry homosexual. I was a budding feminist. Van was either a Marxist or younger than he looked, and he'd discovered Mao. Van liked the little red book. I don't recall what he said about the cultural revolution. We all were against the war.

"And Van was fired from the Model Cities Program, I remember . . ."

"For insubordination. I remember, too, Frederick."

"There was an editorial in the newspaper about that, wasn't there? About how wrong they'd been to fire Van because he wouldn't lie for his boss. Van was a real whistle-blower, wasn't he? Were you proud of him for what he did?"

"Extremely."

There really are moments that by their existence change the way we are and will thereafter be. The night Van was fired, everybody came to our house and it was like a victory party, as if we'd won something important, but later I lay awake while he slept, so scared and mad I could not breathe, and said to myself: never depend on someone else to feed your children. Never again. It wasn't all Van's fault any more than it should have been all Van's responsibility but from now on, it would be my responsibility; I would *make* it mine and nobody's else's, even if I weren't sure how or if I were right. Nor did I care.

"Do you recall exactly when you came looking for work at the radio station, Linda?"

"Vaguely."

It was the day after Van was fired, and I was begging for work, not knowing how to do anything except talk and scribble, if that. Lucky for me Neil was running the station. Older by a dozen years, Neil had come here one month after he'd been graduated from college and two years before Alaska was a state; he'd been working and not working at KJNO ever since. It was a volatile place, where people came and went frequently, even regularly, and not always by choice. Neil was a troublemaker, a smart-talking cynical son of a bitch who partied too hard, drove too fast and had no mercy in him. He claimed to despise everything we believed in. He voted Republican, he said, only because the Tories had no column on the ballot; and still I was crazy about Neil. Van only sort of liked Neil, liked his brains and style, but nothing he thought or said. Van couldn't understand Neil. Sometimes neither could I. But sometimes I couldn't understand Van.

"The first time you and I met, Linda, was when I interviewed Van, your husband."

"And I talked the whole time, didn't I, Frederick?"

"Yes, you did. And we'll be back to talk with Linda some more after we take this call from a listener. Hello. This is *Action Line*. You have a pickup truck you want to sell. Tell us about it."

He was funny and quick-witted and between the three of us, Neil, Frederick and myself, Frederick was always smarter faster. Frederick had grown up in San Diego, raised, as he put it, "by people of Depression values from the Midwest." When I met him, he'd lived in Alaska for only a year. "From the minute I arrived," said Frederick, "I felt I was on Indian land and all the white people were visitors. Or worse." He was twenty-five then. Frederick hated to spin records, finding the technical side of radio more interesting, but that wasn't what the job was and anyway, hating to spin records was how he met Neil. This was before Neil returned to be manager of the station. One day Frederick had been so bored that between records he'd asked, almost as if he were talking to himself except it was over the air, if anyone knew "whatever happened to Patrice Lamumba." The phone rang.

"The niggers in the Southern Congo ate him." Neil was press secretary to the governor of Alaska at the time.

Frederick was at the time (and is now) the kind of person who doesn't go in for sizing other people up so quickly; he likes to wait to see what they turn out to be when they grow up. After Neil came back to work at the station, Frederick watched closely and found he liked Neil a great deal. As Frederick says, "If I have any prejudices, it's against dumb people. I like bright people and people with a badass sense of humor and Neil is both. Also, he despises everybody pretty much equally."

For a conservative, Neil was not at all resistant to change; he was not afraid to let people do things differently than had been done before. He was not afraid, period. And if Frederick's politics were not Neil's, neither were they Van's. It wasn't that black and white. In college, Frederick had thought a lot of the antiwar energy was wasted ("Okay, now we've succeeded in blowing up the administration building and shutting down the university. Okay, now a bunch of kids can't get an education, which means now some of them will have to go to Vietnam. I mean, *what was the point?*"), but in Juneau he believed he'd found a place where one voice could be heard, and you might not always succeed but you could be heard, one person or a farmhouse full of people could make a place noticeably different than if they weren't there. A farmhouse full of people . . .

"You lived in a commune while you were here, didn't you, Linda?"

"It was more of a farmhouse, Frederick."

"Back to the land and all?"

"Not exactly."

He's playing radio with me again. I don't know why we called it the farmhouse; certainly we never grew anything. I suppose because it had been a farm once. Some people called it the hippie farm. Neil always said we were so disorganized we turned anything we did into "a fucking Chinese fire drill." He had a sign made for the place the day we moved in. The Chinese Firehouse, it said, in Chinese. But of course, Neil lived there, too.

"Did it have a purpose, this farmhouse?"

"Yes. We thought if a dozen people could live together in peace and harmony, the whole world could."

"And?"

"And a dozen people couldn't."

Or could they? Was the farmhouse a success or a failure? What did we think we were doing, all of us moving in together like that? Saving money? The world?

"Let's get back to your radio career in Juneau. You started a controversial radio program right here on this station, didn't you?"

"Well, Frederick, it was only controversial because it was here. You have to remember that back then, music was also politics. There were only the two radio stations in town and neither one played rock 'n' roll, not real rock 'n' roll, not the music the whole world was listening to. Not Jagger or Crosby, Stills & Nash, nor Neil Young, not the Grateful Dead, not the Who nor The Band; no Rod Stewart, no John Lennon. They were, if you can believe it, considered too radical to be played on the radio in the capital city of the biggest state in the United States in the year 1971. The only way you heard new music was if someone brought back an album from Down South [to an Alaskan, Seattle, Boston and New Orleans are equally "Down South"] or someone sent you one. We went to the owner of KJNO and said if we can find sponsors, will you let us have the hours from midnight Saturday until six Sunday morning (when the religious programming began) to play our music? And he said yes. At first. So we did that. We sold the time and went on the air with *Blackout*. All things considered, it seemed an appropriate name."

"Where did you get the records?"

"They were our own. But after the first night we were on the air, people began to show up at the station around midnight Saturdays, bringing their own records, saying 'Here, this ought to be heard.' That's weird, when you think about it, Frederick. And kind of neat."

Neat. The second night we were on the air somebody brought us a copy of Lennon's "Workingman's Hero." We put it on and pretty soon John Lennon goes: "We're so fucking crazy we can't follow their rules." Over the air. Well, we didn't know how many times he said "fuck" during the song, so we sat around and said to one another, "He only says it once, right?" Nobody worried about the word having *already* gone out on the air, which, in those days, was a big deal. Done was done, man; the question was, does he say it again in the same song, and we agreed he didn't, but of course he did.

We started another show, too; actually Frederick started it, I named it. Frederick worried there wasn't enough information on radio: there were no book reviews or movie reviews, no local reporting to speak of and no commentary on a regular basis, nothing but middle-of-the-road (lots of Engelbert Humperdinck and Mantovani) junk, like Muzak, only not so inventive, plus a little rip-'n'-read news off the AP wire now and then to meet the FCC news requirement, and commercials, plenty of them, played early and often. He persuaded the station owner to let him put together a magazine of the air, which Frederick called *The Monday Night Magazine of the Air,* a name that struck the rest of us as lacking panache, or as Van put it, balls. Well, not long before, an Alaskan Airlines jet, shooting what passed for an instrument approach at the Juneau airport, had flown into a mountain instead, killing 111 people. It got everybody talking about cockpit tape recorders, and pretty soon there was a list floating around about what you couldn't afford to say in a cockpit anymore because someone might hear it: they were supposed to be common phrases used by pilots and air-traffic controllers; who knows where these things come from? Each phrase was given a code number, so everyone would know what you were trying to say even if you couldn't say it. For instance, #63 meant something like "Gee, I hope the watchamacallit lasts until we land" and #92 was "Tell Mama I said good-bye." But #108 was "Beautiful—just fucking beautiful." We took Frederick's tapes and secretly re-recorded the promos for *The Monday Night Magazine of the Air.* The next day Frederick heard my voice on the air telling everyone to be sure to listen to M-108! Frederick complained people wouldn't know what it meant. People would surely know the "M" stood for Monday, I told him.

"You were fired from KJNO, weren't you, Linda?"

low their rules." Over the air. Well, we didn't know how many
mes he said "fuck" during the song, so we sat around and said
one another, "He only says it once, right?" Nobody worried
out the word having *already* gone out on the air, which, in those
ys, was a big deal. Done was done, man; the question was, does
say it again in the same song, and we agreed he didn't, but of
urse he did.

We started another show, too; actually Frederick started it, I
med it. Frederick worried there wasn't enough information on
dio: there were no book reviews or movie reviews, no local
porting to speak of and no commentary on a regular basis,
thing but middle-of-the-road (lots of Engelbert Humperdinck
d Mantovani) junk, like Muzak, only not so inventive, plus a
le rip-'n'-read news off the AP wire now and then to meet the
CC news requirement, and commercials, plenty of them, played
rly and often. He persuaded the station owner to let him put
gether a magazine of the air, which Frederick called *The Monday
ght Magazine of the Air,* a name that struck the rest of us as
cking panache, or as Van put it, balls. Well, not long before,
Alaskan Airlines jet, shooting what passed for an instrument
proach at the Juneau airport, had flown into a mountain in-
ead, killing 111 people. It got everybody talking about cockpit
pe recorders, and pretty soon there was a list floating around
out what you couldn't afford to say in a cockpit anymore be-
use someone might hear it: they were supposed to be common
rases used by pilots and air-traffic controllers; who knows
here these things come from? Each phrase was given a code
mber, so everyone would know what you were trying to say
en if you couldn't say it. For instance, #63 meant something
e "Gee, I hope the watchamacallit lasts until we land" and #92
as "Tell Mama I said good-bye." But #108 was "Beautiful—just
cking beautiful." We took Frederick's tapes and secretly re-
corded the promos for *The Monday Night Magazine of the Air.*
he next day Frederick heard my voice on the air telling everyone
be sure to listen to M-108! Frederick complained people
ouldn't know what it meant. People would surely know the "M"
ood for Monday, I told him.

"You were fired from KJNO, weren't you, Linda?"

"Vaguely."

It was the day after Van was fired, and I was begging for
work, not knowing how to do anything except talk and scribble,
if that. Lucky for me Neil was running the station. Older by a
dozen years, Neil had come here one month after he'd been
graduated from college and two years before Alaska was a state;
he'd been working and not working at KJNO ever since. It was
a volatile place, where people came and went frequently, even
regularly, and not always by choice. Neil was a troublemaker, a
smart-talking cynical son of a bitch who partied too hard, drove
too fast and had no mercy in him. He claimed to despise everything we believed in. He voted Republican, he said, only because
the Tories had no column on the ballot; and still I was crazy
about Neil. Van only sort of liked Neil, liked his brains and
style, but nothing he thought or said. Van couldn't understand
Neil. Sometimes neither could I. But sometimes I couldn't understand Van.

"The first time you and I met, Linda, was when I interviewed
Van, your husband."

"And I talked the whole time, didn't I, Frederick?"

"Yes, you did. And we'll be back to talk with Linda some
more after we take this call from a listener. Hello. This is
Action Line. You have a pickup truck you want to sell. Tell us
about it."

He was funny and quick-witted and between the three of us,
Neil, Frederick and myself, Frederick was always smarter faster.
Frederick had grown up in San Diego, raised, as he put it, "by
people of Depression values from the Midwest." When I met
him, he'd lived in Alaska for only a year. "From the minute I
arrived," said Frederick, "I felt I was on Indian land and all the
white people were visitors. Or worse." He was twenty-five then.
Frederick hated to spin records, finding the technical side of
radio more interesting, but that wasn't what the job was and
anyway, hating to spin records was how he met Neil. This was
before Neil returned to be manager of the station. One day Frederick had been so bored that between records he'd asked, almost
as if he were talking to himself except it was over the air, if anyone

knew "whatever happened to Patrice Lamumba." The phone rang.

"The niggers in the Southern Congo ate him." Neil was press secretary to the governor of Alaska at the time.

Frederick was at the time (and is now) the kind of person who doesn't go in for sizing other people up so quickly; he likes to wait to see what they turn out to be when they grow up. After Neil came back to work at the station, Frederick watched closely and found he liked Neil a great deal. As Frederick says, "If I have any prejudices, it's against dumb people. I like bright people and people with a badass sense of humor and Neil is both. Also, he despises everybody pretty much equally."

For a conservative, Neil was not at all resistant to change; he was not afraid to let people do things differently than had been done before. He was not afraid, period. And if Frederick's politics were not Neil's, neither were they Van's. It wasn't that black and white. In college, Frederick had thought a lot of the antiwar energy was wasted ("Okay, now we've succeeded in blowing up the administration building and shutting down the university. Okay, now a bunch of kids can't get an education, which means now some of them will have to go to Vietnam. I mean, *what was the point?*"), but in Juneau he believed he'd found a place where one voice could be heard, and you might not always succeed but you could be heard, one person or a farmhouse full of people could make a place noticeably different than if they weren't there. A farmhouse full of people . . .

"You lived in a commune while you were here, didn't you, Linda?"

"It was more of a farmhouse, Frederick."

"Back to the land and all?"

"Not exactly."

He's playing radio with me again. I don't know why we called it the farmhouse; certainly we never grew anything. I suppose because it had been a farm once. Some people called it the hippie farm. Neil always said we were so disorganized we turned anything we did into "a fucking Chinese fire drill." He had a sign made for the place the day we moved in. The Chinese Firehouse, it said, in Chinese. But of course, Neil lived there, too.

"Did it have a purpose, this farmhouse?"

"Yes. We thought if a dozen people could live and harmony, the whole world could."

"And?"

"And a dozen people couldn't."

Or could they? Was the farmhouse a success o did we think we were doing, all of us moving that? Saving money? The world?

"Let's get back to your radio career in Junea controversial radio program right here on thi you?"

"Well, Frederick, it was only controversial bec You have to remember that back then, music There were only the two radio stations in town played rock 'n' roll, not real rock 'n' roll, not the world was listening to. Not Jagger or Crosby, St Neil Young, not the Grateful Dead, not the Who no Rod Stewart, no John Lennon. They were, if it, considered too radical to be played on the rac city of the biggest state in the United States in The only way you heard new music was if someo an album from Down South [to an Alaskan, Sea New Orleans are equally "Down South"] or so one. We went to the owner of KJNO and said sponsors, will you let us have the hours from mi until six Sunday morning (when the religiou began) to play our music? And he said yes. At that. We sold the time and went on the air w things considered, it seemed an appropriate nar

"Where did you get the records?"

"They were our own. But after the first night air, people began to show up at the station ar Saturdays, bringing their own records, saying 'F to be heard.' That's weird, when you think abo And kind of neat."

Neat. The second night we were on the air son us a copy of Lennon's "Workingman's Hero." W pretty soon John Lennon goes: "We're so fuckin

"I like to think of it as my first cancellation, Frederick."

They fired Neil first, mostly for letting us do what we did. The people from the farmhouse had taken turns being disc jockey on *Blackout* and the two groups had further mingled, cross-pollinating, so to speak, through living arrangements and politics, which was always more complicated than matters of who slept where. Or with whom. Neil lived at the farm. Frederick didn't but was usually there. Marvin and Gary did, as did Kirsten, Judy, Jimmy and Peter. And Van and I and our children. One or two others now and then. And, later, Louise.

"You actually found the farmhouse on *Action Line*, didn't you?"

"Yes, Frederick. We found our commune on the radio."

Stole is what you mean. Frederick was hosting *Action Line* back then, too. One Saturday this woman called in with a farmhouse she wanted to rent. I was supposed to put her on hold until Frederick could put her on the air. Instead I got her number and told her we'd call her right back. "Hey, everybody, I've got an idea . . ."

"Before we say good-bye, Linda, what's the purpose of this trip? What are you doing in Juneau?"

"Just visiting."

"The old places?"

"The only ones I know."

Answering his questions is not answering my questions. The road north of Juneau stops after thirty miles, having gone nowhere, but between Juneau and that point are Auke Bay and the Mendenhall Valley, formed by the glacier receding over a brief 150-million-year period. Way out near the glacier itself is a little dirt road that winds around to Auke Bay, and off that little dirt road is a large, yellow farmhouse I want to see again. After leaving the station I get in my rented car and head north. Morning is still fogged in, like my head. None of us knew there was a place like that farmhouse near Juneau; it looked as if it belonged in Montana: the open green meadow, forest and river nearby, the mountains sheltering us from—from what?—from damn little, it turned out.

I drive to the glacier, but there is no dirt road anymore. There are only oil suburbs, mile after gray mile of mostly ugly houses put up during the boom. You can see why the chamber of commerce says there's plenty of housing; maybe one-quarter of these are empty. It couldn't be just good taste, you don't suppose.

I find where I think the farmhouse was and get out of the car to talk to that spot. Commune with it? This is where I loved my life best. This is where I hated my life most. This is where I lost my husband. My marriage. Right here on this spot. Or had it begun before we came to Alaska? Was this where our dreams came to die, or did we kill them in this place. And did we do it to ourselves or was it done to us? Say it. To *us*. Yes, he left you for Louise, but you opened the door, lady. You sure did open *that* door. You and Neil. What was that all about? Lord, what was Neil doing in a commune in the first place? Governor Keith Miller's press secretary, the most conservative governor in the short history of Alaska, in a commune.

Chalk it up to more than the times or even the Harvey Wallbangers ("the drink of the movement," Marvin called it. Orange juice for health. Vodka for the revolution. Galliano for the hell of it); it had as much to do with how Neil was as how we were. He was a *real* conservative; he had no use for a government that interfered in the affairs of a citizen ("That's why we have a goddamned Constitution, I tell you.") and thought it was the duty of every citizen to keep his mouth open at all times. Neil was all for the war in Vietnam, or so he claimed. He hated the whole antiwar, hippie, countercultural horseshit (or so he claimed) but, said Neil, it was well within people's rights to be assholes and entirely correct of them to march, protest, sit in, sit down and in general raise holy hell when people tried to get them to stop being assholes. Generally, he was as mad at government as we were, and for similar, if different reasons. Besides, we had something at that farmhouse Neil wanted. And I don't mean me. Not entirely.

We had our own fairy tale going; we were happy, the lot of us—and if a certain ignorance was indispensable to our happiness, we didn't know that, either. We shared our food, our resources, monetary and otherwise, and for a while, our lives. Everybody had, as Marvin put it, a function. Kirsten, Marvin and

I were the wage earners, until I got fired. Van with his blond hair and droopy outlaw mustaches, wearing cowboy hat, boots and a gaze permanently fixed on the far hills, was our political guru and we were all politicians, but Gary was our candidate. We decided to run him for borough assembly. His platform, as I recall, was basically "free everything." Neil, who didn't agree with a single idea of Gary's but liked Gary personally better than any current member of the borough assembly (and liked even more the idea of messing with their heads), was his campaign manager. The rest of us, plus most of the staff from the radio station, were The Committee to Elect. He got 300 votes. We said it was a moral victory.

Kirsten was our all-round good person. Judy was clothier and patchwork maven. All our jeans had butterflies sewn over rips or were fringed at the bottom, artfully. All our other clothes had pieces missing when Judy was making a quilt. We had a carpenter, two photographers (I have not a single photograph from this time) and Neil, the house hard-ass. And we had Jimmy, who lay on the couch, smoking dope and saying, "Far fucking out," a lot, and not always alone. The children were mine and Van's, but were loved and petted and looked after by the whole group, together and individually, and Magoo, the yellow dog, ate off any plate you turned your back on.

Everybody cooked. We bought our food wholesale by the case, cheap. Gary and Jimmy, being Indians, had gaffing rights for salmon, but they weren't very good at gaffing. I was not with them the day they all went out for deer. Marvin described it to me later. First of all, nobody there, with the exception of Neil, was a real hunter. We weren't into killing or said we weren't, but free meat was attractive; we had little or no money at all times. They went by fishing boat to an island in the channel. According to Marvin, half of them started on one side of the island, the other half on the other. They planned to meet on a ridge in the middle. "We were, in effect, aiming at one another," said Marvin later. As good fortune would have it, no deer were seen and no shots were fired before the two parties joined up.

Then, according to Marvin, "somebody says, 'I hear something.'

The brush moves. All of a sudden ten guns go off. And it was Bambi. Poor deer, poor dear."

We ate him anyway. Neil fried the backstrap for dinner that night. Big Rabbit, we called it, deer season being another season. If living off the land was hard on the conscience, it was easy on the stomach. Bears, though, we left alone after Magoo and Jimmy ran into a large brown one out back of the farmhouse and it was hard to tell whether the yellow dog was riding Jimmy or the other way around; they came through the back door at approximately the same speed and precisely the same time.

To reason with future bears, I bought a shotgun, a 12-gauge, and shells with magnum loads (in case any locomotives tried to follow the bears through the door). Coincidentally (or not), it was about this time Louise, who came from Pennsylvania Quakers and until recently had been known to us only as the woman with the long braid who dispensed brown food at Gandalf's, a health-food and political (everything was connected then, everything) restaurant downtown, moved into the farmhouse.

Louise wrote and published the *Southeastern Sun and Salmon Wrapper*. I remember we were surprised at first; if someone were going to start an underground newspaper, how come it hadn't been us? Van was not surprised. There were many people more serious about "the revolution" than we were, and Louise was one of them. Van, it turned out, was another. I'd pushed us to the left initially, but Van had soon passed me and showed no signs of slowing down. I was angry at him for that, and Van and Louise were spending too much time together. So were Neil and I, even if it weren't quite the same. Neil and I were alike, except for our politics, I told myself. Van and I were different, except for our politics. But Van and Louise were headed where Neil and I weren't, politically and in other ways. And I loved Van.

The revolution trucked on. We were trying to start a community radio station. It was Frederick's idea. Why should people just listen to stuff in their homes and cars, he said, and have nothing to do with what goes out? We'd taken letting The People run things about as far as was possible at KJNO, so maybe what we needed was a brand-new station. What we had in mind was

an all-volunteer operation; there would be something for everyone, which didn't mean if you called up during a political dis-
cussion or Stravinsky (or Coltrane) and wanted to hear the Moody
Blues, you'd get it. You would, but not right then. We'd use
radio for Indians to teach other Indians their language; Tlingit
was fast being lost. We'd use radio to really cover city hall—
and citizen efforts. People would come up with their own ideas
and be able to put them on the radio. We'd use radio to reach
one another, a vehicle for people to be heard by other people.
Capitol Community Broadcasting was formed. I wrote a pam-
phlet. "Tired Ears?" it began. The other radio station in town,
(not KJNO, whose owner simply ignored us) attacked us vehe-
mently on the air, the owner saying how insulted he was by this
"Tired Ears?" campaign, how communist it was and all. Every
time he ranted, Capitol Community Broadcasting got another
250 members.

The Citizens' Participation Committee had found its voice by
now, too, and was raising it regularly. One day, seventy-two-year-
old Cecelia Kunz, Native Alaskan, daughter of the Eagle clan and
natural-born American patriot, marched into the borough assembly meeting and demanded they put a picture of Chief Kowee
right up there between Joe Juneau and Richard Harris. And kept
it up until they did. Details counted, said Cecelia, who, following
her own advice, had brought the picture with her.

By then, Marvin was out in back of the farmhouse, practicing
loading shotgun shells with paper wadding so Neil wouldn't really
kill Van on stage during the play, which Marvin was worried Neil
might, and not by accident, either. Marvin was directing us in
our first (and only) group theater effort. For The People. Joseph
Heller, who wrote *Catch-22*, had also written a play called *We
Bombed in New Haven*, about World War II and not Vietnam, but
the message was no different; it was a morality play and it mixed
reality with what Heller called "irreality." (Heller would have been
very comfortable at the farmhouse.) In the play, a tradition-
bound and quite mad captain repeatedly orders his men to bomb
things, non-military targets, friendly cities, friendly countries,
simply because "my orders say to." The sergeant tries to talk him

out of it; all the men are being killed on these raids, not to mention the people they bomb. There's a nurse who's in love with either the sergeant or the captain, she's not sure. When the sergeant realizes he's due to be killed next, he goes over the hill. The captain finds him and explains it's all a game. Then shoots him. The play ends with the captain forced to pass on new recruits, but every one of them bears his own son's name. By the end of the play, everybody is dead except the nurse, who has run away.

Neil played the captain. Van played the sergeant. The other people at the farmhouse and radio station played the other parts. I played the nurse. The first night Marvin got the right stuffing in the shells, but when Neil fired the gun he missed Van's chest, where the padding was. For several weeks Van sported a large bruise on his stomach, a brief distance north of his private parts. Louise watched everything from the front row.

It's raining harder now. The clouds are murky and lower, the rain the color of tears. You walk back to the car, parked next to where the farmhouse used to be, thinking: if you made this stuff up, nobody would believe you.

Right around the time of the play, Van and Louise began to sleep together each night, upstairs at the farmhouse, in the room and in the bed that had been ours, Van's and mine. It was as though *they* were married now. Van said we would work this out. They were in love, he said. It was a new age; it called for new solutions, he said. Sometimes I was with Neil. Most of the time I slept downstairs, alone, thinking things over, until I could no longer fool myself. "This" was not *workable*. The children and I moved to a small apartment on Douglas Island, across the channel. I got a job at the state legislature. A Republican hired me. I don't know why and neither did he; I expect I looked more than usually needy, but I must have been wearing shoes—it was January. Two months later, Van and Louise left to travel, to look at The Big Picture. Six months later, I left Alaska to go to work for the Associated Press in Dallas. Marvin found an apartment he could afford. Gary and Kirsten got married. The other people went other places. The farmhouse was empty.

Over.

So now you're going to have this reunion. Hail, hail, the gang's all here, well, most of them, and can they tell you what you want to know? *Question:* Was it about changing the world or was it just sex, drugs and rock 'n' roll? *Question:* Did we cause things to change or did they just happen? *Question:* Did the farmhouse collapse of its own weight or because it was a bad idea to begin with, or because it never was an idea?

And did Van leave me or did I leave him? I still want to know.

Yes, but what will you ask them tonight?

You pull away from the place where the farmhouse used to be and drive back to town. On the radio, *Action Line* is still on the air. Frederick's interviewing a man running for the Senate, who has no chance of winning and who says at one point, "You must remember we live in a city whose main government is industry." Frederick's too polite to say, "What the gentleman meant to say was . . ." I'm glad. I like it better his way; it's how I remember things, too.

Right before the party, I stop for a moment, as always, to wish I were thinner, and this night, like all these nights—and days— I also stop for a moment to be grateful I'm sober.

Show time.

Some of us are late arriving. In that, nothing has changed. We tell each other we look just as we did nearly twenty years ago. Gary—and yes, it was his face in the mural—actually does, except for the gray hair which you notice right off no longer comes anywhere near his shoulders. Kirsten's hair is even shorter than Gary's, if not so gray; she doesn't look like the mother of teen-agers, does she? Yes, she does: certain of those tiny lines on her forehead cannot have come from anything else, I know. Kirsten and Gary still look good together and apparently still are. Marvin is just as lanky and wired (on life) as ever. In three years, he tells me, he retires from the state. Dennis and Peter both have beards now, but I can't for the life of me recall—did they have beards then? Judy isn't here; there's some confusion when Dennis says didn't you know? She married one of the Beatles—and I say, she *didn't. Which one?* And they say Arnold, they think—the one from Anchorage.

Oh—*those* Beatles. Frederick circulates, playing the perfect host, telling people where the kitchen is.

Neil settles for vodka and orange drink, refusing orange juice even as a mixer; too healthy, he says. Neil drinks too much. You can tell. I guess you always can when it's somebody you know well. Knew well. No, everybody can tell. As they could with you. When I picked him up at his apartment tonight, he wouldn't let me inside. He doesn't want me to know about his life now. I know about that, too.

Van is not here, of course; nobody's sure where he is right now, maybe Virginia, maybe Texas; Van does not keep to a schedule, or a job, or to one woman. Louise sits by the fireplace, looking at a book of photographs.

"You mean you invited Louise? I don't believe it," someone said before she got here. They'd have to understand: some things are no longer questions. Many moons have come and gone since Van and Louise left Alaska and then returned to Alaska, got married and had Elishka (from Alaska), the half-sister to my children, who looks more like my son than my daughter does. Over the years I saw Louise whenever she and Van came to pick up Josh and Vanessa for their summer visits. We learned, in time, to respect one another, if not to like one another, the way we did when we met. I haven't seen Louise much since she divorced Van several years ago, but sometimes Ellie, their daughter, comes to stay with me and my children. It's a new age, I tell Louise.

"Neil, why did you hire me at the radio station?" I have decided to take the offensive. To get to the bottom of things. Not that this is.

"Because you wouldn't leave me alone."

"Yeah, but there you were, a little to the right of Ghenghis Khan."

"And you to the left of Joe Stalin."

"Oh, I don't know about that." A lively exchange of views would suit me right now.

"And Van to the left of you. When he left you." Neil leers.

Nobody leers like Neil. He puts his whole body into a good leer. But every time someone mentions Van's name, conversation stops and we all look around as if we believe he'd walked in when our backs were turned, or will soon.

"Gee, whatever happened to Magoo?" Kirsten is trying and I am grateful but I know where this one goes.

"The yellow dog died."

"Gee, too bad."

This is exciting. Maybe I should ask what everybody's doing for New Year's. Did I live with these people? *Somebody say something.*

"There's chili in the kitchen," says Terry. "I'm sure Frederick has told you where the kitchen is; it's his idea of graciousness."

"Does the chili have beans in it?" Peter heads for the kitchen.

"Of course it has beans in it. Marvin made it. I hate beans in chili." I will let this ring until someone answers.

"Eaten any Big Rabbit lately, Linda?" Thank God, Marvin has never forgotten that hunting trip.

"Oh, Jesus, the hunting trip," say Gary and Frederick, and begin to talk about it, both at once. Dennis and Kirsten join in. Things are picking up.

"What I remember most is coming back and that rich son of a bitch who owned the boat took his garbage bag and threw it overboard," says Neil.

"And Gary didn't say a word, remember?" says Frederick. "He just took his shirt off, his shoes and his socks, took his wallet out and laid it on the side, then dived in and started swimming around, retrieving garbage floating in pieces in 38° water."

"Did he do that?" Neil, the radical-right environmentalist, has forgotten how impressed with Gary he was that day. We all were. If you've been in 38° water, you are, too.

"Yeah. He did that."

"What I remember," says Neil, "is when you and Marvin decided to put up plywood partitions to make rooms for yourselves in the basement of the farmhouse, a place not intended for human habitation in the first place, not that subdividing a commune wasn't an interesting paradox in itself, but you were doing it wrong, remember?" Neil is looking at Gary, but it's Marvin he's going for, I can tell. I like this.

"Yeah, I remember," says Marvin, "and your kid was visiting and stood around being a pest, telling me what I was doing wrong every five minutes. He was just like you—a pain in the ass."

"And after this happened two or three times," Neil continues, "my son said, 'You're still doing it wrong, Marvin, but don't worry. I won't tell you how.' "

"A real pain in the ass," says Marvin, but he, too, is smiling, and chuckling at the memory of being bested by an eleven-year-old. We all smile and chuckle with him.

"I never lived at the farmhouse," says Frederick, to no one in particular, "but I felt at home there."

"Whose idea was it," I ask, "to do that dumb play as social protest against the Vietnam War?" Now what made me think of that right now? I wonder.

"Yours," says Marvin.

"Are you sure?"

"You know," says Gary, grinning, "it's not every commune can field its own cast."

"Don't forget about the radio people. We were there, too," says Dennis, and then he giggles.

"Only barely. You may as well have been furniture. You died in the play. Early in the play." Gary is starting to giggle, too.

"So did you."

"We all died in the play," says Neil.

"Everybody died in the play," says Frederick, for the record.

"Bombed, you mean," says Marvin, for the laugh.

"In New Haven," says everybody, together, finally.

Gary looks bewildered. "We must have made a whole fifty dollars a night from the play. Who did we give it to? I remember we donated it to some cause but I can't remember *which* cause."

"There were so many." Kirsten tastes a cookie.

"I remember it had to do with our politics," says Gary.

"It doesn't matter," says Marvin. "It was something that needed to be said. The play, I mean. They were killing American soldiers faster than you could make them, using them for cannon fodder over there. There was no right about it. It was all wrong, totally wrong."

"Yep, those were our politics," says Gary.

"What were our politics?" Peter is returned from the kitchen, bearing chili.

"Polarization. The politics of how to piss 'em off."

We all stop talking to eat; in that, too, nothing is changed. When we are done, someone brings out a camera. Kirsten says, "You should be grateful to that play, Gary. And to the commune."

"What do you mean?" I ask. Are we about to get into what it all meant?

Kirsten gives her husband the sweetest look: "Gary thought he was a politician. He found out he was an actor."

Everybody laughs. Ronald Reagan has come into this conversation, somehow. We are floor-sprawling relaxed now, most of us; we have eaten, we have taken photographs: the radio gang, the farmhouse gang, several complex mixtures of the two, but Louise will not be in any of our class pictures. She says she has to go now. We all say good-bye, and to give our best to Ellie. It's quiet for a moment after she leaves.

Gary continues. "You can laugh if you want, but these days two, count 'em, two theaters right here in Juneau have the honor of supporting me full-time. I always have work now."

Well, it's something, I say to myself. Gary found work he could love a lifetime. That's something for anybody.

He tours, too, he tells me. They go to the schools and perform the stories, the legends, the Tlingit history, and you should see them, Linda, those kids are so far ahead of me, of my generation, so far ahead of us. Those kids are getting so much more information about our native culture—and they're getting it from kindergarten on. *And getting kindergarten, too.*

Maybe it's more than something.

"Do you still have the Citizens' Participation Committee?"

"No, but we have the Alaska Native Land Claims Settlement. A billion dollars of our own changed a lot of things around here."

"And do the young people of today appreciate their good fortune?"

"Of course not," says Neil, scowling almost as well as he leers. "You young people never do." His words slur a little, not much.

"*You* young people? Come on, old man," I say, "you gotta admit, these twenty-five-year-olds today—we were better than that, better than them. Better then this Dumbo generation."

"Better, I don't know, but more interesting, yes. You were more interesting."

And Van, wasn't he the most interesting of all of us, my cowboy-poet, lover, organizer, *revolutionary*? We don't say that word tonight but that is the word, and whether we acknowledge it or not, we said it then. Maybe we were only half serious, or not all, but we said it. Revolution, we said. Van is the only one of us who still says that word. Or believes it. But he was right about so many things, wasn't he? Especially the wrongs. Van was always right about the wrongs. It was solutions that gave him trouble. Still, what's so wrong with peace, love and happiness—and all power to the people? And if you can't take it apart when it's broken, how can you ever figure out how to put it back together so it works? Of course, nobody likes the ones who take *everything* apart (and some things couldn't be put back together, could they, Van?). I look around the room at my old friends, people I used to live with, people I've loved. Love.

"I didn't want to be married to Van. I wanted to be him. I was so envious of the damn purity of his commitment. The height and breadth of his dreams. His ability to lead. I was furious. Even before we came to Juneau, I think, and of course later, when he married Louise, and especially when he took *her* name. I had his and he had hers. It was all so crazy."

"I always thought Van was a little manipulative," says Marvin.

"In that case, Linda, you *are* like Van," says Neil, gruffly.

"I learned a lot from Van." Frederick, always the fairest.

"What did we learn? It happened just the way Van said it would, didn't it? We didn't change things; things just changed. Things happened, but we didn't make them happen."

"You can't ever know that, Linda. Maybe we did."

"This is beginning to sound like *The Big Chill*. Do we have to do this?" Marvin is getting bored.

"No, really," says Frederick. "Remember community radio? Tired Ears? Well, maybe you don't know this, but Capitol Community Broadcasting became K-TOO radio. It went on the air in 1974. And from that eventually came public *television* station K-TOO."

"You're kidding. All-volunteer radio? And television, too? Wow." I am genuinely pleased to hear this. "You mean we actually accomplished something?"

"Yes," says Dennis.

"And no," says Frederick.

I ask what he means.

"The all-volunteer part didn't last. Neither did the open mike. Things got more organized, the way they do, I guess. Now it's all NPR and PBS and very hard to get something on if you're local, because it wouldn't be PBS quality, which is a damn shame; the only way we'll ever get people involved in television is if they can produce it themselves, on a shoestring. People ought to be involved in television. It shouldn't be passive." Frederick, bless him, still has his new frontiers.

"So we didn't accomplish anything?"

"Yes, we did. It just didn't stay the same as we meant it. Nothing does."

"Is anything else changed because of us?"

Marvin grins. "How about you? You became a hotshot reporter and that started here. I remember when you covered the Salmon Derby for the radio station and it wasn't just 'where did you catch it and how did you catch it'; it was 'and what was your motivation for going out today?' Strange questions to ask fishermen, but you always wanted to know *why* anybody did anything. You with your bloody questions."

"There has to be more than that." Surely I haven't come this far to find out my time living here was nothing more than Introduction to Journalism 101. "There must be something that was changed by us."

"Well, I don't know about you but I never understand any politician now," says Marvin, proudly, and then tells us how he plans to donate his mink coat to the Republican running for governor in hopes the man, if elected, will make Marvin head of the state unemployment office.

"It's an old coat and these days I don't dare wear it anyway—all those creepy people with fake blood and pictures of animals chewing their privates off."

Marvin, Marvin. You are always a man of your time.

"I'll tell you another legacy of our time together," says Kirsten. "Gary and I always have people staying in our house, and we always have. I guess we got used to having other people close to us. In our lives."

We compare notes. We all have people around, living or almost living with us most of the time, except for Neil with his secrets, and maybe Jimmy for practical reasons having to do with sudden flight and yes, Van, for reasons of his own.

"You want to know what it all meant?" says Gary. "I'll tell you what it all meant." He stands up, stretches, yawns, and smiles at me.

"What, Gary?" Does he know or is he even serious?

"Most of us can't cook for one anymore. Or even two. *We're not loners.* That's what it all meant. Go ask Neil. Go ask Van. They both hate it, but they know it's true, especially Van."

Gary is serious. Right, too, I expect.

It's late. Neil is nodding. He truly doesn't look well. I will drive him home. On the way he asks me to stop and buy him a bottle of vodka. Early the next morning, Frederick calls. After I left, everybody talked and decided something had to be done for Neil. Before he died. Frederick and Gary are going to pick him up and check him into the hospital for a physical exam. Will I drive? I understand; they want me to help kidnap Neil. They want to save Neil. I'm new at this sobriety stuff myself, one year sober, and not at all certain I ought to be telling Neil anything. Or that I can. But he does need hospitalization; he's malnourished, his cough is awful—I saw him spit by the car and it was brown—his skin is jaundiced and, yes, he is dying. At his apartment, we tell Neil we're taking him for coffee. In the car, on the way to the hospital, we tell him the truth.

"You're meddling again," he says, but he goes with us and in fact, seems relieved. At the hospital, the doctor says we were right to bring him and that he will need to be there at least a week, if he lives. Frederick calls the local alcohol rehabilitation center to see what can be done when Neil is ready to leave the hospital. I call the local number of a national organization with which I am acquainted. They say Neil has to want to talk to them. We go back to Neil and tell him he wants to talk to them. Neil agrees, he'll talk to them. Listen to them.

"You never stop, do you?" Ashen-faced and connected to several machines, Neil says this to Frederick, Gary and me from his bed in intensive care. "You just never stop, any of you." He stops. "Thank you. Maybe."

And now you're alone, driving your rental car too fast out the road, past the McDonald's, past KJNO, all the way out to Eagle River Beach, crying the whole time—for Neil, for Van, for somebody, you maybe, crying because so much seems lost, and what's not lost, *hidden*. This whole trip, this idea, this quest, has been like trying to bite a basketball.

Don't ask questions of a fairy tale.

We had fun. We didn't see why changing the world couldn't be a party, and so party we did. Remember the afternoon forty or fifty of us got together right here on this beach? Remember that? Someone mentioned arm wrestling and the next thing you knew, Van and Neil were lying there on the lead-colored mud flats where we'd just finished playing football ("Touch? What are you, some wussy Kennedy?"), lying there belly to the mud, and you'd have thought it was more than a game with them, which it always was, but never black and white, always gray vs. gray, and this time was no different. Van was bigger than Neil, but Neil just would not give. Neither man would give. They had strained and pushed at one another as hard as they could until their faces were red and Van's eyes stood out like a dragon's (or a dragon slayer's) and Neil's arm would not go down, Van could not make it go down. Finally all of Neil's body began to rotate, but the arm never went down.

You had to love them both; they were *all* our opposite sides, those two.

You did love them both, Linda.

We picked the carrots that grew wild near the river that day, washing them in it for cleanliness and to add flavor; it was salty where the river met the channel. We fished. I showed Vanessa a salmon, swimming under the clear water.

"What color is the fish?" she asked.

"What color do you see?"

"Green."

"Look again."

"Blue."

"Look again."

"Black."

"Look again."

"White."

"Look again."

"Silver now."

Her father caught that salmon, and when it was on the bank, Vanessa could see the fish was gray. But it was also dead.

In the afternoon, we built a fire and baked several king salmon, stuffing their insides with wild onions, and later we sang. Everybody had brought something to make music; there were lots of kazoos and rubber-band-constructed instruments, but also enough guitars, flutes, banjos and even violins to make it sound almost like music now and again. "... *aanndd ... aaannnddd ... aaaannnnnnnddddddd ... you put the load right on meeee.*" All of us harmonizing, all right together. For once. It was as fine as picnics get. As fine as days get. As life gets. And it was raining the whole time.

You know what? It may have been a kazoo commune and a rootie-kazootie revolution, but it really was worthwhile to live when love was all you thought you needed. Or had.

Now you stand in cool, gray sand, feeling a cool, gray wind blow the tears across your face and off, away, lost in the air, history. Look out there. Aren't there more shades of gray out there than you ever saw or thought possible? It's not that some questions cannot be answered; it's that some questions have no answer. Was it true or false? Right or wrong? Beautiful or ugly?

Hell, in the end, not even the questions turn out to be that simple, that black and white. Order will not be brought to the whole. Be content with some unsolved riddles in your life. Be content with questions. With gray. We cannot get grace from answers; they're like the fish on the banks, dead, with nothing more to tell us.

When you get back to New York, go find the hunting knife they gave you the first time you left Alaska. What you knew about Juneau is carved right into the blade, have you forgotten? "108, Baby" it says on that blade; and you don't know any more now than you did then. You haven't and never will get your answers or even understand half the things you do know about what happened in this life, and it doesn't matter, not one damned bit, because it's all still beautiful—*just fucking beautiful*. And sometimes that's enough. Look out there. This is the land where gray comes alive. Gray's land.

MOVE ON

I want to explore the light.
I want to know how to get through,
Through to something new,
Something of my own.
Move on.

—STEPHEN SONDHEIM

Rayon makes you stupid. I might have figured this out sooner if circumstances had been different, but I never finished college so I never learned until the day I found myself on this commencement platform as a speaker what happens when somebody puts on a rented, one-size-fits-most, black rayon robe (yes, robe; gowns are for balls and brides, which this isn't and I'm not, lately), then tries to tell the truth about anything. Imagine my shock sitting on this stage watching one person after another stand up, fiddle with the microphone, then open his mouth to begin a speech containing the important truths of our time, only to find himself *rayoned* into near idiocy before completing the first sentence. Lordy, did they sound stupid, all that bilge about the hills of tomorrow. Is it really the rayon? Or is it that people who are asked to make these commencement addresses generally can't find the truth with both hands?

Or is it that lying is necessary to the day?

I know all about that. I've had lots of practice lying to the young. I'm a mother. When it comes to filling the hearts and minds of children with a passel of pretty lies they are young enough to believe, nothing, nobody, not even The Church, can beat your average loving mother. Commencement addresses? I gave one to my daughter when she was six. She gave me one thirteen years later. Hers was shorter.

Mine first.

It was early September, the time of year my mother called dark-cotton season. She meant it was too warm to wear wool and too late to wear pink. It was just after sunrise, the time of day my father called the possibility hour. He meant it was too early to fail and too good to last. It was the morning my daughter started first grade. *Real* school, she called it, having gone to kindergarten in Houston, which she said was not real; this opinion, however, had little to do with school and a lot to do with her relatives, most of whom lived in Houston and many of whom never enjoyed more than a nodding acquaintance with reality. Unhappily for my daughter, I, too, was one of her relatives from Houston. I thought about this as I braided her hair, telling her to stand still after I'd already told her I wasn't going to tell her to stand still again, dammit. I thought about it because I was worried for her; it's not helpful to have a mother who thinks *The Wizard of Oz* is a travelogue. I continued to mess with Vanessa's hair, all the while considering certain facts of life that really weren't, never mind that I'd sort of assured her they were. Facts like happy endings. Facts like liberty and justice for all. And the contradictory rest of it: mind your elders but think for yourself but look to the rainbow but don't bite off more than you can chew but go for the gold but come home for dinner but stand up for your rights but sit down when the bell rings but dream your dream but keep your feet on the ground and don't cry, Bambi's mother didn't die, it was only a movie.

Plus the one that goes, "Of course you're going to love school."

I was almost ashamed of myself. What kind of mother would deliberately mislead her own child, then stand there smiling like your ordinary natural-born fool while the kid goes skipping out the door to reality?

"Gee, this place isn't quite as nice as Mommy said it was. What should I do now?"

Good question. But what could I have done differently? Should I have made sure she knew that puppies die and people you love lie and some stories never end happily and, well, Bambi's mother dies every day because this simply isn't a fair world, my child, starting with school. Maybe I hoped the world would have changed for her. Maybe I hoped she wouldn't notice it hadn't. There she was, my shiny girl-child, braided and ready to climb those pretty hills of tomorrow. There I was, guilty, scared and suddenly quite determined to fix everything with one perfect, last-minute warning. The right warning would protect her—so what if there were only fifteen minutes left before school started? An all-pupose warning would come to me any moment now. There was plenty of time before the bell rang and the slaughter began. Nothing came to me.

We got in our car, an ordinary balky Fiat my daughter, inoculated with my fancy tales, had named Roxanne Mountain Jeep. Nothing came to me. If it's true that when the student is ready, the teacher appears, it's also true that when the student appears, sometimes the teacher is not ready.

But Vanessa was so ready, for anything. For everything. She could already read and loved it that she could. Every night she read me a bedtime story. On Saturday nights I got two stories. Vanessa knew other stuff, too, elemental, vital information, and if she'd learned some of it from me, she'd also learned some of it from Slattery, a man with an industrial-strength brain and a pixie heart, who was always our friend and, yes, our teacher. (I had my mother's friend Gladys. Vanessa had her mother's friend Slattery.)

Slattery taught all of us all the time; he couldn't help it. It was Slattery who taught me how to point. I'd asked him to tell me what love is. Slattery had answered his way by asking me to tell him what a chair was. A chair? Easy, I said. It's a piece of furniture meant to be sat upon. A chair has four legs and a bottom. No, four equal legs and not a bottom, exactly—a sitting place. No, wait—a chair doesn't need to have four legs or a bottom, but, wait, yes it does—or does it? A chair is a contrivance upon which one might . . . oh, to hell with it, Slattery. I give up. What's a chair?

Slattery turned to the ladderback in the corner. He aimed his bony forefinger, his left arm, half his should-have-been-a-dancer body and both his curious, odd eyes at the ladderback. "*That* is a chair."

"Yes, that is a chair, I can see that. But what I want to know is, what is *love?*"

Body, arm, finger, eyes and smile swiveled in my direction. He made a motion with his finger to include me, him and the space between. "That is love."

"What?"

"That."

"What that?"

"Linda, think chair. What is a chair?"

"Dammitall, Slattery, the only way I can define a chair is by pointing to it." I thought for a moment. "I get it."

"Now do you know what love is?"

"No, Slattery, but I can point to it." I pointed.

"Right. Except for one thing."

"What."

"You're pointing at the chair."

Slattery played other games, taught other lessons; he would ask Vanessa to bring him two things exactly alike. She would return with two pennies. Slattery would ask her to look closely. Was one penny more tarnished than the other? More rubbed down by fingers? Was it made in a different year? She'd try two shoes, two forks, her own two eyes, until finally she caught on.

"What do you know?" asked Slattery.

"I know no two things are exactly alike."

"Right."

"Except for . . ."

"Except for what?"

"Except for itself. A thing is exactly like itself."

"Oh, dear," said Slattery.

Vanessa and I drove down the hill to the school. Still nothing. She got out, leaned back in the window, kissed me and turned away, heading for the first grade, picking up speed as she went. Nothing? See here, you must know *something* useful.

"Vanessa, wait!"

She stopped when I yelled, turned back around and stood there looking at me, even loving me, but itchy, impatient.

"What, Mama? What?"

Did I mention to you this habit grown-ups have of couching any really useful information, when and if they finally get around to giving some, in terms guaranteed to make no sense to anyone but the grown-up who is at that moment speaking? How else can I account for the fact that I sent my daughter off to school with these words: "Kid . . . keep your powder dry."

It would be years before my daughter understood what I'd tried to tell her in that school parking lot, a split second this side of the first grade, but it wasn't ten minutes before I realized what had happened. I'd given her a commencement address—an apology, an attempt to atone for years of God-knows-how-many lies by rising at the last minute to sound a generally incoherent warning, hoping it would rattle loud enough to be heard over the noise made by the winds whistling through the hills of tomorrow, knowing it wouldn't, and sounding like a fool for trying. If that's what a commencement address was, I said to myself, then I didn't need to give another; nobody in my family needed to go out of her way looking for new methods to make a fool of herself. That afternoon when my daughter came home from her first day of school, she was not grinning, she was sagging and doing so with a mighty dignity. She had a piece of paper in her hand.

"Mommy, I'm in trouble. My teacher wants to talk to you. That's what it says here." And it did. It said Vanessa wasn't cooperative, that she'd "interfered with the educational process." *On her first day?* Vanessa, what happened?

She told me her teacher had given each child a card on which were drawn two apples and one orange, then told them to circle which two things were exactly alike.

Oh, dear.

Vanessa never did get the hang of school, in fact she dropped out when she was fifteen, entered college when she was sixteen, and later quit that for her music, but she never stopped reading and she never stopped learning. Last summer, while she was reading *War and Peace,* something I've never been able to do

(Vanessa says it's best not to worry about sorting out characters in the beginning; just keep reading and after a couple of hundred pages, they either sort themselves out or you don't care), she ran into some college students, one of whom asked her what that big book was.

"*War and Peace*," said Vanessa.

"Warren who?" said the student. "What else did he write?"

"Oh, dear," said Vanessa.

It's discouraging to know that schools haven't gotten any smarter. But it's nice to know Vanessa is one thing that's still exactly like itself. Slattery would be proud.

Thirteen years after I drove down that hill to Vanessa's first day of school, I discovered another kind of commencement address: the one my daughter gave me. It was another one of those possibility mornings in September, only this time my daughter handed me a slip of paper and on it was written: *222 MacDougal Street.* She was nineteen and she'd rented an apartment. It was just a few blocks away and she promised everything would be almost the same as it was before. Almost. The word tore a hole in my heart. She hoped I'd understand; she had things to do, that was all. Back when she'd started first grade, I'd told myself to stay calm, she wasn't really leaving home. Now she was telling me to stay calm, she *was* really leaving home.

222 MacDougal Street

That is a *real* commencement address.

It hurt, oh, it hurt. She was ready to move on. I wasn't. I wanted to grab her, to stop her, to . . .

I sit on this stage listening to that man, that idiot, telling these soon-to-be-graduates about the big wide world out there, telling them what he thinks they can expect (everything), thinking about the day Vanessa left home—and from that I make the natural leap to thinking about the day she arrived.

It's 5:33 in the morning of the fourteenth day of March, 1969. Yellow, that's what I remember. She was wrapped in a yellow blanket, dusted off or dipped or whatever they do when one person leaves another person to begin her journey. It was a buttercup blanket, not yellow like a school bus, but not like lemon yogurt, either. Sunny-day yellow, maybe. Her eyes were open. She scared the hell out of me. I was prepared to be nervous (and wrong) about holding and not dropping, feeding and not poisoning, bathing and not breaking. But no one prepared me for her eyes. No one warned me that some babies are born with a look they will carry all their lives, and so will I.

She looked at me. She looked right through me and she knew. Right then Vanessa knew that I was a draftee who would, if it were all the same to everyone, rather be in Guadalajara painting, or writing in London, getting stoned in Taos or maybe even back in Nashville, Tennessee, a freshman at Vanderbilt, a *tabula rasa* where my memories were concerned. I would write to you often, I told myself, hugging you close, crying tears on your brand-new face. I would draw and write (and send you) pictures and stories about a man who sold silver balloons. I would be that sad, mysterious woman in the photograph by your bed, the one who came to visit but never when she was expected. I would be the high, green wind that blew in and out of your childhood, and I would miss you all my days, but you knew it would be worse if I stayed.

I meant to go. I told you so, Vanessa, and those eyes heard me, talked for you and agreed: I would be a spotty mother at best, a mother who would run scared of you, drink too much, marry too often, make too much money and leave you too much alone—until the day you left me. We did not lie to each other that day, my daughter. And in some ways each has been a disappointment to the other; I suspect that is true even among those families which, from the outside, appear to be made in Happyland. (Did I tell you what you did for me? Did I tell you how you changed my life forever and made me see more of myself than I cared to see?)

We sat on a sofa and cried the night you moved out. I saw your real face. So often we wear our masks around each other, while our hearts dance a funny dance that never ends. I will not forget the face I saw that night. Your first woman-face, a preview of you at thirty or fifty, or even next year.

A little yellow blanket. I wonder what became of it? And the woman with one foot out the door and a built-in aversion to children on grounds of a built-in lack of responsibility, with her dream about seeing the world, having adventures, meeting strangers and getting lost—what happened to her?

Would you and Josh have been better off if I'd run off and joined the circus? Would I have been? Only this I know: raising, supporting, caring for and in general trying to figure out what to do with these human beings who arrived without instructions, growing with the two of you, hurting with, for and because of you, surviving you and seeing you survive me—well, you don't get that at your average circus. The irony is that, like Dorothy, I found a good deal of adventure in my own backyard. The bitch is I think I lost the red shoes.

I do not worry whether you, my children, forgive me for my sins, real and questionable, against you; if you don't, you will. You've begun already, and when you turn around to meet your own strengths and weaknesses, you will know that you are looking backward, forward and straight ahead. As for me, well, mothers just naturally tend to forgive anything short of matricide. But becoming mothers does not mean we get halos that can be seen or hurts that can't; forgiving you two was and is a rigorous workout, metaphysically speaking. So what? I do. You do. We don't. We will.

Here's my first worry: once grown, you'll discover you really don't enjoy me, my company, conversation—or our connection. My second worry is that the same thing will happen in reverse.

By the way, Vanessa, would you like to know why I didn't run away the day you were born? It was your fault. You began to cry when I put you down so I could get dressed. You certainly weren't crying for me. We were strangers who went to the same gene pool together, that's all. You were crying because you were one day new in this world and you were alone, lying next to nothing, frightened of open spaces, not knowing their beauty. I was half-way out the door, heading for those same open spaces. I rang for the nurse, planning what I would say to get her to take you and leave the room long enough for me to leave all my rooms. As fortune would have it, the nurse didn't show up. So I held you, only temporarily, I said, and then, tired still from your coming, we both fell asleep—you feeling safe, me feeling you, finally knowing in some way, even in sleep, that my circus had come to town.

But what about the people they leave behind them, these near-grown kids? What about their parents? What about us?

Two years ago we began remodeling our house before it fell on us, but to the professional renovator, it's a crime against nature to complete a six-month job in less than three years, if at all. Soon it was December; we were still waiting for the lazy house to let us back inside, and every time I thought about Christmas I got the urge to be somewhere else. It wasn't only the house. This year my children no longer lived at home; worse, they had Christmas jobs instead of Christmas vacations. Both would be working Christmas Eve and Christmas Day, which meant there would be no one to help me hang the stockings there was no place to hang anyway. Christmas dinner. What would we do for Christmas dinner? Vanessa said not to worry, she'd just make a pot roast or something for Christmas.

"Pot roast? I don't know how to make pot roast. How do you know how to make pot roast? Who taught you to make pot roast?"

"Bugs Bunny."

"Excuse me?"

"No, really, Mom. Josh and I—we've watched every Looney Tunes cartoon ever made. Remember the one where the two Frenchmen are chasing him and one falls into a pot and Bugs says, 'Lessee. Hmmm. Oh, yes: one cup of water for each pound of Frenchman, cook one half hour for each pound of Frenchman, add carrots, peas, onions, potatoes, salt and pepper and stir.' Remember that one?"

"Uh, what has this got to do with pot roast?"

"I figure if it worked with Frenchmen, it would work with roast beef."

"Why?"

"Bugs Bunny never lied to me yet."

Pot roast for Christmas. Maybe it was time to blow off The Family Christmas. But how could I—when it came to matters of sentiment, our family was never wishy-washy; we gave a great

Christmas. When I was very little, we had The Family Christmas at my grandmother's house. Candles in the window, cakes on the table, presents in the closet, pallets on the floor, silver bells, silly secrets, sweet surprises and all the black olives you could eat.

When my grandmother got old, The Family Christmas moved to my mother's house. Colored lights around the front door, poinsettias on the patio, a crystal bowl of eggnog on a mahogany table, silver dishes of divinity fudge in the front room, silly secrets, sweet surprises and all the black olives you could eat.

For the past ten years, The Family Christmas has lived at my house. Packages with no tags, puppies with no manners, a tree too tall for the room, a crèche with a missing baby Jesus, silver candlesticks on a Formica table, silly secrets, sweet surprises and all the black olives you can eat.

Three generations of The Family Christmas. My stocking was stuffed with memories. But everything was changed now. Why didn't I just go skiing instead? That's what Rolfe said we should do. Go skiing. Just the two of us. We'd been working hard; the vacation would be good for us, a romantic interlude. (Rolfe also said it would be an aerobic interlude, but I was decent enough to overlook that.) The more I thought about it, the more I liked the idea, only how could I explain to my children there wasn't going to be a Family Christmas this year because Mother was tired? I knew they wouldn't understand. When they did, I cried for an hour.

Ungrateful, unfeeling little humanoids, they were. Creatures with memory banks instead of memories. Well, they could eat pizza for Christmas dinner. From a can.

We went skiing in Colorado. And we went to the Hotel El Dorado, which has suffered still more changes, still with her same old dignity, and she's still a hotel. The little swimming pool is gone, too, now. So is the "dorm" where I lived that summer. The inside of the hotel has been painted an institutional cream color, the big rooms divided to make small rooms. In the dining room, cut in half to make space for a much larger bar and cocktail lounge, they serve "fresh-caught Colorado trout" from Idaho, blackened, naturally. Down the long, empty, memory-filled hall came the sound of John Denver on the radio in the cocktail lounge. That same week that very same local radio station, once a rock 'n' roll and news station, had been changed "to fit the times" (translation: it wasn't making enough money). People were fired and a satellite-fed, New-Age Muzak called "The Breeze" had taken over, but a woman disc jockey, on the day of the change, had defied orders and broadcast instead "The Last Rock 'n' Roll Show on KSNO." *Then* she quit. Leaving us John Denver. I remembered knowing a woman like that once in Alaska.

We skied in Aspen. When I was there in 1962, they said progress had ruined everything. They said this in a town with one paved road. All the roads are paved now, but reality still has to boogie to stay in the race. The stakes are bigger now; there are more players and some of them are guys named Mohammed Hadid, Donald Trump and Ritz Carlton. But in the *Aspen Daily News,* I read the following story: "A man who had a bad day attacked a public bus, kicking rocks at it. A deputy gave him a ride home." I thought of the old school bus I'd climbed inside so many summers ago to see what it felt like to sit in the back of the bus. I've ridden plenty of buses since then and had some bad days myself; and I've seen more than one bus I'd like to kick, but I've met damn few deputies who'd drive me home afterward. In the long run, Colorado will be okay, I think.

The day before Christmas, my son called. He wanted to know where you buy those redberry candles, how long you cook the average goose, and when do you know you've found the perfect tree? I asked my son why it mattered. He said they wanted The Family Christmas to be just like the ones they used to know. Family Christmas? What Family Christmas?

"Why," he said, "the one my sister and I are making for each other and five of our friends."

That family Christmas. Oh.

Vain. Stupid. Those were two of the words that came to mind. I had forgotten the really important part; I had forgotten that with or without me, they are a family. That's what happens when memory only works backwards. So there I was in Colorado, skiing a little, crying some, smiling some, thinking about my children who were back home in New York City, celebrating The Fourth Generation Family Christmas. Everything was changed but nothing was different, I realized. And I never knew how right I was about that until after Christmas, when my son and I, discussing the passage of time and Christmases and families that go on, sometimes in spite of themselves, both began to cry and admitted to one another that although torches passed were probably the most beautiful, we weren't as ready as we'd thought; the truth was, in the end, we'd hated being apart Christmas. We needed each other. Still.

There is a small play I go to see every year, called *The Fantasticks*. It is the longest-running musical in America, the longest-running play in the world, and possibly the most popular. If you've seen *The Fantasticks,* I don't have to explain what accounts for this kind of endurance, and if you haven't, I'm not sure I can. This is a tough play to describe, short but not sweet, fancy but plain. The story begins and ends in September, just before a rainfall, and is about a girl who doesn't want to be normal, a boy who doesn't want to be understood, their fathers, (who prefer vegetables because you know what you get when you plant a vegetable), a handsome stranger promising adventure, an ancient actor who wants you to try to see him "in light," an Indian who dies well and a cardboard moon.

It's about life on the banks.

Will Durant said civilization is a stream with banks. He said the stream is sometimes filled with blood from people killing, stealing, shouting and doing the things historians usually record, while on the banks, unnoticed, people build homes, make love, raise children, sing songs, write poetry and even whittle statues. He said historians (and journalists) are pessimists, because they ignore the banks for the river, but the story of civilization, he said, is the story of what happened on the banks. I go to see *The Fantasticks* because at least once a year I need to be reminded in the strongest and simplest way possible about the importance of what goes on on the banks, and how to get back to them. Deep in December, when you're skiing in Aspen and your children find they are a family without you, it's nice to remember.

The rest of the time, it's necessary.

I wish I could tell this to the parents sitting out there whose own children are about to move on. I know what you're thinking, I'd say to them. The time goes so fast. They told us it would but we didn't believe them.

It's harder for me to measure time now. If you asked me now how long one day is, I'd say it depends. If a baby is two days old, one day is half its life. If a baby is one year, one day is one three-hundred-sixty-fifth of its life. So nobody can say exactly how long one day is. I tried to persuade Josh of the logic of my definition of time, but he has no respect for my grasp of scientific theory. I tried telling him about another scientist, the one who said when you sit next to a nice girl for two hours, you think it's only a minute, but when you sit on a hot stove for a minute, you think it's two hours. And that, said Albert Einstein, is relativity. Was my son persuaded? Yes, but not until last September, when the boy noticed that somehow summer was shorter than it used to be. How do you make time stay? I asked once. Now I know better; time stays, we go.

It was ten minutes to midnight and I was in my house in Greenwich Village, sitting in that old beat-up brown corduroy chair I'd carried around with me for so many years, the one on which babies had dribbled, kittens had sharpened their claws and puppies had chewed (or worse). The one little boys had climbed over, big girls (including me) had cried in and two white mice had once lived under. The chair I refused to throw away, despite pointed hints from those with a less sentimental heart or a more refined sense of smell. In ten minutes, I would be forty-six.

Well, what did you think it would be like? *I don't know, but I didn't think it would be like this.* Change. That's what I'd said I wanted. What a long time ago that had been. Anything could happen, I'd said. Anything. Trouble was, it did. And it had changed me, changed what and who I was.

People said I was a maverick, and until recently I believed them, assuming it was just one more fact of life, maybe the only one nobody had to explain to me twice, but now I think people are full of it, because the truth—which I've finally come to see as different from facts—is that I'm no maverick. What am I? Either I'm a woman of my time or I'm a mutant.

If you ask me, I'm not a mutant. So I must be . . .

Technically, I suppose you could say my time as a woman began on March 24, 1957, when, during volleyball practice, I noticed blood on the back of my gym suit, but that does not make me a woman of the fifties, any more than selling my fur coat and moving into a commune made me a woman of the sixties, or chucking it all to work for large corporations made me a woman of the seventies, or earning a million dollars and falling in love with a man seven years younger made me a woman of the eighties. I've lived and bled my way through *The Power of Positive Thinking,* the poodle skirt, *The Catcher in the Rye,* the first date, the way of Zen, the New Frontier, the Great Society, one giant step for mankind, the light at the end of the tunnel, our long national nightmare, the energy crisis, the "me" generation, the Cinderella Syndrome, the farmer in the White House, the actor in the White House, the Rainbow Coalition, the decade of greed, dead dreams, live television, and, yes, five networks, four marriages and two children.

And I'm still counting. What's more, as crusty but lovable Benjamin Disraeli once said, I feel a very unusual sensation—if it's not indigestion, I think it must be gratitude. I count my blessings. I'm grateful George Bush continues to breathe uninterrupted and that nobody ever died from a fractured syntax, and that on the worst day of his life Robert Redford never looked like Dan Quayle. I'm grateful Jessica loved Roger Rabbit for his soul and Ed Meese found another line of work. I'm grateful Mickey Mouse can still boogie at sixty. If Mickey can, I will. I'm grateful ET is alive and able to phone home from inside my VCR. I'm grateful for Steven Spielberg. Also Garry Trudeau, Ella Fitzgerald and NPR. I'm grateful I live in America, where a kid can grow up dreaming that one day Imelda Marcos and Leona Helmsley will share a cell somewhere. I'm grateful Jim Henson lived at all and that Kermit will live always. I'm grateful that (so far) I still have enough canned goods in the pantry to afford to say no to producers who tell me what I ought to do is host A Talk Show With

Substance. Finally, I'm grateful steroids don't make you write faster. One can just say no to just so much in this life.

I'm grateful for so much, but what do I know now that I didn't know then? What have I learned through all these changes in and around me? I've learned to do things my own way, even if I'm wrong, which often I am, but only dead fish swim with the stream. I've learned that if you don't want to get old, don't mellow. I've learned always to set a place in life for the unexpected guest. And to be content with questions. I was right all along; questions are better.

Most of all, I've learned that a good time to laugh is any time you can.

I've also learned the easier a change is to make, usually the less it matters, and that the older we get, the harder it is to choose change, which makes it even more necessary to do so from time to time. Change is one form of hope; to risk change is to believe in tomorrow. Hope is a gift we need later more than sooner. As has been said, only the young can afford hopelessness. Only they have time for it. Maybe what we need are old memories and young hopes. I remember when my mother first came to live with me in New York City, a move she agreed to make only because it was me or the nursing home. There she was, a sixty-eight-year-old Native Texan, swept into the air like Aunt Em's house, then plunked down with a great thud in a city which in no way could be described as Emerald or even, if you wanted her opinion, inhabitable. Not by *nice* people. It was an Oz where all witches were bad, all munchkins were muggers and no roads were yellow, although some of them were brick, which was not what *she* was accustomed to, she'd have you to know. Brick? There were no brick streets in Houston, not in her part of town, she was sure. Brick streets were not modern.

Mama was not a happy cowgirl.

I tried to interest her in the New Yorkness of it all: Broadway. Little Italy. Soho. Washington Square. Small, interesting shops on small interesting Village streets. Brownstones. Fruit stands. Pocket-size parks. Neighborhood restaurants. *Nothing.* All she could talk about was how much she missed Houston, how she missed going to the Post Oak Shopping Center, the Galleria and the other larger, newer malls. She'd enjoyed just walking around in those stores, even when she didn't buy anything, she said. There was something about big stores, she said, something comforting. I will not lie to you. I will not tell you that my mother ever stopped missing Houston or ever came to love New York City, but she did come to like it, eventually, and the day I think she began to change her mind was the Sunday she finally decided to read *The New York Times*. I remember the look on her face when she saw the full-page ad. Mama began to smile. The smile got bigger.

"Oh, Linda, look! Saks Fifth Avenue has a store *here*, too!"

Yes, Mama. *Just because everything is changed, it doesn't mean everything is different* (just ask Josh).

Mama's gone now, but me, I'm still here, still trying at times to choose change (I have to work at it now) and still trying to survive those times change chooses me. My fortune's not all been told. Who knows? I may yet play third base for the New York Yankees (I figure my chances have improved considerably with Steinbrenner out) but I'll never go to another baseball game with my daddy or eat another ice-cream cone with Mama, or Gladys. Those days are gone. Those people, too, forever. Learning to live with that has not been easy.

In the movie *Bang the Drum Slowly*, the second-best baseball movie ever, Michael Moriarty says to Robert De Niro, a plumb-dumb catcher who's dying, and whom he has come to love, "Everybody knows everybody is dying. That's why people are as good as they are." Yes. I've come to believe that if death is not open to appeal, neither is it a monument to human impotence, nor a punch line to a sick cosmic joke. As a species, we may have greasy hair, smelly socks and a tendency to overthrow home plate, but we are not terminal losers. That we always die in the end does not mean we're fools to live as though our living might mean something.

It means we won after all.

We shine, we do. We plant a tree that won't be big enough to climb until we're too old to climb trees, we write constitutions to protect the rights of people who won't be born for another hundred years and may not be worth the trouble anyway, and we try to take care of our sick, though we all suffer from a disease for which there is no cure and no hope for one. We will not last and we know we will not—and still we write, carve, build, paint and plant to last. We are, it seems to me, very, very brave.

Yes, we stand alone, but sometimes we stand alone together; we are even brave enough to love other humans, knowing we must lose them, brave enough to give birth to more humans, knowing we must lose them, too. Everybody dies. Everybody knows everybody dies. To live as if this were not so makes us giants. What we lack in distance we make up for in height, and once in a while we stand tall enough to touch the sky, look the sun straight in the eye and laugh. To me, this laughter is the finest sound there is. It is the sound of the human spirit, the sound of life. It's the best thing about us and it lasts until the game is called on account of darkness.

> *And the way you catch the light,*
> *And the care, and the feeling,*
> *And the life—*
> *Moving on.*

Those children (and to me they are children) here to listen to me speak know nothing of this yet, nor do they want to hear of it. Endings are not interesting to beginners. They believe anything is possible. I used to believe that, too. It's not true; anything is not possible. However, more things than ever I dreamed of, both good and bad, turn out to be possible, and if $2+2$ hasn't yet equaled 5, in my life, as in most lives, it has often equaled twenty-two.

—but hey, they wouldn't understand that, any more than I would have understood at their age. Happy endings? Sure, they may know some stories are happy, and they've learned some stories are sad, but what they don't know yet is that most stories are both.

I'm not going to try to tell them that today, either.

So here I am, robed, and ready to lie to them front to back. They'd better be prepared to hear about those damned hills of tomorrow and what a well-equipped lot of campers they seem. I'll smile a Pope smile and send them on their way, sprinkling on their heads a generous shower of trite, thrice-blessed words about the sanctity of life, the beat of different drummers and the need for peace on earth, beginning with the Democratic party. In academic circles (a redundancy, I suspect), this is what regularly passes for a commencement address. I'm tempted to drop a hint about keeping your powder dry. Yes, I might . . . but I doubt if I will (blame it on the rayon). Tell them yourself. You can never tell anybody anything, but tell them anyway. Tell them Linda Jane said move on.